An Introduction to Discourse Analysis

New edition

Malcolm Coulthard

Longman

London and New York

Longman Group UK Limited
Longman House, Burnt Mill, Harlow,
Essex CM20 2JE, England
and Associated Companies throughout the world.

*Published in the United States of America by
Longman Inc., New York*

First published 1977
Second edition 1985
Sixth impression 1990

ISBN 0-582-55379-2

British Library Cataloguing in Publication Data
Coulthard, Malcolm
  An introduction to discourse analysis. —
  New ed. — (Applied linguistics and language study)
  1. Discourse analysis
  I. Title II. Series
  415 P302

Library of Congress Cataloging in Publication Data
Coulthard, Malcolm.
  An introduction to discourse analysis.
  (Applied linguistics and language study)
  Bibliography: p.
  Includes index.
  1. Discourse analysis. I. Title. II. Series.
  P302.C68 1985   401'.41   85-4262

Illustration on page 113 reproduced by kind permission of Academic Press, New York

Set in 10/12pt. Linotron 202 Erhardt

Produced by Longman Singapore Publishers Pte Ltd
Printed in Singapore

Applied Linguistics and Language Study

General Editor: C. N. Candlin

APPLIED LINGUISTICS AND LANGUAGE STUDY

General Editor
Professor Christopher N. Candlin, Macquarie University

Error Analysis
Perspectives on second language acquisition
JACK C. RICHARDS (ED.)

Stylistics and the Teaching of Literature
HENRY WIDDOWSON

Listening to Spoken English
GILLIAN BROWN

Language Tests at School
A pragmatic approach
JOHN W. OLLER JNR

Contrastive Analysis
CARL JAMES

Language and Communication
JACK C. RICHARDS AND RICHARD W. SCHMIDT (EDS)

Learning to Write: First Language/Second Language
AVIVA FREEDMAN, IAN PRINGLE AND JANICE YALDEN (EDS)

Strategies in Interlanguage Communication
CLAUS FAERCH AND GABRIELE KASPER (EDS)

Reading in a Foreign Language
J. CHARLES ALDERSON AND A.H. URQUHART (EDS)

Discourse and Learning
PHILIP RILEY (ED.)

An Introduction to Discourse Analysis
New edition
MALCOLM COULTHARD

Computers in English Language Teaching and Research
GEOFFREY LEECH AND CHRISTOPHER N. CANDLIN (EDS)

Bilingualism in Education
Aspects of theory, research and practice
JIM CUMMINS AND MERRILL SWAIN

Second Language Grammar: Learning and Teaching
WILLIAM E. RUTHERFORD

The Classroom and the Language Learner
Ethnography and second-language classroom research
LEO VAN LIER

Vocabulary and Language Teaching
RONALD CARTER AND MICHAEL McCARTHY (EDS)

Observation in the Language Classroom
DICK ALLWRIGHT

Listening in Language Learning
MICHAEL ROST

Contents

Preface

From the response received to the first edition of Malcolm Coulthard's pioneering *An Introduction to Discourse Analysis*, it is clear that our hope that it would 'put discourse analysis on the map' has been amply fulfilled. The references to the book in the linguistic literature would be evidence enough to this were it not also for the corroborative impact it has made on a range of applications: language teaching and acquisition, stylistics, reading and writing studies, speech pathology and many others. It would not be an exaggeration to say that it stands even now as a key work of reference for many teachers and students throughout the world.

Why then a second edition? Principally, because if you take the broad view in making connections between language form and language use, bringing together as Coulthard does appropriate work from a range of disciplines: linguistics, social anthropology, philosophy, psychology, there is inevitably the need after eight years to review judgements and to bring to a new generation of students and scholars something of the excitement of more recent research. The 'time-bomb' of meaning, referred to in the first edition, has long since exploded and its effect on the narrowness of earlier models of linguistics has been fundamental. Taking the wider focus is now a way of life. Not that this development has been unproblematic; there remain the issues of description and analysis in discourse and pragmatics to which much of the first edition was dedicated. What has changed is a general perception that the bold integration of different disciplines, subject to overriding principles of descriptive and explanatory adequacy, offers the most promising avenues for attack.

It would be gratuitous to list here the additions and deletions, the changes in organizational structure which practice with the book has dictated: perhaps most noteworthy among these, however, are the entirely new Chapter 5 on *Intonation* and Chapter 6 *A Linguistic Approach* which bring up-to-date the highly influential work of the author and his colleagues at the University of Birmingham. All sections of the book have, however, been revised, and where necessary and appropriate, made current and more clearly interconnected. As an aid to the reader, however, it may be valuable to provide a summary view of current positions on the analysis of discourse; a way in to the richness of the reference provided here.

Any approach to discourse analysis and pragmatics has, presumably, to represent two distinguishable but related discourse worlds in the pursuit of its objective, namely the characterization of speaker/writer meaning and its explanation in the context of use. On the one hand, more nomothetically, discourse analysis must portray the structure of suprasentential text or social transaction by imposing some framework upon the data, explicitly or implicitly. On the other hand, more hermeneutically, discourse analysis should offer us a characterization of how, in the context of negotiation, participants go about the process of interpreting meaning (whether this is reciprocal as in conversation or non-reciprocal as in reading or writing need not detain us here, suffice that the process is interactive).

In their structure-portraying role discourse analysis and text linguistics have much in common, as in fact does the ethnography of speaking, concerned as it is with the display of sequenced episodes in some social encounter. In its interpretation-characterizing role, on the other hand, discourse analysis is involved in the assessment of the communicative function of momentary messages, drawing upon general and specific background knowledge in the process of making inference. The object of the first type of discourse analysis is the determination of interactive acts, siting them within some larger interactional frame; the objective of the second type of discourse analysis, on the other hand, is more the capturing of illocutionary force, drawing upon general pragmatic principle, an understanding of contextual expectations in the activity type under discussion, together with knowledge of how information may generally be structured, and procedures of natural analogy. All this is an attempt to display coherence.

So far, then, we have two different approaches to discourse analysis, one concerned with sequential relationships, the other with interpretation; the one working for 'rules' which will capture generalizations about intersential structure wherein the 'function' or 'value' of the utterances is in a sense taken for granted, the other working for 'procedures' where 'function' or 'value' is not a product based on intuitive understanding of the utterances in question, but a matter of negotiative process among a variety of contextual factors all of which taken together lead to the establishment (or the revelation) of specific social relationships between the interlocutors, themselves, of course, powerful sources of clue to illocutionary value. Rather than providing rules to account for relationships between product and form, in this second view procedures are introduced for the tracing of the negotiative process. One approach to discourse analysis is thus emphasizing organization and mapping, the other emphasizing social relationships and interaction.

Here, however, lies the paradox in our account: the organizational and the interactive (the structural and the procedural) each implies the other and cannot easily be abstracted from each other in any effective study of the discourse process, and for two reasons. Firstly, following studies in conversational analysis (amply documented by Malcolm Coulthard in Chapter 4), discoursal 'place' provides an orientation for participants in their evaluation of illocutionary force. Secondly, taking such an integrated view enables us to see language forms as the surface realization of those communicative strategies involved in the interactive procedures working amongst those various social, contextual and epistemological factors we have identified as crucial to the process of communicative inference and coherence. An example of such an integrated view exists in the work of Brown and Levinson (1978) where strategies of message construction are a key locus for an understanding of the interconnection between discourse structure and social structure. Their strategies of face redress, for example, act as a mediator between communicative intent and the circumstances or social relationships holding between the interlocutors. It is via these strategies that the degree of modification of the impact of communicative intent on the addressee is negotiated between the intentions themselves and the social relationships, traced then in the appropriately chosen form.

It would seem, then, as this book makes abundantly clear, the characterization of utterance function cannot be left to the tender mercies of linguistic form. How, then, can we map action to utterance? Following the suggestions outlined in Coulthard's *Introduction*, we can turn to a range of resources, all of which, we must acknowledge, are to be hedged around by the natural processes of contextual negotiation, participants' history and naturalized ideologies which makes easy identification and labelling very difficult. We can marshal our knowledge of speech events, themselves of course culturally-specific constructs, and apply to them (if we are aware of them as *outsiders*) the specific inferencing procedures relative to the event in question, using our framework of expectations about the nature of the speech events to which they contribute. We can make use of our knowledge of social role which is itself a negotiable 'good', if one takes a critical view of discourse. Furthermore, we can apply our understanding of the maxims attaching to various pragmatic principles and examine with care the placement of the utterance in question in the often quite lengthy, sometimes discontinuous and certainly very complex patterns of conversational structure. One could go on ... the point is that we are dealing with an immensely complex inferential process that makes use, as this book amply shows, of information of many kinds. If we do not take this into account, if we underestimate the quantity of text needed to make judgements of value, if we fall into the trap of failing to acknowledge culturally-biased presupposition, if we fail to embed utterances in the context of speech events, if we fail to make the connection between the formations of discourse and the formations of society, then we will take a too simplistic view of the subject-matter of this book. What is more, if we do not review our methodologies and the reasons why we undertake the research then we shall neither have access to adequate data nor have any social warrant for their collection or their analysis.

In explicitly acknowledging Malcolm Coulthard's contribution to an awareness of the caveats presented here, I can do no better than repeat the final appreciation of the first edition: 'the crucial matter has been to have seen the connections between disciplines concerned with describing and explaining human communication and to have suggested a synthesis'.

Christopher N. Candlin   *Lancaster*
General Editor   *1985*

Author's preface

In some ways it is more difficult to rewrite than to write — a second edition is necessarily constrained by the first. I have tried to retain the organization and as much as possible of the content of the first edition and thus, with the exception of Chapters 5 and 6 which have been totally rewritten, most of the new material occurs in the second halves of chapters.

The intention behind the book remains the same — to introduce those interested in the analysis of verbal interaction to relevant research in a variety of fields. This of course means that few of those whose work is presented here would regard themselves as Discourse Analysts and that for purposes of presentation I may have linked together researchers in what they and their followers feel are totally inappropriate ways. The prime example is Labov, brilliant but unclassifiable, who has worked in a whole series of areas: in the last edition he appeared with Ethnographers of Communication and Conversational Analysts — I have rectified this, but now he appears with Speech Act Philosophers!

Textbooks cannot be written in a vacuum; most of the excisions and additions I have made result from teaching Discourse Analysis to many groups of students sadly too numerous to be named. It is, however, possible and appropriate to acknowledge my debt to Dave Willis and Ken Hyland, whose theses I supervised and from whom and which I learned more than they will ever believe. In final place because he knows its real significance, Mike Hoey, a stimulating colleague and a true friend, without whom both content and form would have been more flawed.

Birmingham
August 1984

1 Introduction

Although it is now many years since J. R. Firth urged linguists to study conversation, for there 'we shall find the key to a better understanding of what language is and how it works' (1935), the serious study of spoken discourse is only just beginning and currently much of the work is being undertaken not by linguists but by sociologists, anthropologists and philosophers. The explanation is not hard to find. While all linguists would agree that *human communication* must be described in terms of at least three levels — meaning, form and substance, or *discourse, lexico-grammar* and *phonology* — there are disagreements over the boundaries of *linguistics*.

Firth (1951) asserted that 'the main concern of descriptive linguistics is to make statements of meaning'. Part of the meaning of an utterance is the result of contrasts in the levels of phonology and syntax, and Firth accepted that in order to isolate meaningful contrasts in these levels 'we make regular use of nonsense in phonetics and grammar', but, he argued, language is fundamentally 'a way of behaving and making others behave' and therefore ultimately the linguist must concern himself with the 'verbal process in the context of situation'. For Firth language was only meaningful in its context of situation; he asserted that the descriptive process must begin with the collection of a set of contextually defined homogeneous texts and the aim of description is to explain how the sentences or utterances are meaningful in their contexts.

Firth himself did not in fact explore the relation between form and meaning and his exhortations to others were ignored, because Bloomfield led linguistics away from any consideration of meaning to a concentration on form and substance, by observing that linguists 'cannot define meanings, but must appeal for this to students of other sciences or to common knowledge' (1933). The utterance 'I'm hungry' could be used by a starving beggar to request food or by a petulant child to delay going to bed; Bloomfield argued that linguistics is only concerned with those phonological, lexical and syntactic features which the utterances share — he felt it was no concern of linguistics to explain how identical utterances can have different functions in different situations, nor how listeners correctly decode the intended message.

For a generation American linguists concentrated massively and highly successfully on problems within phonology and morphology — on the existence of the phoneme and the validity of unique phonemic descriptions; on discovery procedures for isolating phonemes and morphemes in languages not previously described; on the mechanical identification of morpheme boundaries and word classes. When Chomsky redirected linguistics towards the study of sentence structure, the concerns were still pre-eminently with the formal features of language: 'the fundamental aim in the linguistic analysis of a language L is to separate the *grammatical* sequences which are sentences of L from the *ungrammatical* sequences which are not sentences of L and to study the structure of the grammatical sequences' (1957). In arguing the independence of grammaticality from meaningfulness Chomsky produced the most famous example of 'nonsense' in linguistics — 'colourless green ideas sleep furiously'.

Earlier linguists, while concentrating on formal aspects of language, had used collections of speech or writing as a source of examples. Chomsky suggested that not only was a corpus unnecessary, it was actually counterproductive. No corpus, however large, can be adequate because it will never contain examples of all possible structures and will actually contain misleading data, *performance* errors, caused by 'such grammatically irrelevant conditions as memory limitations, distractions, shifts of attention and interest and errors (random or characteristic) in applying knowledge of the language in actual performance'. The prime concern of linguistic theory, Chomsky argued, is with the underlying knowledge, the *competence* of the ideal speaker-hearer. The underlying competence is the same for all native speakers and therefore can be studied in the productions of any one individual, usually the linguist himself, who proceeds by introspection, checking potential sentences for grammaticality against his intuitions.

The insights achieved by transformational grammarians were enormous, but as time passed the problems became more serious. It became evident that there was not in fact a uniform native speaker competence; it became necessary to talk of degrees of grammaticality or acceptability; crucial examples were attacked as ungrammatical and defended as 'acceptable in my idiolect'. Meanwhile the timebomb *meaning* was ticking away: in the late 1960s Ross, McCawley and G. Lakoff began arguing that one cannot in fact describe grammar in isolation from meaning, that powerful syntactic generalizations can be achieved by making lexical insertions at an early stage in the generation of a sentence. By 1972 Robin Lakoff was arguing that 'in order to predict correctly the applicability of many rules one must be able to refer to assumptions about the social context of an utterance, as well as to other implicit assumptions made by the participants in a discourse'. Thus the results of empirical investigation have forced many transformational linguists to recognize the importance of context and to join a series of disciplines converging on the study of situated speech.

There is as yet, however, no single discipline which concerns itself with the study of interaction; in writing an introduction to discourse analysis I am not, paradoxically, describing only the work of researchers who consider themselves discourse analysts — many of those mentioned here would be bemused or annoyed by the label. Rather, what I have tried to do is draw together in the first six chapters research from many disciplines — philosophy, psychology, sociology, sociolinguistics, conversational analysis, anthropology, ethnography of speaking, phonetics and linguistics — which is useful to anyone interested in the analysis of situated speech or *spoken discourse*. Labels are always difficult; I have chosen to maintain a distinction between spoken *discourse* and written *text*, but this is by no means a universally accepted distinction; many German writers use 'text' to refer to speech as well, while Hoey (1983) and Widdowson (*passim*) use 'discourse' to refer to writing, and to complicate matters further 'pragmatics' as defined by Leech (1983) and Levinson (1983) overlaps substantially with discourse analysis as I conceive it.

Early attempts at discourse analysis

Although Firth urged linguists to study the total verbal process in its context of situation he did not do so himself, choosing rather to concentrate on phonology. In the period up to the late 60s there were only two isolated attempts to study suprasentential structure, one by Harris (1952), the other by Mitchell (1957).

Harris's article, although it has the promising title 'Discourse Analysis', is in fact disappointing. Working within the Bloomfieldian tradition he sets out to produce a formal method 'for the analysis of connected speech or writing' which 'does not depend on the analyst's knowledge of the particular meaning of each morpheme'. He observes that in grammar it is possible to set up word classes distributionally and produce a class of adjectives A which occur before a class of nouns N; such a statement captures a powerful generalization, even though it is possible to show that a particular member of the class A, 'voluntary', may never occur before a particular member of the class N, 'subjugation'.

Harris suggests that a distributional analysis can be successfully applied to a whole text to discover structuring above the rank of sentence. As an example he creates a text containing the following four sentences:

> The trees turn here about the middle of autumn.
> The trees turn here about the end of October.
> The first frost comes after the middle of autumn.
> We start heating after the end of October.

The aim of the analysis is to isolate units of text which are distributionally equivalent though not necessarily similar in meaning; that is *equivalences* which have validity for that text alone. From the first two sentences above one establishes the equivalence of 'the middle of autumn' and 'the end of October', not because they are similar in meaning but because they share an identical environment, 'the trees turn here'. The next step is to carry over the equivalences derived from the first two sentences into the next two and this allows us to equate 'the first frost comes' with 'we start heating' and of course both with 'the trees turn here' which provided the original context. Thus, in terms of equivalence classes, all four sentences have identical structure, class X followed by class Y. The analyst progresses in this way through the text creating a chain of equivalences and occasionally, as required, introducing a new class until the whole of the text has been divided into units assigned to one or other of the classes.

Harris points out that in evaluating his approach the only relevant questions are 'whether the method is usable and whether it leads to valid and interesting results'. In the thirty years since the article was published no one has adapted or developed his method for the analysis of discourse, though the idea of 'transformation', introduced to handle the equivalence relations, became, in a modified form, a central feature in Chomsky's Generative Grammar. It may well be, of course, that any purely formal analysis of structure above the sentence is impossible.

In marked contrast, Mitchell's 'Buying and selling in Cyrenaica' presents a semantically motivated analysis. Working in the Firthian tradition he specifies the relevant participants and elements of situation in detail and divides the buying-selling process into *stages* purely on content criteria, admitting that 'stage is an abstract category and the numbering of stages does not necessarily imply sequence in time'. He describes three major categories of transaction — market auctions;

other market transactions; shop transactions — although the second
and third are distinguished mainly by situation because they share the
following five stages:

1. salutation
2. enquiry as to the object of sale
3. investigation of the object of sale
4. bargaining
5. conclusion

This is an ideal structure: sometimes stages 1 and 2 do not occur and
stages 3 and 5 may be realized non-verbally. The following is an example of a shop transaction:

Personality	Translation	Stage
BUYER:	Have you a bed to sell?	2
SELLER:	I've got one but it's rather expensive.	2
BUYER:	Let me have a look at it then.	2
SELLER:	Certainly.	
	If you want it for yourself I will make you a reduction.	4
BUYER:	How much is it?	4
SELLER:	£4.	4
BUYER:	What's your last price?	4
SELLER:	Believe me if it were anyone but you I'd ask him five.	4
BUYER:	I'll make you a firm offer of £3.50.	4
SELLER:	Impossible, let it stay where it is.	4
BUYER:	Listen. I'll come this afternoon, pay you £3.70 and take it.	4
	(Buyer crosses threshold of shop on his way out.)	
SELLER:	It still wants some repairs.	5

While this analysis captures the structure of the transaction it is ar-
guable that it is not a linguistic analysis at all — the stages are defined
and recognized by the activity that occurs within them rather than by
characteristic linguistic features and, with the possible exception of
stage 4, which when opened by the buyer apparently begins with the
formula 'How much?', there are no *linguistic* markers of transitions
between stages. However, once the stages have been isolated non-
linguistically Mitchell then *characterizes* them linguistically by providing examples of the kinds of phrases and clauses, often ritual, which
occur within them.

Discourse units and discourse function

The fact that Mitchell did not offer any internal structure for his
stages must not be taken to imply that spoken discourse has no structure and consists simply of a string of grammatically well-formed utterances. The following examples from Labov (1970), the first from

an interview with a schizophrenic patient, the other fabricated, are grammatically unexceptional yet noticeably odd:

A: What is your name?
B: Well, let's say you might have thought you had something from before, but you haven't got it anymore.
A: I'm going to call you Dean.

A: I feel hot today.
B: No.

In both examples B's contribution obviously breaks rules for the production of coherent discourse, and one of the major aims of discourse analysis is to discover these rules and to describe the conversational structures they generate. Obviously an initial and fundamental question is the nature of the units whose structure and occurrence the sequencing rules will describe.

Harris (1952) observes that traditionally grammatical description has taken the sentence as its upper limit, and it is instructive to discuss the reasons for this. A grammatical description provides the structure(s) of a given unit in terms of allowable combinations of smaller units and an essential feature of any grammatical description is the specification not only of what structures can occur but also of those structures which cannot occur. Thus a grammar of English would allow the following sentences:

I bought these chairs yesterday.
Yesterday I bought these chairs.
These chairs I bought yesterday.

but not:

Yesterday these chairs bought I.
These chairs bought yesterday I.
I these chairs yesterday bought.

and a speaker's decision about which of the possible grammatical options to select on a particular occasion will then depend on cohesive and stylistic considerations. Once one comes to look at choices above the sentence, however, there are no parallel restrictions on combinations of units and all the decisions a speaker or writer makes are stylistic ones — there is no way of describing *paragraph* structure in terms of allowable combinations of simple, complex or compound sentences because any collection of sentence types in any sequence can constitute a paragraph and 'rules' about paragraph writing therefore take the form of advice about 'topic sentences' and the alternation of long and short sentences.

However, while it appears that structure describable in terms of formal grammatical units ends at the sentence, we can explain the Labov examples in terms of patterning of *functional* units which certainly does occur above the sentence and across utterance boundaries. In the following example it is impossible to describe or even contemplate constraints on B's utterance in grammatical terms but in functional terms his options are highly restricted:

A: Where's the typewriter?
B: In the cupboard.
 Is it in the cupboard?
 Look in the cupboard.
 I think it's in the cupboard.

In other words, whereas we cannot provide a meaningful structural description of a conversation in terms of 'declarative followed by moodless clause', or 'interrogative followed by declarative', it is possible to provide a meaningful structure in terms of Question and Answer, Challenge and Response, Invitation and Acceptance. Thus Labov (1972a) argues that the first and most important step is to distinguish '*What is said* from *what is done*', and stresses that the unit of analysis is not the grammatically defined clause or sentence but a functional unit, which may of course be *realized* by a single clause or sentence.

Any attempt to characterize discourse structure in terms of functional units must confront the problem of grammatical realization — how do the four major clause types, 'declarative', 'interrogative', 'imperative' and 'moodless', realize a multiplicity of different functions, and how can a hearer correctly interpret which function is intended?

Labov (1970, 1972a), taking as given that question-answer is a basic interactive structure, focuses on *answers* and sketches out a series of *interpretive rules* to explain how a second utterance comes to be heard as an answer to a question. The simplest relationship is between a question and an elliptical answer:

A: Are you going to work tomorrow?
B: Yes.

Here a simple rule can account for the relation:

If A utters a question of the form Q (S_1) and B responds with an existential E (including *yes, no, probably, maybe* etc.) then B is heard as answering A with a statement (E) S_1.

A more complex relationship holds between the following pair of utterances:

A: Are you going to work tomorrow?
B: I'm on jury duty.

Grice (1975) argues that there is an underlying constraint on all conversationalists to 'be relevant' and for this reason A will assume, at least initially, that there is a proposition known to both which connects B's response to his question, i.e. 'if someone is on jury duty he cannot go to work'. To account for this type of relationship Labov proposes the following rule:

> If A makes a request of B of the form $Q(S_1)$, and B responds with a statement S_2, and there exists no rule of ellipsis which would expand S_2 to include S_1, then B is heard as asserting that there exists a proposition known to both A and B, of the form
> If S_2, then (E) S_1
> where (E) is an existential operator, and from this proposition there is inferred an answer to A's request: (E) S_1.

This rule makes clear the crucial importance of *shared knowledge* in conversation; not simply shared rules for the interpretation of linguistic items, but shared knowledge of the world, to which a speaker can allude or appeal. Labov notes that this rule is invariant: A *must* inspect B's utterance to see if he can detect an underlying linking proposition and 'failure to locate such a proposition may reflect a real incompetence'. Younger members of a social group may not be able to find the proposition being asserted:

LINUS: Do you want to play with me, Violet?
VIOLET: You're younger than me. (*shuts the door*)
LINUS: (*puzzled*) She didn't answer my question.   (Labov 1972a)

There are two possible 'solutions' to this joke — one is that Linus, unlike the reader, is unable to derive the underlying proposition 'If you are younger than me THEN NOT I want to play with you'; the other, more subtly, is that his previous experience or self-esteem lead him to conclude that the underlying proposition is not in fact coherent and that therefore Violet has not provided an answer. In either case the question had set up the next utterance as a potential answer and the questioner had used inferring strategies to evaluate the utterance as a possible meaningful answer.

These first rules are concerned with explaining how statements following questions come to be heard and interpreted as answers, but in these instances there is an expectation that an answer will follow; much more difficult to explain is how some utterances, declarative in form, come to be heard as questions. Labov presents the following extract from a therapy session,

THERAPIST: Oh, so she *told* you.
PATIENT: Yes.
THERAPIST: She didn't say for *you* . . .
PATIENT: No.
THERAPIST: And it never occurred to her to prepare dinner.
PATIENT: No.

and observes that it consists of a series of pairs where 'the first utterance is a statement and the second is "yes" or "no", and it seems that a statement is functioning as equivalent to a yes–no question'. Labov suggests that the statements in the therapy extract are acting as *requests for confirmation* and have the same compelling force as requests made in question form; but how 'is it that we regularly and reliably recognize these as requests and not as assertions', because it is certainly not the case that *any* statement can be followed by 'yes' or 'no'.

A: I don't like the way you said that.
B: *Yes.

A: I feel hot today.
B: *No.

The proposed interpretive rule depends again on shared knowledge. Whenever there are two participants, A and B, in a conversation, Labov observes, one can distinguish 'A-events', things that A alone knows about, 'B-events', things that B alone knows about, and 'AB-events', things that are known to both. Using this terminology he states a simple interpretive rule:

If A makes a statement about a B-event it is heard as a request for confirmation.

The interpretation of such utterances as requests for confirmation depends crucially of course on speaker A's assumptions about speaker B's knowledge being correct. In the following example the assumptions were wrong and A's intended request for confirmation was heard as a statement of new information.

A: There's no playgroup next week then.
B: Oh, isn't there?

This brief discussion of a part of Labov's suggestive work has raised some of the questions which discourse analysis sets out to answer — how does one characterize and label the basic unit of interaction; how many different functions are there; how are these functions realized lexico-grammatically and what structures do these basic units combine to form? Succeeding chapters present a variety of answers and in evaluating them it is useful to bear in mind the four criteria to which Sinclair (1973) claims all linguistic descriptions must conform:

1. The descriptive apparatus should be finite, or else one is not saying anything at all, and may be merely creating the illusion of classification.
2. The whole of the data should be describable; the descriptive system should be comprehensive. This is not a difficult criterion to meet, because it is always possible to have a 'ragbag' category into which go all items not positively classified by other criteria. [Of course] if we find that 95% of the text goes into the ragbag we would reject the description as invalid.

While making apparently innocuous demands — that the system should have a demonstrably finite number of items and be able to handle the whole of a specified corpus — these two criteria cannot be applied to all of the descriptions presented in succeeding chapters. Indeed, as Labov (1972a) notes, Sacks and his colleagues believe it is inappropriate to attempt to describe all the data at this stage, and Labov himself only attempts to handle fragments.

3. There must be at least one impossible combination of symbols.

This is the basic notion of linguistic structure to which we were appealing in our earlier discussion of the status of paragraphs, and is one which Levinson (1983, pp. 291–4) uses to criticize the descrip-

TABLE 1.1   Categories of interaction analysis

Hymes	Sacks	Scheflen	Sinclair
event	conversation	presentation	interaction
	topic	position	transaction
			sequence
	sequence	point	exchange
	pair		
act	turn		move
		sentence	
			act

tion proposed in Sinclair and Coulthard (1975). Of course this rule presupposes an interest in the *structure* of interaction — speech act analysis for instance is concerned only with the functional meaning of individual utterances. Those descriptions that *are* concerned with structure vary in the number of analytic units they propose from two (Hymes 1972a) to six (Sinclair and Brazil 1982). Table 1.1 matches roughly in terms of size the category labels from four different descriptions, Scheflen's being based on non-verbal aspects of interaction.

4. The symbols in the descriptive apparatus should be precisely relatable to their exponents in the data . . . if we call some phenomenon a 'noun' or a 'repair strategy' or a 'threat' we must establish exactly what constitutes the class with that label.

The problem can be approached from either end: one can write *re-alization* rules to show how functions are related to their lexico-grammatical realizations, or *interpretive* rules to show how particular stretches of speech are understood as having particular significances. Subsequent chapters have examples of both approaches but it looks as if interpretive rules will ultimately be preferred.

The other major concern of discourse analysis, which the Labov examples do not highlight, is the relationship between the discourse and the speakers and hearers by and for whom it is produced — a concern with how speakers take and relinquish the role of speaker, how social roles affect discourse options in terms of who speaks when and what they can talk about, how non-verbal signalling works and how the actual form of utterances is conditioned by the social re-lationships between the participants.

The research reported in the succeeding chapters comes from a wide range of disciplines with differing ideas on what constitutes rel-evant and acceptable data. As we saw above Firth argued for a text-based description, Chomsky for a total reliance on intuition. Lyons (1968) suggests that there are in fact three degrees of idealization between raw data and the idealized sentences of Chomsky's competence.

The first stage is *regularization* in which the analyst ignores such phenomena as slips of the tongue, hesitations, repetitions, self-editing and so on. The second stage is *standardization* in which one ignores variation and treats whatever data one is examining as homogeneous — thus at the phonemic level, different pronunciations of the same 'word' are treated as if they were the same; at the level of discourse, variants of a *misapprehension sequence* are all regarded as occurrences of the same unit. This is an essential step in any classificatory system, for in the final analysis all utterances can be shown to be unique. However, there are currently disagreements among linguists over the degree of standardization and the amount of variation which can be successfully described (Sankoff 1974). The third stage of idealization involves *decontextualization*, which separates sentences from their contexts of use or occurrence and treats them as self-contained and isolated units.

Much of the work described in the following chapters is based on transcripts which are in an unregularized form, but in fact analyses the data as if it were both regularized and standardized. The work by philosophers on speech acts, however, is based entirely on decontextualized fabricated data and all approaches make some use of fabricated examples to make points and arguments clearer.

2 Speech acts and conversational maxims

While linguistics restricted itself for a generation to a concentration on form, the study of meaning was left to linguistic philosophers, who concentrated on the sense, reference and implications of sentences and parts of sentences. In 1962 J. L. Austin observed that while it had long been the assumption of philosophers that 'the business of a "statement" can only be to describe some state of affairs or to "state some fact", which it must do either truly or falsely' (p. 1), more recently they had come to realize that this was not always the case. There are sentences which look like statements, or as Austin prefers to call them *constatives*, that are not intended to record or impart information about facts: some, for example, like 'the King of France is bald' are strictly nonsense, despite unexceptional grammatical form; others, *ethical propositions*, are 'perhaps intended, solely or partly, to evince emotion or to prescribe conduct, or to influence it in special ways'. Austin focuses on a third group of sentences which he labels *performatives*, in which the saying of the words constitutes the performing of an action:

'I name this ship the *Queen Elizabeth*' — as uttered when smashing the bottle against the stern.
'I do' (take this woman to be my lawful wedded wife) — as uttered in the course of a marriage ceremony.
'I give and bequeath my watch to my brother' — as occurring in a will. (p. 8)

In saying 'I name this ship the *Queen Elizabeth*' the speaker is not *describing* what he is doing, nor stating that he is doing it, but actually performing the action of naming the ship; from that moment the ship is named. A confirmation that it is in saying the words that one performs the action is that very frequently one can insert the word 'hereby' — 'I *hereby* name this ship ...'. The uttering of the words alone is, however, not sufficient — while the performative utterance is 'usually a, or even *the* leading incident' in the performing of the acts of naming, marrying or bequeathing, it is rarely if ever the 'sole thing necessary if the act is to be deemed to have been performed'. Austin stresses the conventional nature of the performative act and the fact that an agreed procedure must be followed. There are four conditions which must be satisfied if the performative act is not to *misfire:*

1. There must exist an accepted conventional procedure, having a certain conventional effect, that procedure to include the uttering of certain words by certain persons in certain circumstances. (p. 26)

By this condition Austin draws attention to the fact that there is a limited number of performative acts and one cannot arbitrarily adapt a procedure in order to perform what appears to be a similar act — there is a procedure for christening babies but not dogs, for naming ships but not houses. For some acts procedures differ in different countries — no one, whatever his religion, can divorce his wife in England by saying 'I divorce you; I divorce you; I divorce you', while some acts are possible in one language community but not in another — there is no formal procedure in Modern English for insulting someone, to match that used by German students to initiate duels in the inter-war years. This is not, of course, to say that one cannot insult someone in English, but simply that one cannot insult them by saying 'I insult you'.

2. The particular persons and circumstances in a given case must be appropriate for the invocation of the particular procedure invoked. (p. 34)

This condition emphasizes the fact that the uttering of the correct and appropriate words is insufficient to achieve the successful performance of the act: the words must be uttered by the appropriate person — the blacksmith in Gretna Green may read the marriage service as well as any parson, but the ceremony is still invalid; while even the appropriate person cannot utter the appropriate words in inappropriate circumstances — one of the umpires in the Test match when Leonard Hutton scored his record 364 claimed later that Hutton was technically out lbw at 332, but, as no one on the fielding side appealed, the umpire was unable to pronounce him out.

3. The procedure must be executed by all participants both correctly
4. and completely. (pp. 35–6)

These conditions cover misfires which occur despite the existence of a conventional procedure and the presence of the appropriate participants in the appropriate circumstances. The problems may be verbal or non-verbal. The marriage ceremony includes yes/no questions, 'Do you take this woman . . .' but 'yes' is not an acceptable answer and the ceremony has a fixed point for the ring to be placed on the finger — failure to produce the ring or placing the ring on the finger at a different point in the ceremony would again cause the act to misfire.

So far we have seen that the uttering of certain words by appropriate people in appropriate circumstances can constitute the performing of certain conventional acts; an obvious next question is what formal features mark utterances as performative? All Austin's initial examples have the verb in the simple present active form with a first person singular subject, e.g. 'I name this ship', and this is apparently significant since neither 'I am naming this ship', nor 'he names/named this ship', nor 'this ship is named by me' is an acceptable substitute. However, it soon becomes apparent that there are some performative utterances with the verb in the passive — 'passengers are requested to return to their seats'   and others which have no subject or verb at all — 'guilty' pronounced by the foreman of a jury or 'out' by an umpire — and Austin is forced to conclude reluctantly that there are in fact no linguistic features which reliably and unambiguously distinguish performative from non-performative utterances.

The achievement so far has been to isolate 'a class of utterances, linguistically quite heterogeneous, which have in common that, in virtue of non-linguistic conventions, to issue them (happily) *counts* as *doing* this or that' (Warnock 1973). In one important sense these performative utterances are idioms — the meanings of the individual words are not of great importance and synonyms cannot be substituted — it is the uttering of *predetermined* words in a fixed sequence in a few highly conventionalized and at times ritual situations, which constitutes the performing of the action. If performative utterances were restricted to such situations their existence would be an interesting but not particularly significant fact about language use. However, Austin noticed that the concept of the performative utterance, of doing something by saying something, had a more general application, for in saying 'I promise', 'I apologize', 'I warn you', one actually performs the acts of promising, apologizing and warning. Thus these utterances also are performative, but are crucially distinct from the first group in that there are no rule-governed conventions restricting their use — anyone can make a promise to anyone in any place at any time.

This extension of the concept to ordinary language situations is very exciting but it raises enormous descriptive problems because, although the performative utterance may be *explicit*, for example 'I warn you that p', it is much more likely to be *primary*, simply 'p' — there are, as Strawson (1964) points out, cases in which 'to utter the words "the ice over there is thin" to a skater is to issue a warning . . . without its being the case that there is a statable convention at all, such that the speaker's act can be said to be an act conforming to that convention.' This, of course, raises the crucial question of how one recognizes a given utterance as performative. There are even problems with utterances containing explicit performative verbs:

> I promise only when I intend to keep my word.
> On p. 49 I protest against the verdict.

but these can usually be sorted out with the 'hereby' test discussed above. Much more problematic are the utterances without a performative verb. Austin suggests that the problem is not, in fact, too difficult, because

> any utterance which is in fact performative should be reducible or expandable or analysable into a form with a verb in the first person singular present indicative active ... Thus 'out' is equivalent to 'I declare, pronounce or call you out', 'guilty' is equivalent to 'I find, pronounce, deem you to be guilty'. (p. 62)

The discussion has now come full circle. We first established that there was a set of utterances of the form 'I + present simple active verb' which were performatives; then it became apparent that not only were there constative utterances with the same grammatical form, but also performatives with other grammatical forms which often did not even include the performative verb. We then suggested, however, that those utterances which were actually performative, but did not have the form 'I + present simple active verb' were 'reducible, expandable or analysable' into that form. This revives the question of how one decides whether an original or transformed utterance of the form 'I + present simple active' is performative or constative. In the following table the first column contains explicit performatives and the third column constatives, while the status of those in the middle column is doubtful.

TABLE 2.1

Performatives	?	Constatives
I thank you	I am grateful	I feel grateful
I bid you welcome	I welcome you	
I apologize	I am sorry	I repent

(Austin 1962, p. 79)

Austin suggests four tests for deciding which way utterances in the middle column are being used:

1. Does the saying of the words constitute the performing of an act? This can be tested by asking 'did he really' of a particular utterance. It is not possible to dispute whether a person actually bid another welcome, the uttering of the words constitutes the action, but one can ask, following the utterance 'I welcome you', 'Did he really welcome him?', and the answer and therefore the classification of the utterance is likely to depend on the circumstances.

2. Could the action be performed without uttering the words? One can be sorry just as one can repent without saying anything but one cannot apologize silently.

3. Is the action something that can be done deliberately and voluntarily? One can be 'willing to apologize' but not 'willing to be sorry' — one is either sorry or not, though one can be willing to *say* that one is sorry.

4. Can the utterance be literally false? Austin sees this as a crucial distinction between constatives which can be true or false and performatives which can only be happy or unhappy. Despite saying 'I am sorry' it need not be true that one is sorry; if one says 'I apologize', however, it cannot be false that one has apologized — the apology may be insincere and the speaker may have *abused* the procedure but that is another matter.

Using these criteria it is possible to assign utterances of the form 'I + present simple active verb' to the class of explicit performatives or of constatives, the one being subject to a test of happiness, the other to a test of truth.

However, yet again in the argument, having taken two steps forward we must take one back. Austin now recognizes a class of utterances which he labels expositional performatives or *expositives* where 'the main body of the utterance has generally or often the straightforward form of a statement', and which are therefore subject to a test of truth. However, prefacing the statement is a verb phrase like 'I argue/conclude/testify/admit/predict' which in fact satisfies all the criteria for performatives:

I argue that there is no backside to the moon.

and it doesn't take long to realize that even 'I state' satisfies the performative test. This is initially very disconcerting because the whole drift of the argument so far has been concerned with distinguishing performatives from constatives, but it is now evident that all utterances previously labelled constative, even those with the grammatical form 'I + present simple active verb', are in fact primary performatives which are 'expandable or analysable into a form "I state that . . ."'. There is now an elegance in the description — instead of claiming two classes of utterance, one performative and the other constative, Austin now asserts that in saying anything one is performing some kind of act.

Having demonstrated that in fact all utterances are performative Austin reconsiders the senses in which 'to say something may be to do something' and concludes that in 'issuing an utterance' a speaker can perform three acts simultaneously: a *locutionary* act which is the act *of* saying something in the full sense of 'say'; an *illocutionary* act which is an act performed *in* saying something, the act identified by the explicit performative; and a *perlocutionary* act, the act performed *by* or as a result of saying. Thus:

> *Act A or Locution*
> He said to me 'Shoot her' meaning by 'shoot' shoot and referring by 'her' to her.
> *Act B or Illocution*
> He urged (or advised, ordered, etc.) me to shoot her.
> *Act C or Perlocution*
> He persuaded me to shoot her. (p. 101)

It is not Austin's intention to suggest that in speaking one has the option of performing one or other of these acts; one usually performs all three simultaneously, but it is useful for analytic purposes to distinguish them.

Austin first distinguishes locutionary and illocutionary acts. While 'to perform a locutionary act is in general, we may say, also and *eo ipso* to perform an *illocutionary* act' (p. 98), the interpretation of the locutionary act is concerned with *meaning*, the interpretation of the illocutionary act with *force*. Austin glosses 'meaning' unhelpfully as the use of language with 'a certain more or less definite "sense" and a more or less definite "reference"', but Strawson (1973) clarifies things by asking what a listener would need to know, so that he could be said to know 'the meaning of precisely what was said' on a given occasion. He points out that a complete mastery of the linguistic system, syntax and semantics, is almost always insufficient: any stranger listening to a tape-recording of the utterance 'John will get here in two hours from now', would know neither the person referred to by 'John' nor the time and place designated by 'here' and 'now'. Thus meaning must be seen as an amalgam of textual *and* extra-textual information, and it is the function of the locutionary act to transfer this meaning from speaker to listener. There is still a sense in which the listener may, however, not have understood 'how what was said was meant', that is whether the illocutionary *force* of the locution concerning John was assertion, prediction or warning.

The locutionary/illocutionary distinction is not an easy one. It could be argued that in explicit performative utterances like 'I warn you there's a bull in that field', to know the meaning of the locutionary act is already to know the illocutionary force; and Cohen (1969) asks 'in what way does the illocutionary force of such an utterance differ from that part of its meaning which belongs to it in virtue of its performative prefix', going on to argue that illocutionary forces do not in fact exist. Strawson (1964) accepts that in *explicit* performative utterances the meaning may exhaust the force but points out that in primary performatives the meaning 'though it limits does not exhaust the force', while Searle (1969), in a similar vein to Cohen, argues that 'where a certain force is part of the meaning, where the meaning uniquely determines a particular force, these are not two different acts, but two different labels for the same act', and reaches the conclusion that there are only illocutionary acts. These criticisms are in fact unhelpful and appear to pun on the meaning of 'meaning', for as Forguson (1973) observes, 'even if there are cases in which meaning completely *determines* force it isn't the *same thing* as force'.

Austin himself expected the distinction between illocutionary and perlocutionary acts to give more trouble. Basically an illocutionary act is a *linguistic* act performed in uttering certain words in a given context, while a perlocutionary act is a *non-linguistic* act performed as a consequence of performing the locutionary and illocutionary acts. The illocutionary act being achieved through the uttering of certain words is potentially under the complete control of the speaker: provided he uses the correct *explicit* performative in the appropriate circumstances he can be certain that the act will be 'happy' — no one can prevent someone from warning or advising them except by refusing to listen. The associated perlocutionary act, however, is the causing of a change in the mind or behaviour of the listener, so that he becomes 'alarmed', 'convinced', 'deterred'. Thus the act is the effect of the utterance on the listener, but because this is not an effect governed by convention — there is no conventional or reliable way of linguistically 'convincing' or 'deterring' someone — I may warn you hoping to deter you but in fact succeed only in encouraging or even inciting you.

For this reason, Austin feels it necessary to distinguish between perlocutionary *object*, basically the intended result of the illocutionary act, and perlocutionary *sequel*, an unintended or secondary result. It is in this way that Austin solves the problem raised earlier of accounting for those actions like 'insult' for which there is no performative verb, therefore no illocutionary act and therefore no perlocutionary object; some perlocutionary acts can only be sequels: 'thus I may surprise you or upset you or humiliate you by a locution, though there is no illocutionary formula "I surprise you by . . .", "I upset you by . . .", "I humiliate you by . . ."' (p. 117). Unfortunately

Austin did not pursue the investigation of perlocutionary objects and sequels, but such a study could reveal persuasive and oratorical techniques and form the substance of a companion volume *How to achieve things through words*.

From the discussion so far it will be evident that Austin attaches considerable importance to speaker's intention — he argues in fact that if a listener misinterprets an utterance the speaker should be regarded not as having (accidentally) produced a different illocutionary act but as having produced no act at all: 'the performance of an illocutionary act involves the securing of *uptake*', that is *intended* uptake.

This position creates two major problems. First, the unstated assumption is that each locution has only one illocutionary force; but, as Searle (1965) argued persuasively, primary performatives are not only potentially ambiguous but often deliberately so:

> suppose at a party my wife says 'It's really quite late'. That utterance may be at one level a statement of fact; to her interlocutor, who has just remarked on how early it was, it may be (and be intended as) an objection; to her husband it may be (and be intended as) a suggestion or even a request ('Let's go home.') as well as a warning ('You'll feel rotten in the morning if we don't.').

Second, there is the problem of discovering what the speaker's intention was, something literary critics have long regarded as a fruitless endeavour, and of deciding what in fact *has* happened if no illocutionary act has been performed. However, as those analysing language in use have discovered, there is, fortunately, no real need to concern oneself with the speaker's intention because interaction proceeds according to the listener's *interpretation* of the force of an utterance. Edmondson (1981) actually suggests a 'hearer-knows-best' principle according to which,

> H's interpretation of S's behaviour may be said to determine what S's behaviour counts as at that point of time in the ongoing conversation: this allows of the possibility of course that S may self-correct — i.e. the hearer-knows-best principle may be applied sequentially. (p. 50)

Subsequent developments

Austin's theory is suggestive, but he died before he was able to develop it. One significant gap is that whereas he proposed four conditions governing the 'happy' production of ritual or archetypal performatives, he suggested no conditions or rules for other performatives. Searle (1965) attempts, through a detailed discussion of one conventional illocutionary act, 'promise', to explicate the notion of illocutionary act by stating a set of necessary and sufficient conditions for the performance of a particular kind of illocutionary act and extracting from it a set of semantical rules for the use of the expression (or syntactic device) which marks the utterance as an illocutionary act of that kind.

He chooses not to separate an utterance into locutionary and illocutionary acts, preferring to see it as consisting of two (not necessarily separate or even separable) parts: a *proposition*, and a *function indicating device* which marks the illocutionary force. In each of the following utterances, Searle suggests, the speaker expresses the same proposition, that John will leave the room — that is, he predicates the action of leaving the room of John, though only in the second does he perform the illocutionary act of 'asserting':

Will John leave the room?
John will leave the room.
John, leave the room!
If John will leave the room I will leave also.

The function-indicating devices in English include word order, stress, intonation contour, punctuation, the mood of the verb and finally the set of so-called performative verbs, but in the 1965 article he confines his discussion 'to full-blown explicit promises and ignores promises made by elliptical turns of phrase, hints, metaphors, etc'. In other words, his concern is not with deciding whether and how a potentially ambiguous utterance is interpretable as a promise but with how an utterance of the form 'I promise that p' can 'happily' secure uptake as a promise.

Before he can clarify the nature of the rules which govern the linguistic realization of illocutionary acts, Searle needs to distinguish the two major types of rule, *regulative* and *constitutive*. Regulative rules, as the name implies, are concerned with conditions on the occurrence of certain forms of behaviour — 'Children are forbidden to play football on the grass'; whereas constitutive rules define the behaviour itself — 'A player is offside if . . .'. If the children ignore the notice they will be playing football, though incidentally breaking the law; if they ignore the offside rule they are technically no longer playing football, for football has no existence apart from its constitutive rules.

In the study of language use both sets of rules are important. All interaction has regulative rules, usually not explicitly stated, which govern greetings, choice of topic, interruption and so on, and as Hymes (1972a) points out, the rules vary from community to community. Constitutive rules in speech are those which control the ways in which an utterance of a given form is heard as realizing a given illocutionary act. Searle's aim is to describe the constitutive rules for the illocutionary act of *promising*. He suggests that five rules govern the making of a promise:

propositional content rule — in a promise, a future act must be predicated of the speaker himself; he cannot promise to have done something nor promise that someone else will do something.

preparatory rules (a) — a promise is defective if the promiser doesn't believe that the promisee wants the act performed or even if the thing promised is, unbeknown to the promiser, something the promisee doesn't want done — otherwise whatever his intention the speaker will be uttering a warning or threat.

(b) — a speaker cannot promise to do something he would (be expected to) do anyway — as Searle observes, any husband who promises his wife not to be unfaithful during the next week is likely to provide more anxiety than comfort.

sincerity rule — the speaker must intend to perform the action. It is of course possible for someone to make a promise with no intention at all of honouring it, but then, Searle contends, he is abusing the procedure.

essential rule — the uttering of the words counts as the undertaking of an obligation to perform the action.

A major difference between Austin and Searle lies in the assignment of the illocutionary force of an utterance — as we saw above for Austin, it is the successful realization of the speaker's intention, but for Searle a product of the listener's interpretation. Preparatory rule (a) makes this clear and provides for the speaker saying 'I promise I'll be there by three o'clock', feeling certain in his own mind that he has committed himself and yet unwittingly having performed the illocutionary acts of 'warning' or 'threatening', because the hearer doesn't in fact want him to be there by three o'clock.

Searle observes that for his analysis to have any general interest the analytic framework should be adaptable to the description of other speech acts, and in Searle (1969) he offers an analysis of 'request', 'assert', 'question', 'thank', 'advise', 'warn' and 'order'. For ordering, the *propositional content* must be a future act by the hearer,

the *preparatory* conditions include that the speaker should be in a position of authority over the hearer, the *sincerity* condition is that the speaker wants the ordered act done and the *essential* condition has to do with the fact that the speaker intends the utterance as an attempt to get the hearer to do the act. (p. 64)

In analysing this set of illocutionary acts Searle noted that certain conditions recurred, and this led him to question whether there were 'some basic illocutionary acts to which all or most of the others are reducible'. Austin had in fact tentatively proposed *grouping* his performative verbs into five major classes: *verdictives*, typified by the giving of a verdict by a jury, arbitrator or umpire — acquit, grade, estimate, diagnose; *exercitives*, which are the exercising of powers, rights or influence — appoint, order, advise, warn; *commissives*, which commit the speaker to doing something, but also include declarations or announcements of intention — promise, guarantee, bet, oppose; *behabitives*, a miscellaneous group concerned with attitudes and social behaviour — apologize, criticize, bless, challenge; and *expositives*, which clarify how utterances fit into ongoing discourse, or how they are being used — argue, postulate, affirm, concede.

However, there are problems with this classification, as Searle (1976) points out: 'there is no clear or consistent principle or set of principles on the basis of which the taxonomy is constructed', and therefore 'a very large number of verbs find themselves smack in the middle of two competing "categories"' — for example, Austin lists 'describe' as both a verdictive and an expositive. However, the fundamental weakness of Austin's classification of illocutionary verbs is that it is just that, a classification of illocutionary verbs. As Searle comments, 'Austin seems to assume that a classification of different verbs is *eo ipso* a classification of kinds of illocutionary acts.' In other words, Austin's classification is essentially a folk-linguistic one — it relies on the English language for its descriptive labels and therefore includes speech acts which the language happens to lexicalize, omitting those for which there is no lexical label. This means that on the one hand 'I order you to', 'I request you to', 'I beg you to', 'I entreat you to' are necessarily regarded as different illocutionary acts, though all could be expansions of the same primary performative 'put down that gun' uttered by speakers with differing status relative to their addressee; while on the other hand, whereas one can report both 'I complimented her' and 'I insulted her', only the former can be classified as a report of an illocutionary act.

Searle argues that it is much more reasonable to think of speakers as performing a limited number of illocutionary acts and to see the illocutionary *verbs* as semantic complexes carrying other information in addition to force — thus request/beg/entreat are concerned with differences in the relative status of speaker and hearer, suggest/propose/insist with variation in the strength with which the illocutionary point is presented, and boast/lament and congratulate/console with 'differences in the way the utterance relates to the interests of the speaker and hearer'.

One exciting consequence of this proposal, which Searle himself does not mention, is that it provides a solution to the problem of expanding primary performatives. The hearer or analyst doesn't have to decide which of more than 1000 performative verbs is the correct expansion, but only to which class the utterance belongs; all the other information will either be available in the context or co-text or situationally unimportant — thus there is now a principled explanation for the synonymy in Austin's expansion 'I declare, pronounce, give or call you out'.

Searle argues that there are three major ways in which speech acts can vary:

1. They can differ in the way in which they fit words to the world — he notes that some 'illocutions have as part of their illocutionary point to get the words (or more strictly their propositional content) to match the world, others to get the world to match the words. Assertions are in the former category and requests in the latter'.
2. They can differ in terms of the psychological state they express — here he uses 'believe', 'want' and 'intend' as primitives, arguing that stating or explaining involves 'believing that p', promising involves 'intending that p' and ordering 'wanting that p'.
3. They can differ in terms of point or purpose — this is the most important criterion of the three and corresponds to the *essential* condition in his earlier analysis.

Using these three dimensions, Searle proposes five macro-classes of illocutionary act: representatives, directives, commissives, expressives and declarations. For *representatives*, the point or purpose is to 'commit the speaker to something being the case' — in other words, it is an utterance in which the speaker fits his words to the world and which incorporates his 'BELIEF that p'. The degree of belief can obviously vary between 'swear', 'suggest' and 'hypothesize' and affective features can be incorporated as in 'boast' and 'complain'.

Directives are all attempts by the speaker to get the hearer to do something — in this class the speaker is WANTING to achieve a future situation in which the world will match his words and thus this class includes not simply 'order' and 'request' but, more subtly, 'invite', 'dare' and 'challenge'. *Commissives*, a category taken over intact from Austin, are like directives concerned with altering the world to match the words, but this time the point is to commit the speaker himself to acting and it necessarily involves INTENTION.

The fourth class, *expressives*, is much less well defined — there is no dynamic relationship between words and world and no primitive psychological verb. Instead 'the illocutionary point of this class is to express the psychological state specified in the sincerity condition about a state of affairs specified in the propositional content'. As examples he offers 'thank', 'apologize' and 'deplore'.

The fifth class, *declarations*, consists of acts which in their uttering alter the world and includes many of those which Austin first considered as performatives. They typically require an extra-linguistic institution which provides rules for their use — a court, committee, church, rule book — except for the special case of declarations concerned with language use itself: 'I define, abbreviate, name, call or dub'. Leech (1983, p. 180), however, argues that there are good reasons for regarding most of these as not illocutionary acts at all because 'they are conventional rather than communicative acts: the linguistic parts of ritual'.

Any attempt to apply this classification to spoken texts immediately throws up problems. First, as Willis (1983) points out, at the beginnings and ends of many interactions and at strategic points during them participants produce utterances which are basically *structuring* — should one see 'hello' as a directive requiring a second 'hello' (but in that case how does one categorize the second one), or as an expressive (but expressing what)? Rather, it is a propositionally empty item with a range of alternative realizations marking a beginning. Second, many representatives are acknowledged by the hearer:

A: It's raining again.
B: Yeah.

and in these cases the second utterance appears to function merely as an overt signal of 'uptake'. Third, and most problematically, Searle regards questions as directives but it is difficult to see which words the addressee is being asked to change the world to match — it seems much more insightful to see questions as a separate category which functions interactively to elicit instances of the other four major classes:

a) What time is it?   It's four o'clock.   REP
b) What can I do to help? Open the door.   DIR
c) Can you help us?   I'll give a cake.   COM
d) How do you feel?   I'm so happy.   EXP

It is interesting that Leech (ibid.) in his development of Searle's proposals decided to set up a category of *rogatives* and thus to separate out questioning items from directive ones.

Searle's proposals are obviously a first but very suggestive attempt at classification — Leech, as we have seen, adds one category; Willis (ibid.) proposes three more and suggests more detailed sub-classification at secondary delicacy while Stiles (1981), using a different basis for classification, also proposes a division into eight categories. All these proposals represent a significant step forward as they free speech act analysis from dependence on acts that happen to have been labelled by speakers, and open the way to a more soundly-based contrastive analysis and thus to applications in the field of language teaching and language acquisition.

Indirect speech acts

Searle's classification of illocutionary acts suggests that the problem of interpreting primary performatives may not be as great as had originally been thought, but it certainly doesn't solve the problem. (The discussion at this point is complicated by the fact that different descriptive categories are used — even for Searle (1975) the directive category doesn't include questions, and representatives and commissives are apparently subsumed under statements.) Searle formulates the problem of primary performatives as one of explaining how and when the grammatical moods declarative, interrogative and imperative do *not* realize the macro-functions statement, question and directive. For illustrative purposes we will concentrate on directives:

1. Can you pass the salt?
2. Would you pass the salt?
3. I'd like the salt.
4. You ought to pass her the salt.

Sentences 1–3 are representative of a large set of utterances which Sadock (1974, 1975) has maintained are in fact primary performative versions of 'I request you . . .' — an analysis he justifies by the fact that they can all co-occur with 'please'. Sadock argues that in such cases we are in fact dealing with *idioms*, and thus that the initial interrogative or declarative item should not be broken down but treated unanalysed as one conventional way of conveying a request. Certainly there is some intonational support for this — as we point out on p. 131, in many occurrences of such utterances the initial phrase is marked intonationally as uninformative by being unstressed or *nonprominent* (see pp. 102–4 for an extended discussion of the significance of prominence).

However, there are major problems with an attempt to explain indirectness in terms of idioms. First, it cannot cope with all the data — examples like 4, where the requested action is implied or hinted at, must be explained in other ways. Second, the list of idioms is worryingly long. Third, as Levinson (1983, p. 270) points out, 'idioms are by definition non-compositional and are therefore likely to be idiosyncratic to speech communities . . . however, most of the basic . . . structures translate across languages'. Finally, and as Searle himself points out, most importantly, the addressee can respond to both the surface form and the underlying force:

>   1a. Can you pass the salt? Sure. (*passes the salt*)

These examples are easy to instance and accept, but Searle goes on to generalize, suggesting that 'the man who says "I want you to do this" literally means he wants you to do it'; this leads him to argue that when such sentences are uttered the literal illocutionary act is also performed, and thus he talks of *indirect speech acts*, that is, speech acts performed indirectly through the performance of another speech act.

As supporting evidence for his claim of simultaneous performance, Searle cites speakers' reports of utterances, observing that 'Can you pass the salt' can be reported by an utterance of 'he asked me whether . . .', but this is an unreliable criterion because mothers can frequently be heard complaining 'I've asked you three times to . . .' when they have been heard by all present to use straight imperatives. Also, the following teacher directives don't seem to admit verbal responses easily:

T: How many times have I told you to . . .	P: ? Seven, sir
T: Who's talking now	P: ? Me, sir
T: Can I hear someone whistling	P: ? Yes, sir

The debate continues, but in fact one doesn't need to accept the claim of simultaneous performance to appreciate Searle's analysis of the options available for indirectly directing. He suggests that the possible realizations can be grouped into six categories:

1. Sentences concerning hearer's ability;	Can you pass the salt?
2. Sentences concerning hearer's future action;	Are you going to pass the salt?
3. Sentences concerning speaker's wish or want;	I would like (you to pass) the salt.
4. Sentences concerning hearer's desire or willingness;	Would you mind passing the salt? It might help if you passed the salt.
5. Sentences concerning reasons for action;	I don't think you salted the potatoes.
6. Sentences embedding either one of the above or an explicit performative.	Can I ask you to pass the salt?

Searle observes that the first three types refer to the three felicity conditions on directive illocutionary acts which he proposed in 1969, respectively *preparatory*, concerned with the hearer's ability; *propositional content*, concerned with the futurity of the action; and *sincerity*, concerned with the speaker wanting the hearer to perform the action. He combines groups 4 and 5 arguing, not entirely convincingly, that 'both concern reasons for doing A ... since wanting to do something is a reason par excellence for doing it'. He is then able to show that a speaker can make an indirect directive by:

1. either asking whether or stating that a preparatory condition concerning H's ability to do A obtains;
2. either asking whether or stating that the propositional content condition obtains;
3. stating that the sincerity condition obtains though *not* by asking whether it obtains (interestingly, though, questioning the sincerity condition can function to request the hearer to desist: 'Do you think I enjoy listening to you whistling?').
4. either stating that or asking whether there are good or overriding reasons for doing A, except where the reason is that H.wants or wishes, etc. to do A, in which case he can only ask whether H wants or wishes, etc. to do A.

These generalizations represent a powerful description of the data — they categorize and circumscribe the available ways of producing an indirect directive — but there is no attempt to *explain* why these are the options and the only options, nor how a hearer faced with an utterance like 'Can you pass the salt' sets about deciding whether the speaker intends it as a request or a question. Indeed, Searle admits that the hearer 'needs some way of finding out when the utterance is just a question about his abilities and when it is a request', but observes unhelpfully that 'it is at this point that the general principles of conversation (together with factual background information) come into play'.

It is interesting at this point to compare Searle's description with that proposed from a different perspective by Labov and Fanshel (1977). They begin first by characterizing the prerequisites for an utterance imperative in form to be heard as a valid directive, or in their terms a *request for action*:

If A addresses to B an imperative specifying an action X at a time T_1 and B believes that A believes that

1. a) X should be done for a purpose Y (*need for the action*)
   b) B would not do X in the absence of the request (*need for the request*)
2.   B has the *ability* to do X

3.   B has the *obligation* to do X or is *willing* to do it
4.   A has the *right* to tell B to do X,

then A is heard as making a valid request for action. (p. 78)

Imperative utterances which fail to satisfy one or more of these pre-conditions are, in Austin's terms, infelicitous, and may be variously interpreted as cheeky, insulting, joking or simply irrelevant.

The rule so far only covers those utterances in which there is a close fit between intended function and formal realization, that is imperative directives; but as Labov and Fanshel observe, these are the minority of cases. They therefore offer a rule for *indirect requests*:

If A makes to B a *request for information* or an *assertion* about
a) the existential status of an action X to be performed by B
b) the consequences of performing an action X
c) the time T₁ that an action X might be performed by B
d) any of the pre-conditions for a valid request for X as given in the Rule for Requests
and all other pre-conditions are in effect, then A is heard as making a valid request of B for the action X. (p. 82)

They cite as an example an utterance from a therapy session, 'well-youknow, w'dy'mind takin' thedustrag an' just dustaround?', and explain that this is interpreted as an indirect request through being recognized as a request for information about the third pre-condition for valid requests, B's willingness. They go on to observe that although they are in the main concerned with 'the text as it actually occurs' their discourse rules represent 'a general grammar of possible speech actions and possible ways of executing them'. Thus while the indirect request to 'dustaround' actually occurred in the form quoted above, there are many alternative ways in which it could have been realized by questioning or asserting other pre-conditions:

a) *Existential status*	Have you dusted yet?
	You don't seem to have dusted this room yet.
b) *Consequences*	How would it look if you were to dust this room?
	This room would look a lot better if you dusted it.
c) *Time referents*	When do you plan to dust?
	I imagine you will be dusting this evening.
d) *Pre-conditions*	
1a. need for the action:	Don't you think the dust is pretty thick?
	This place really is dusty.
1b. need for the request:	Are you planning to dust this room?
	I don't have to remind you to dust this room.

2. ability:	Can you grab a dust rag and just dust around? You have time enough to dust before you go.
3a. willingness:	Would you mind picking up a dust rag? I'm sure you wouldn't mind picking up a dust rag and just dusting around.
3b. obligation:	Isn't it your turn to dust? You ought to do your part in keeping this place clean.
4. rights:	Didn't you ask me to remind you to dust this place? I'm supposed to look after this place, but not do all the work. (p. 83)

Obviously the examples above are just a few of the large number of indirect formulations of this particular request: as Labov and Fanshel observe, there is an 'unlimited number of ways in which we can refer to the pre-conditions and this poses a serious problem if we want to make firm connections between these discourse rules and actual sentence production' (p. 84). Of course, a given indirect request can be made in an 'unlimited number of ways' only if it is considered in isolation; in reality, the constraints of the preceding discourse, the current topic, the facts of the situation and the current speaker's intentions for the progress of the succeeding discourse will all reduce the choice enormously.

The situation is not quite as simple as Labov and Fanshel suggest — the following is a counter-example to their claim that in producing an utterance following their rules, 'A will be heard as making a valid request of B':

c: Malcolm, can you open this for me.
m: I don't know.
c: No, I was making a request.

In fact, the Labov and Fanshel analysis has the same problem as Searle's: both need, as Levinson (ibid.) points out, an associated inference theory to explain how a listener comes to reject the direct interpretation and select the indirect one — the most convincing proposals are those of Grice (1975).

Conversational maxims

As Garfinkel (1967) observed, it is never possible to say what one means in 'so many words' — speakers require hearers to 'work' to a greater or lesser extent to derive their message from the words uttered. Grice (1975) offers an unremarkable example:

Suppose that A and B are talking about a mutual friend, C, who is now working in a bank. A asks B how C is getting on in his job and B replies *Oh quite well, I think; he likes his colleagues, and he hasn't been to prison yet.*

Grice observes that in addition to what B has said he has *implicated* something else — he has provided information from which A can deduce extra information.

In setting out to explore this phenomenon of *conversational implicature* Grice suggests that conversationalists are oriented to and by an over-arching *co-operative principle*:

Make your conversational contribution such as is required, at the stage at which it occurs, by the accepted purpose or direction of the talk exchange in which you are engaged.

This principle implies decisions in four major areas, *relation, quality, quantity* and *manner*, and their significance is spelled out by *maxims*:

1. relation   be relevant

2. quality   a) do not say what you believe to be false
              b) do not say that for which you lack adequate evidence

3. quantity   a) make your contribution as informative as is required (for the current purposes of the exchange)
              b) do not make your contribution more informative than is required

4. manner   a) avoid obscurity of expression
              b) avoid ambiguity
              c) be brief
              d) be orderly

It is important to realize that these maxims do not represent a descriptive statement of how conversational contributions are: firstly, there will always be occasions when a speaker decides to 'quietly and unostentatiously VIOLATE a maxim' — he may lie, he may not give as much of the relevant information as he could, or he may, like the Delphic oracle, offer utterances which are only later seen to be ambiguous; secondly, and much more importantly, there will be occasions when a speaker is seen to break a maxim either because he has been faced with a CLASH between two maxims making it impossible, for instance, for him to be as specific as he ought to be and still to say nothing for which he lacks adequate evidence, or because he has chosen to FLOUT a maxim, 'that is to say he may blatantly fail to fulfil it'. In such instances the conversational maxims provide a basis for the listener to *infer* what is being conversationally *implicated*.

Grice exemplifies the process with reference to his example about C not having been to prison yet:

> in a suitable setting A might reason as follows: 1. B has apparently violated the maxim 'Be relevant' and so may be regarded as having flouted one of the maxims conjoining perspicuity, yet I have no reason to suppose that he is opting out from the operation of the CP; 2. given the circumstances I can regard his irrelevance as only apparent if and only if I suppose him to think that C is potentially dishonest; 3. B knows that I am capable of working out step (2). So B implicates that C is potentially dishonest.

Thus what is being claimed is a two-stage process — firstly recognition of the apparent irrelevance, inadequacy or inappropriateness of the utterance, which secondly 'triggers' (Levinson 1983) the subsequent inferencing.

This theory obviously supplements the descriptions proposed by Searle and by Labov and Fanshel and allows for occasions when the trigger fails and the listener takes the utterance at its face value, but it still has two crucial weaknesses. Firstly, there is no attempt to explain why a speaker might choose one form of flouting rather than another, given that there is an infinite set of possibilities though Brown and Levinson (1978) and Leech (1983) make interesting attempts to explain some of the selections in terms of extra maxims concerned with politeness; secondly, and more worryingly, although Grice is centrally concerned with hearers' inferencing, his examples are always *explanations* of one interpretation rather than a discussion of how an utterance with a series of potential implicatures comes to have in the context only one. As Sadock observes:

> the Co-operative Principle has been very believably invoked, e.g. by Searle (1975), to account for the fact that an utterance of 'it's cold in here' can convey a request to close a door. But it can also convey a request to open a door or to bring a blanket or to pay a gas bill. In fact it is difficult to think of a request that the utterance could NOT convey in the right context.

Thus we are left with the conviction that only a theory of inference can cope with the way in which speakers derive meaning from indirect utterances, but also with the knowledge that Grice has only taken a first step towards the solution.

3 The ethnography of speaking

Chomsky set the goal of linguistic theory as the description of the ideal speaker-hearer's competence, his knowledge of *grammaticality*, or whether or not putative sentences are part of his language. In emphasizing a concern with the grammatical rather than the appropriate, Chomsky was willing to demonstrate simply the grammatical relationships between 'he hit me', 'it was me that he hit', 'it was him that hit me', without attempting to explain why one and not another might be appropriate to a particular situation. Hymes (1971) argues that Chomsky's definition of competence is too narrow — linguistics ought to concern itself with *communicative* competence, the speaker's ability to produce appropriate utterances not grammatical sentences.

He suggests that 'an adequate approach must distinguish and investigate four aspects of competence: *systematic potential*; *appropriateness*; *occurrence*; *feasibility*'. By *systematic potential* he refers to 'whether and to what extent something is not yet realized' and suggests that 'it is to this that Chomsky in effect reduces competence'. *Appropriateness* includes 'whether and to what extent something is in some context suitable, effective or the like'. These two features can vary independently: schizophrenic's talk is often marked by grammatical but inappropriate utterances, as in this example already quoted from Labov (1970),

A: What is your name?
B: Well, let's say you might have thought you had something from before, but you haven't got it any more.
A: I'm going to call you Dean.

while Albert (1972) reports that among the Burundi appropriate but ungrammatical utterances occur frequently in certain situations — differences in rank require a peasant-farmer to make 'a rhetorical fool of himself' when his adversary is a prince or herder although at other times he 'may show himself an able speaker'.

A speaker's competence also includes knowledge about *occurrence*, 'whether and to what extent something is done'. This theoretical dimension provides for the fact that members of a speech community 'are aware of the commonness, rarity, previous occurrence or novelty of many features of speech, and that this knowledge enters into their definitions and evaluations of ways of speaking'. The final dimension *feasibility* is concerned with 'whether and to what extent something is possible'. Hymes (1972a) refers to the experience of J. R. Fox working among the Cochiti of New Mexico, who was unable to elicit the first person singular possessive form of 'wings' on the grounds that the speaker, not being a bird, could not say 'my wings' — 'only to become the first person able to say it in Cochiti, on the grounds that "your name is Robin"'.

Any utterance, or extended piece of discourse, can be described in terms of these four dimensions. Thus Hymes suggests that Leontes' speech in Act II of *The Winter's Tale* is ungrammatical, appropriate, individual and difficult, while the bumbling speech of the Burundi peasants is ungrammatical, appropriate, common and awkward. Even if the scope of linguistics were expanded to cover these four aspects of competence Hymes feels it would still be too narrow and in his dissatisfaction feels the need to propose 'a second descriptive science of language', the *ethnography of speaking*, concerned not simply with language structure, but with language use, with 'rules of speaking . . . the ways in which speakers associate particular modes of speaking, topics, or message forms, with particular settings and activities' (1972a). Any description of 'ways of speaking' will need to provide data along four interrelated dimensions:

1. the linguistic resources available to a speaker — how many different styles he can choose from;
2. supra-sentential structuring — how many differently structured linguistic events, like trials, religious ceremonies, debates, songs, are recognized;
3. the rules of interpretation by which a given set of linguistic items comes to have a given communicative value;
4. the norms which govern different types of interaction.

Obviously, any attempt to produce a description in these terms would be an enormous and perhaps impossible undertaking, and thus all the work so far attempted within this framework is necessarily partial.

The speech community

The initial task is to delimit the group of speakers for whom one is going to produce 'rules of speaking'. Hymes (1972a) stresses that it is not adequate to define a group as all those who have access to a particular language or dialect; he argues that it is possible for speakers to share formal linguistic features, phonology, grammar, lexis, but still to be unable to interpret accurately each other's messages. For example, Labov (1972a), in a discussion of aspects of language use among adolescent New York negroes, presents utterances like 'your momma's a peanut man', or 'your mother's a duck', which are superficially intelligible but whose real significance as *ritual insults* is not available to most English speakers.

Speakers who apparently share the same language may also have different 'norms as to greetings, acceptable topics, what is said next in a conversation', how speaking turns are distributed and so on. For example, Sacks, Schegloff and Jefferson (1974) suggest that for American English there is a conversational rule that only one speaker speaks at a time, whereas Reisman (1974) observes that in Antigua 'the start of a new voice is not in itself a signal for the voice speaking to stop or to institute a process which will decide who is to have the floor'. Any group which shares both linguistic resources and rules for interaction and interpretation is defined as a *speech community* and it is on such groups that ethnographers of speaking concentrate.

Although the limiting criterion of a speech community is the sharing of one linguistic variety, most communities have several between which they switch. Blom and Gumperz (1972) report an investigation in the Norwegian village of Hemnesberget where all the residents speak both the standard language, Bokmål, and the local dialect Ranamål. Bokmål is the language of formal education, official transactions, religion and the mass media, but the local dialect still enjoys great prestige, and by 'identifying himself as a dialect speaker both at home and abroad, a member symbolizes his pride in his community'. In any interaction speakers have a choice of two varieties; Blom and Gumperz were interested in the factors which influenced the use of one rather than the other. After close observation and analysis of tape recordings of free speech they concluded that locals would typically use local dialect except in situations 'defined with respect to the superimposed national Norwegian system'. Even then, in the community administration office, where the standard language prevailed, clerks were observed to switch depending on topic and, 'when residents step up to a clerk's desk, greetings and inquiries about family affairs tend to be exchanged in the dialect, while the business part of the transaction is carried on in the standard'. In other words, it appeared that topic could only cause speakers to switch *from* standard *to* dialect — whereas in a standard language situation talk about family affairs might be conducted in dialect, in a gathering of friends and kin speakers would *never* switch to the standard language, even if the topic were national or official matters.

To test their hypothesis Blom and Gumperz arranged to tape-record the conversation of two groups of local residents, both self-recruited and consisting of close friends and relatives. On both occasions the investigators first stimulated discussion among the group and then as the conversation progressed interjected questions and comments feeling that the greater the range of topics the greater the chance of a switch to the standard language. In fact, as predicted, 'in several hours of conversation . . . marked by many changes in topic, [they] found a number of lexical borrowings but not a clear instance of phonological or grammatical switching'.

At this point it would seem possible to write rules for the speech community of Hemnesberget to predict the choice of one or other speech variety for one type of speech event, conversation. However, Blom and Gumperz recorded conversations among two more groups, one composed of members of a formerly active peer group who had spent the past few years away at university, returning only in the summer, the other comprising three speakers from families who tended to dissociate themselves from the local community. The students claimed to be pure dialect speakers, but for them topic *was* a significant variable: non-local topics evoked 'a tendency to switch towards standard phonology while preserving some morphophonemic and lexical' features of the dialect. For the other group the local dialect was only used for local anecdotes, humour, and attempts to provide local colour and the standard language was the normal speech style. Thus, what appeared to be one speech community sharing two dialects was now seen disturbingly to be three, distinguished by different selection rules.

Dorian (1982) raises a different question about membership of a speech community — what is the status of semi-speakers or near-passive bilinguals? In the community she investigated, whereas they said very little and produced grammatically deviant utterances, they were culturally fluent: 'unlike the linguist-guest [they] were never unintentionally rude. They knew when it was appropriate to speak and when not; when a question would show interest and when it would constitute an interruption; when an offer of food was mere verbal routine . . .' Hymes (1982a) appears to accept that such are members of the speech community and thus to go along with Corder's (1973) definition of a speech community which Dorian quotes: 'people who *regard themselves* as speaking the same language' (p. 53).

Labov (1972a) argues for a different definition;

the speech community is not defined by any marked agreement in the use
of language elements so much as by participation in a set of shared norms;
these norms may be observed in overt types of evaluative behaviour and by
the uniformity of abstract patterns of variation which are invariant in respect
to particular levels of usage. (pp. 120–1)

This then allows him to see the whole of New York City's population
as a single speech community because they react in similar ways to
phonological variation despite the acknowledged major differences in
grammatical usage and norms of interpretation which he highlights
elsewhere (1969, 1972b).

As these three examples make clear, the speech community, though
a very useful and powerful concept, is an idealization: in fact speakers
do not fall neatly into categories, but just as we can say very useful
things about languages and dialects even though isoglosses don't fall
neatly one on top of another, so we can make useful generalizations
about language use in speech communities, and just as some linguists
have restricted themselves to statements about their own idiolects, so
some ethnographer of speaking may eventually produce detailed rules
for two-member speech communities.

Speech styles

Any ethnography of speaking must describe the linguistic options
open to the speech community. As we have seen, the residents of
Hemnesberget had a choice of two major varieties, the local dialect
and the standard language. Ferguson (1959) suggests that speakers
of Swiss German, Arabic, Greek and Tamil are faced with a similar
choice, this time between two standard languages — a *high* form typically used in sermons, speeches, lectures, news broadcasts, and a *low*
variety used in conversations, political and academic discussion, 'folk'
literature. By contrast Americans, according to Joos (1967), have a
choice not between major varieties but between five different degrees
of formality within the one standard language; Labov (1968) provides
supporting evidence, from the differential occurrence of post-vocalic
/r/, of four degrees of formality.

Geertz (1968) reports that Javanese has three major styles which,
unlike those suggested by Joos and Labov for English, are recognized
and named by speakers of the language — 'krama', 'madya', and
'ngoke', high, mid and low. These styles share some linguistic features
with other levels, but also have unique lexical items and grammatical
constructions. In addition there is a set of 'honorifics', mostly referring
to 'people, their parts, possessions and actions', which occur inde-

TABLE 3.1

Level	are	you	going	to eat	rice	and	cassava	now	Complete sentence
3a	menapa	pandjenengan	badé	dahar	sekul	kalijan		samenika	*Menapa pandjenengan badé dahar sekul kalijan kaspé samenika?*
3	menapa	sampéjan	badé	neda	sekul	kalijan	kaspé	samenika	*Menapa sampéjan badé neda sekul kalijan kaspé samenika?*
2	napa	sampéjan	adjeng	neda	sega	lan	kaspé	saniki	*Napa sampéjan adjeng neda sekul lan kaspé saniki?*
1a	apa	sampéjan	arep	neda	sega	lan		saiki	*Apa sampéjan arep neda sega lan kaspé saiki?*
1	apa	kowé	arep	mangan	sega	lan	kaspé	saiki	*Apa kowé arep mangan sega lan kaspé saiki?*

(Geertz 1968, p. 284)

pendently of the first style-defining set of choices and raise the style 'half a notch'. These honorifics can only occur with the low and high styles, at least in the usage of the educated townsman, who thus has five recognizably distinct varieties to choose between. Thus the question 'are you going to eat rice and cassava now?' could have any of the five realizations on page 38 depending on the context and relative status and familiarity of the interlocutor — a townsman would use low with a friend, mid with a non-intimate and high to a high official from whom he would in turn receive low.

Halliday, McIntosh and Strevens (1964) suggest that it is possible to make much finer distinctions than this and argue that a speaker's linguistic repertoire consists of a large number of varieties, or *registers*, distinguished according to use. This is an intuitively attractive concept, for speech communities within the same language area could then be distinguished by the range of registers they had available, but registers prove difficult to isolate and define. Halliday *et al.* observe that a sports commentary, a church service and a school lesson are 'obviously linguistically distinct', and suggest that there is a register appropriate to each. This raises the question of how different registers can be recognized and isolated and they suggest that while there will be grammatical differences the major distinctions between registers will be lexical. However, the claim that

> some lexical items suffice almost by themselves to identify a certain register: 'cleanse' puts us in the language of advertising, 'probe' of newspapers, especially headlines, 'tablespoonful' of recipes or prescriptions, 'neckline' of fashion reporting or dressmaking instructions,

is worryingly naive. In fact there are no restrictions on the concept: a register can apparently vary in size and importance from that of dressmaking to that of scientific English (Huddleston *et al.* 1968); and registers are circularly defined: the language used in dressmaking patterns is the register of dressmaking and the register of dressmaking is that used in dressmaking patterns.

Hymes (1974) suggests that it is more useful to see a speech community as comprising a set of *styles*, where style is used in the neutral sense of 'a way or mode of doing something'. Whereas style has often been used as a concept to account for variation according to author, setting or topic it has never been used as the general basis of description. This, Hymes suggests, is now possible if one exploits the long recognized fact that a linguistic item can be described along two axes, vertical and horizontal, *paradigmatic* and *syntagmatic*, or choice and chain. For example, for the noun group 'the dog', one of the things a description must do is account for the other items which could occur as paradigmatic choices instead of 'the'; the other thing a description must do is to characterize the set of items which can occur following 'the'.

Drawing on Ervin-Tripp (1972) Hymes suggests that the concept of syntagmatic relations can be generalized to handle the *co-occurrence* of items over larger stretches and this will allow one to 'characterize whatever features go together to identify a style of speech in terms of the rules of co-occurrence among them'. The concept of paradigmatic choice can be similarly generalized to one of *alternation* to cope with the choice between styles.

The concept of style may seem very close to that of register but there is a crucial difference: registers are mainly defined and recognized by topic and context-specific lexis — the register of sermons is the language used in giving sermons; styles, however, as the rules of alternation emphasize, are not mechanically connected to particular situations — speakers may choose among styles and their choices have *social meaning*. One of the most reliable ways of making people laugh is to adopt a style inappropriate to a particular context or message.

It is of course one thing to define a style as a set of co-occurring choices; it is another to isolate different styles. As Hymes observes, 'the relevant speech styles of a community cannot be arrived at mechanically, for one could note an infinite number of differences and putative co-occurrences'. The aim, therefore, is to isolate *significant speech styles*, that is ones that speakers can distinguish and use.

Hymes accepts that some stylistic features may be present in a piece of discourse without defining a significant style; their presence may simply convey a 'tinge or character', but not be an organizing principle and this is close to the everyday definition of style. However, Hymes recognizes two kinds of groupings of stylistic features which do constitute organized use — those which colour or accompany the rest of what is done, *stylistic modes*, and those which can be said to define recurrent forms, *stylistic structures*. A principal aspect of *stylistic modes* is a set of modifications entailed in consistent use of the voice in a certain way, as in singing, intoning, chanting, declaiming. As an example of the importance of mode Hymes refers to the basic distinction among the Wolof of Senegal between 'restrained' and 'unrestrained' speech, distinguished principally by paralinguistic features; restrained speech being characterized as low pitched, breathy, slow, soft with final pitch nucleus, unrestrained as high pitched, clear, fast, loud with initial pitch nucleus.

Stylistic structures, as the name implies, are verbal forms organized in terms of defining principles of development or recurrence. One kind of structure is the organization of sentences and utterances into larger units such as 'greetings', 'farewells', 'prayers'; the other is the systematic exploitation of arbitrary linguistic features which Sinclair (1971) calls *latent patterning* — at the rank of word poets frequently use such features as initial consonant, final syllable, positioning of stress to add an extra layer of patterning which we recognize as alliteration, rhyme and metre respectively. Repetitions at regular intervals of these patterns create structures we call verse forms.

Hymes calls these structures *elementary* or *minimal genres*, and observes that both kinds of groupings of features, modes and structures, enter into more complex groupings called *complex genres*. A church service would be an example of a complex genre, containing the elementary genres of 'hymn', 'psalm', 'prayer' and 'sermon', and evidencing the stylistic modes of singing, chanting and perhaps declaiming.

The work of Bricker (1974) on Mayan provides a useful exemplification of Hymes' concept of style. She notes an initial division into formal and informal genres, the formal comprising 'myth', 'prayer', 'song', 'contemplation', 'planning', 'war', 'argument', and 'frivolous talk', the informal three other types of 'frivolous talk', 'gossip' and 'discussion'. All the formal genres 'are structurally alike: they are expressed as semantic couplets'; the informal genres have no common structure, but specifically avoid couplets. The following prayer illustrates the couplet structure,

> Well grandfather,
> Lord:
>
> How long have you been waiting here for my earth?
> How long have you been waiting here for my mud?
>
> I am gathering together here;
> I am meeting here.
>
> I see the house of poverty;
> I see the house of wealth
>
> Of His Labourer,
> Of His tribute-payer.
>
> Holy Esquipulas, thou art my father;
> Thou art my mother.

Obviously the organizing principle is the highly marked semantic and syntactic parallelism. These couplets happen to be from a prayer but apparently could just as easily come from a song, for songs closely resemble prayers in their context, content and function — the crucial distinction is in the stylistic mode, 'prayers are simply recited, while songs are sung to a musical accompaniment'. Naturally some genres will have a more rigid and overt structure than others — indeed until recently many considered that conversation had no identifiable structure at all. Hymes suggests that for conversation the distinctive modes and structures are simply more difficult to identify, and the work of Sacks, Schegloff and Jefferson, described in detail in Chapter 4, provides growing evidence of a high degree of structuring in conversation.

Speech events

Hymes stresses that it is essential to distinguish a *genre*, which is a unique combination of stylistic structure and mode, from the 'doing' of a genre. In order to emphasize the distinction between genre and performance, a distinction frequently obscured by users of a language, who often employ the same label for both, Hymes suggests the categories of *speech event* and *speech act* to parallel complex and elementary genres. All genres have contexts or situations to which they are fitted and in which they are typically found. Some genres, like 'conversation', can occur appropriately in a wide range of situations, some, like 'prayer', are highly restricted; however, it is a defining criterion of a genre that it is a recognizable style and therefore can be used in inappropriate situations. The cultural implications of an inappropriate use of a particular genre like prayer may of course differ; in one culture the result may be laughter, in another death.

Speech events occur in a non-verbal context, the speech *situation*, which may or may not affect the choice of genre and 'it is for speech events and speech acts that one writes formal rules for their occurrence and characteristics'. Speech events are the largest units for which one can discover linguistic structure and are not necessarily coterminous with the situation; several speech events can occur successively or even simultaneously in the same situation, as for instance with distinct conversations at a party. The relationship between speech events and speech acts is hierarchical; 'an event may consist of a single speech act, but will often comprise several'.

One ultimate aim of the ethnography of speaking is an exhaustive list of the speech acts and speech events of a particular speech community, though the descriptive framework is currently 'heuristic' and 'quite preliminary'. However, any researcher attempting a description in these terms faces several major problems. Firstly, unlike Austin and

Searle, Hymes doesn't offer a list of speech acts, even for English, although 'request', 'command', 'statement' and 'joke' are used informally as examples. Even Hymes (1982b), reporting on a study of classroom interaction and admitting that 'a general theory of speech acts would appear to be central' (p. 32), does no more than discuss critically more recent formulations of Searle (1976) and Dore (1979). In the absence of any clear direction those working within the framework of the Ethnography of Speaking appear to develop their own categories ad hoc. Saville-Troike (1982, p. 146) quotes a student dissertation which analyses the opening of Japanese door-to-door sales encounters as a sequence of six acts: 'greeting'-'acknowledgement'-'identification'-'question about purpose'-'information about purpose'-'expression of disinterest/interest'.

A second linked problem is that Hymes, although warning that acts are not 'identifiable with any single portion of other levels of grammar', does not discuss how acts are related to the lexis and grammar which realize them; thus, when Saville-Troike reports another study in which an event opens with the sequence 'greeting'-'acceptance of greeting' (p. 156) the reader does not know whether this is equivalent to 'greeting'-'acknowledgement' or significantly different. In other words, unless one knows the set of analytic categories and how they relate to the data one is in fact creating the 'illusion of classification' (Sinclair 1973). However, to be fair, no one else has proposed a non-contentious list of acts, though Chapters 2, 4 and 6 discuss partial solutions from different perspectives.

A third difficulty arises from the fact that whereas other descriptions have at least three units of analysis, Hymes proposes only two and this places great strain on *act*. There is a massive consensus among researchers that some kinds of event contain utterances which typically occur in pairs with the first constraining the occurrence of the second, but although Hymes gives 'greeting' as an example of a speech act he has no way of showing that greetings typically consist of two paired utterances — indeed it is not at all clear whether he would regard the two utterances as a composite realization of the act 'greeting' or whether each utterance itself is an act.

Components of speech events

So far the discussion of speech acts and speech events has concentrated on stylistic mode and structure and for many acts and events these are the defining criteria — a song is a song whoever sings it; at least in our culture. However, some genres are performed for specific purposes in specified places with particular participants. An Anglican baptism traditionally takes place beside the font with seven essential participants — the parson, the unbaptized baby, the parents and three godparents — and the definition and description of the speech event requires participants and situation, as well as style, to be specified.

In fact, Hymes recommends that for every speech event the ethnographer initially provides data on *structure, setting, participants, purposes, key, topic, channel* (spoken, written, whistled, drummed) and *message form*, so that knowing the possible parameters one can check whether an apparently irrelevant one is in fact irrelevant. Hymes reports that Arewa and Dundes (1964), investigating the uses of language among the Yoruba, observed that proverbs were used only by adults and were always spoken, but pressing the point discovered they could also be drummed, though in a slightly altered form, and used by children as part of a formulaic apology. In other words, by being aware of the *possible* parameters the ethnographer can more easily and successfully discover the constraints on the performance of genres, and the defining criteria of particular speech events.

Setting

All speech events occur of necessity in time and space — sometimes it is one of the defining criteria of an event that it occurs at a specific time or in a specific place. Foster (1974) describes a series of fifteen agricultural festivals which the Iroquois celebrate at appropriate points during the year. At two of the festivals two speech events concerned with asking the Creator for successful crops occur, the Tobacco Invocation and the Skin Dance, while at the other thirteen, the major speech event is the Thanksgiving Address. Salmond (1974), by contrast, reports a speech event among the Maori, the Encounter Ritual, which can occur at any time but only in a 'marae', a complex consisting of a carved meeting house and a courtyard for orators. Closer to home we also have speech events tied to a particular time — special church services for Easter, or the Queen's Christmas message; or to a particular place — there is a very restricted number of places where marriages can be solemnized or litigation occur. Even when a speech event is not restricted to a particular setting, the setting may affect either the stylistic mode — people tend to speak in hushed tones in church; or the stylistic structure — Geertz reports that the Javanese 'would be likely to use a higher level to the same individual at a wedding than in the street'.

Hymes stresses that the ethnographer must also take note of the *psychological* setting of an event — the cultural definition of an occasion as formal or informal, serious or festive. Frake (1972) compares litigation among the Subanun and the Yakan. For both litigation is 'an integral speech event concerned with settling disputes by means of a ruling formulated by neutral judges'; the major difference is not in the event itself but in its place in the overall structure of the culture. The Subanun divide activities sharply into festive and non-festive; litigation is festive behaviour and often accompanied by eating, drinking and merrymaking. The festive nature of the occasion conditions the choice of style — both litigants and judges employ esoteric legal language, often arranged into verse form and sung to the tunes of drinking songs. Yakan litigation on the other hand occurs in a very informal atmosphere and the process is initially indistinguishable from 'a group of people talking together'. The underlying structure of both speech events is very similar, but the psychological setting and resulting style very different.

Participants
Traditionally speech has been described in terms of two participants, a speaker who transmits a message and a listener who receives it. However, while in the majority of situations the person who is speaking is also the addressor or the author of the 'sentiments that are being expressed and the words in which they are encoded' (Goffman 1979), the labels 'spokesman' and 'porta voz' witness that there are times when *speakers* act as mouthpieces for others. Similarly, although there are no parallel labels like 'listenman' or 'porta ouvido', reports like 'the Soviet ambassador was summoned to the Foreign Office to hear the views of . . . . .' recognize the role.

For this reason Hymes argues that there are at least four participant roles, *addressor, speaker, addressee* and *hearer* or *audience*, and that while conversation may require only an addressor and an addressee, other speech acts require different configurations. Labov (1972a) reports that ritual insults require three participant roles, one being an audience whose function is to evaluate each contribution. When one considers the necessary participants for a whole speech event the situation is often more complex. Sherzer (1974) describes a speech event among the Cuna called 'chanting' in which two chiefs perform a ritualized interaction in front of an audience — one chief chants, and at the end of each verse the other responds 'thus, it is so'. The responder is essential; a chief cannot chant on his own. Then, when the chanting is over a third participant, the chief's spokesman, addresses the audience directly and interprets for them.

There are some speech events which have only one human participant — for instance in our culture some forms of prayer. Sherzer
(ibid.) describes disease-curing events among the Cuna where the
participants are the curer and a group of wooden dolls, 'stick babies',
which are considered to carry out the actual business of curing once
they have been told, as addressees, what to do. Hymes points out that
non-humans can also be taken as addressors, citing an occasion when
following a clap of thunder an old Indian asked his wife if she had
heard what the thunder had said.

Any comprehensive description of a speech community must include data on who and what can fill the participant roles, and in what
speech events and speech acts. Some speech events simply require
that certain participant roles be filled — anyone can act as audience
to a play or ritual insult; other events require participants of a particular age, sex, kinship relation, status, role or profession — only
Cuna chiefs can chant; initiation or puberty rites are almost invariably
sex specific; while in most Maori tribes only male elders can deliver
speeches on the 'marae'. In other events turns to speak are regulated
by relations between particular participants — Albert (1972) reports
that among the Burundi turns to contribute to a debate are strictly
controlled by relative status, with the most important speaking first,
the least important last; while the Wolof have a rule that in greetings
the lower status speaker begins first (Irvine 1974).

What has been said so far may have implied that assigning the roles
addressor, speaker, addressee, hearer, audience to participants is unproblematic; this would be a mistake. Two major problems arise:
firstly, there are many situations in which participants change roles
frequently and rapidly; and secondly, the definitions of the roles are
not entirely clear. For instance, must a spokesman be selected or del-
egated to express sentiments that are not his own, or can he select
himself: there are radio interviews when the interviewer reads questions sent in by listeners, evidently acting as a spokesman, but then
he may ask supplementary questions — is he still in the role of spokesman? A lecturer may give a lecture about Marx with extensive readings
from the works — is he a spokesman during the whole of the lecture,
during the parts when he is directly quoting, or is he, because he is
teaching about Marx rather than teaching Marx, in fact an addressor
in his own right? Again, if a lecturer chooses to read a pre-prepared
text is he in fact a spokesman for himself as addressor — because the
same text could be read, if he were ill, by someone else — and if he
makes impromptu glosses on his own text does he then revert to
being an addressor because, interestingly, spokesmen and readers

of other people's lectures can't interpret, they can only convey the information in the text.

The problems with addressee and hearer/audience are even more complex. As Goffman (ibid.) points out, in any conversation between more than two participants there will be times when not all the 'ratified hearers' are being directly addressed and the movement in and out of the addressee role can be rapid and short term. One can also differentiate between speech events according to whether the ratified hearers have the option to switch into the addressor role — there are certain events in which they don't, when they are generally regarded by native speakers as an 'audience', but in fact there are two kinds of audience, which the label obscures — one which is directly addressed and another which in some sense overhears, this being one of the features which distinguishes a lecture from a play. But then again, actors can 'break frame', as at the end of *Murder in the Cathedral*, and address the audience directly. Yet again there are pseudo-addressees — in a political interview the politician can treat his interviewer as hearer and address the voters directly, at times even attempting to make eye-contact with them. (The whole question of the role of eye-contact and other non-verbal signals in participant role definition is a fascinating one and is treated at some length in Gosling (in preparation).)

For completeness Goffman argues for the recognition of 'by-standers', unratified hearers who nevertheless hear, and he subdivides them into 'overhearers', who acknowledge they are listening in, and 'eavesdroppers', who don't. The transition from eavesdropper through overhearer to ratified participant is one we are all familiar with, particularly at parties: 'I couldn't help (over)hearing what you were just saying . . .'

Purpose

All speech events and speech acts have a *purpose*, even if occasionally it is only phatic. Sometimes several events share the same style and are distinguished only by purpose and participants or setting. Hymes notes that among the Wai Wai of Venezuela the same genre, the 'oho chant', is used for a series of speech events which are distinguished according to their function in marriage contracts, trade, communal work tasks and invitations to feasts.

Frake (1972) reports four speech events among the Yakan, distinguished by purpose — *mitin* 'discussion', *qisum* 'conference', *mawpakkat* 'registration', and *hukum* 'litigation'. Initially, to the outsider there is no difference — no special setting, clothes or paraphernalia, no activity other than talk. *Mitin* is the most general and apparently refers to unfocused, purposeless conversation in which all participants have equal speaking rights. *Qisum* is a discussion with a purpose; some issue such as when to plant rice has to be decided and again all participants have equal speaking rights, but this time the event has a recognizable end when a decision is reached. *Mawpakkat* is a negotiation over a disagreement; its purpose is to reach a settlement, and now the participants are divided into two protagonistic sides. Finally, *hukum* is concerned with a disagreement arising over an offence; the purpose is to reach a legal ruling based on precedent and this requires additionally a court comprising a set of neutral judges.

Hymes observes that 'the purpose of an event from a community standpoint may not be identical to the purposes of those engaged in it'. At every level of language individuals can exploit the system for personal or social reasons or artistic effects. Irvine (1974) describes a speech event among the Wolof, the 'greeting', which 'is a necessary opening to every encounter, and can in fact be used as a definition of when an encounter occurs'. Relative rank determines who greets whom — it is customary for the lower ranking party to greet the higher and there is a proverb 'when two persons greet each other, one has shame, the other has glory'. However, individuals do not always wish to take the higher status position because along with prestige goes the obligation to contribute to the support of low status persons. For this reason a higher status person may indulge in 'self-lowering' by adopting the opening role, and Irvine observes that no one ever asked her for a gift if they had not first managed to take the lower status role in the interaction.

Key

Within *key* Hymes handles the 'tone, manner or spirit' in which an act or event is performed. He suggests that acts otherwise identical in setting, participants, message, form, etc., may differ in key as between mock and serious, perfunctory and painstaking. Sacks has observed that the first question one must ask of any utterance is whether it is intended seriously and Hymes emphasizes the significance of key by observing that when it is in conflict with the overt content of an act, it often over-rides it. Thus 'how marvellous' uttered with a 'sarcastic' tone is taken to mean the exact opposite.

The signalling of key may be non-verbal, by wink, smile, gesture or posture, but may equally well be achieved by conventional units of speech like the aspiration and vowel length used to signal emphasis in English. The Wolof greeting discussed above has paralinguistic features associated with each role classifiable on the dimensions of 'stress' and 'tempo/quantity':

	Stress	*Tempo/Quantity*
Noble	s (− high, − loud)	t (− rapid, − verbose)
Griot	S (+ high, + loud)	T (+ rapid, + verbose)

Thus the opening greeting normally has the associated paralinguistic features ST, the response st. However, if a speaker wishes to indicate that the status assigned by his role is at variance with his true status he does this by using an inappropriate stress pattern — a speech style sT will sometimes be used by a noble who has taken the role of initiator but wants to indicate that (he knows) he is being polite. He is showing deference (initiator role and T) even though he doesn't have to (s).

Channels

Under *channel* the description concerns itself with the 'choice of oral, written, telegraphic, semaphore, or other mediums of transmission of speech'. Most genres are associated with only one channel and an attempt to use a different channel, as in the case of the drumming of Yoruba proverbs, necessitates some changes. The development of radio and television has created a situation in which some speech events have enormous unseen and unheard audiences, which subtly affect the character of the event. What is superficially a round-table discussion or a cosy fireside chat can in fact be an opportunity to attempt, indirectly, to sway a nation's opinions. The channel itself has even allowed the creation of new speech events, the sports commentary and the quiz show, with their own highly distinctive stylistic mode and structure, prescribed participants, typical setting and key.

Message content

Hymes suggests that 'content enters analysis first of all perhaps as a question of *topic*, and change of topic'. For many events and acts topic is fully predetermined and invariable, though for others, particularly conversation, topic is relatively unconstrained. In some communities topic may have little effect on style, in others it may be strongly marked. Geertz (1960) observed that the Javanese used lower stylemes 'when speaking of commercial matters, higher ones if speaking of religious or aesthetic matters'; while as mentioned above topic was a condition of code-switching in the village of Hemnesberget.

Message form

Obviously the starting and finishing point of studies of speech events is the form of individual utterances; as Hymes (1972a) stresses, 'it is a general principle that all rules of speaking involve message form, if not by affecting its shape, then by governing its interpretation'. Much of the work so far referred to has been concerned with acts and events that have marked stylistic modes and structures or variation at a macro level involving the selection of a particular dialect or styleme — very little attention has been paid to the grammatical and lexical composition of individual utterances despite Hymes' observation that '*how* something is said is part of *what* is said'.

A notable exception is the work of Brown and Levinson (1978). They begin with the observation that 'in general the abundance of syntactic and lexical apparatus in a grammar seems undermotivated by either systemic or cognitive distinctions and psychological processing factors' (p. 99), and go on, in an exciting way, to suggest explanations for a range of features in terms of modifications to take account of interpersonal factors.

Their starting point is the concept of *face*, which they borrow from Goffman (1976) and define as 'something that is emotionally invested and that can be lost, maintained or enhanced'. They suggest that many interactive acts constitute a threat to face and that many aspects of utterance form can be explained in terms of speakers attempting to defuse or mitigate a Face Threatening Act (FTA). Face, they argue, can usefully be seen as consisting of two aspects: *positive face*, 'the positive, consistent self-image . . . crucially including the desire that this self-image be appreciated', and *negative face*, 'the . . . claim to . . . freedom of action and freedom from imposition'. Thus an act may threaten positive face by belittling and/or negative face by imposing. Brown and Levinson predispose us to think of face as a property of the hearer by the way they discuss it and categorize the options open to speakers, but it is important to realize that such acts as 'confessions', 'apologies', 'offers' and 'invitations' threaten the speaker's positive or negative face.

On any occasion when he decides to make an FTA a speaker has four major options: he may do it indirectly, or 'off record', so that if challenged he can deny, however implausibly, that he meant it:

CHILD: Can you fix this needle?
ADULT: I'm busy.
CHILD: I just wanted to know if you can fix it. (Sacks MS)

Alternatively, a speaker may perform the act explicitly, or 'on record', either with some mitigation directed to negative face or positive face, or 'baldly' with no mitigation at all. Brown and Levinson see these options as ordered from most to least 'polite', though politeness as they use it is much broader than it is in its usual ordinary language use.

Bald on record acts are defined as ones which are in strict conformity with Grice's maxims (see pp. 30–32 for a discussion of the maxims), and in which there is no linguistic concession to face. Such acts are not frequent; as Brown and Levinson observe, 'the majority of natural conversations do not proceed in this brusque fashion at all'. Archetypal examples are direct imperatives, 'sit down and shut up', and warnings, 'your icecream is dripping', utterances used when a threat to face is unimportant or overridden by other considerations such as urgency. Paradoxically, when it is the speaker's face that is being threatened, as with an invitation, the significance can be reversed — in most circumstances 'the firmer the invitation the more polite it is': 'do come in/again', 'have another cake'.

A second option is for the speaker to take account of the hearer's positive face, his need to feel appreciated. Brown and Levinson discuss fifteen strategies, only some of which can be touched on here. One set of strategies is not linked to individual FTAs at all, but rather concerned more generally with creating a better emotional environment for future FTAs through complimenting the hearer, 'what a fantastic garden you have' (p. 109), claiming shared interests and needs, 'you must be hungry, it's a long time since breakfast' (p. 108), and indulging in gossip and small talk to show that the hearer is valued for himself and not just his usefulness.

At individual act level Brown and Levinson draw attention to the preference to emphasize agreement and to play down disagreement,

A: That's where you live, Florida?
B: That's where I was born. (p. 119)

which may stretch as far as 'white lies'. Another technique is to organize the presentation of an imposition so that it seems hearer-centred, 'We ought to eat now so you can get to your class on time.' And finally there are techniques depending on the manipulation of single lexical items. One pervasive technique is the exploitation of terms of address which can be used in a formal situation to increase or stress rank — traffic police are used to being addressed as 'sergeant' or even 'inspector' (strangely, Brown and Levinson treat such *deference* as an aspect of negative face though the intention seems to be to make the hearer *feel* better); in informal situations speakers can

use items like 'mate', 'luv', 'chief' to claim a familiarity that may not
exist but which makes the FTA easier, while inclusive pronouns and
verb forms, 'we', 'us', 'let's', involve speaker and hearer in a joint pro-
jected action — thus an infant teacher was able to say 'now children,
let's all gather round me'.

By contrast negative politeness is an attempt to mitigate the incon-
venience caused by the FTA. One major strategy is to minimize the
content by 'diminutives', which often have a regular morphological
form in some languages, or by lexical misrepresentation:

> Could you have a *little* look at this?
> Could I *borrow* an egg?

A second strategy is to minimize the strength of the threat or
imposition:

> I *think* you *may* be wrong.
> Mend the kettle *if you can/have time.*

And a third is to minimize the speaker's apparent involvement with
and therefore responsibility for the FTA by attributing it to others,
to a general rule or to no agent at all:

> Teacher wants us to . . .
> All passengers must . . .
> Please sir, it broke.

In some circumstances, of course, speakers acknowledge the imposition and even apologize for it:

> I know this is a bore . . . (p. 193)
> I'm sorry to bother you . . .

In certain situations a speaker may decide to perform his FTA 'off
record', and it is in such circumstances that the inferencing procedures based on Grice's maxims come into play. However, as we
noted above, for an FTA to be 'off record' there must be more than
one valid interpretation and this is not predictable from form alone:
'"on record" and "off record" are categories that do not precisely
coincide with categories of linguistic forms but only with linguistic
forms in context' (p. 139). Thus, Brown and Levinson argue, utterances like 'can you pass the salt' are not in fact 'off record' at all
because they are by no stretch of the imagination inquiries about ability to pass the salt but are rather examples of 'conventional indirectness' and as such another kind of on record negative politeness
because they indicate a 'desire to be indirect'. Real indirect utterances
depend on two factors, a *trigger*, the breaking of a Gricean maxim, and

an *inference*. Brown and Levinson exemplify the triggers as follows, but are no nearer explaining the inferencing procedures than anyone else:

relevance: the soup's a bit bland (pass the salt) (p. 220)
quantity: what do you think of Harry? nothing wrong with him
            (c.i. I don't think he's very good) (p. 223)
quality: this isn't exactly my idea of bliss (p. 227)
manner: mature people sometimes help do the dishes (p. 231)

We have so far thought in terms of four degrees of politeness ranging from 'bald and record' to 'off record', but as Leech (1983, p. 109) observes it is quite insufficient to note 'a correlation between indirectness and politeness: we must be able to say not only *how* polite an utterance is but why a particular device of indirectness contributes to a particular illocutionary goal'. On the first point, Brown and Levinson note that 'some simple compounding of hedges and indirectness . . . increases the relative politeness of expressions', and the following is not an unusual combination: 'I'm *sorry* to *trouble* you again but *could* you *possibly lend* me a *tiny* cup of sugar.' Leech himself argues that the following examples become progressively more polite as the utterance is increasingly biased towards the negative choice, thus making it more and more easy for the hearer to say no:

Answer the phone.
I want you to answer the phone.
Will you answer the phone?
Can you answer the phone?
Would you mind answering the phone?
Could you possibly answer the phone? (p. 108)

Brown and Levinson suggest that suiting a particular formulation to a specific occasion requires a calculation of the *weightiness* of the FTA and this depends not simply on the seriousness of the threat or imposition but also on the *social distance* and relative *power* of speaker and hearer. It is, however, one thing to recognize these as relevant variables and quite another to combine them to predict a context-specific utterance form. One complicating problem for foreigners is that speech communities differ in the relative weight they give to positive and negative politeness and the amount of politeness they require in informal situations. To the amusement of foreigners, English emphasizes negative face using 'please' and 'thank you' extravagantly, even between intimates, and the culture enshrines the practice in stories for children like *The Bad Baby* whose crime was that 'he never once said please'.

Brown and Levinson confess that in their analysis 'a satisfactory account of interactional setting has been grossly neglected', but their insights are obviously relevant beyond individual utterances; for instance, many of what Sacks (*passim*) has called *pre-sequences* are structures concerned with avoiding FTAs. Invitations, for example, expose speaker and hearer to the risk of a rejection; the use of a pre-sequence in example (1) below allows the invitation to be made safely, in (2) to be avoided, and in (3) to be acknowledged and dealt with:

1. are you busy later   no, I'm not   would you like . . .
2. are you busy later   I'm going out   how exciting . . .
3. are you busy later   I'm afraid I am   that's OK . . .

Rule breaking
A successful ethnography of speaking will describe the normative structure of all the speech acts and events of a given speech community by detailing for each act and event the necessary configuration of components and style. Norms, of course, are not always adhered to and each community has its own rules for interpreting rule-breaking. When Blom and Gumperz replayed the tape of the Hemnesberget students' discussion to other residents they at first refused to believe that the speakers were members of the same speech community and then, when they recognized the voices, expressed disapproval of their 'artificial speech'. On this occasion the rules were apparently not broken deliberately — some of the participants were themselves surprised at their own code-switching — but very frequently rule-breaking is deliberate and for specific effect.

Salmond (1974) suggests that the main justification for writing a detailed description is that 'only when the rules are laid down as economically as possible and all the options are made clear can an outsider appreciate the manipulation that people practise'. She reports that at the Maori 'rituals of encounter' deliberate rule-breaking results in a great loss of or gain in prestige — the unsuccessful contender leaves the 'marae' in utter humiliation, the successful is greatly honoured having proved himself above the constraints that bind ordinary people.

On one famous occasion a Maori group from a part of the country where women were allowed to speak was visiting another where women were not. The hosts opened the oratory but when it came to the guests' turn there was a problem, for the most senior in rank was an old chieftainess. After a moment's hesitation she began to speak. Immediately there was a protest from the hosts but the chieftainess calmly ignored them, continued her speech to the end and then said

"You Arawa men, you tell me to sit down because I am a woman, yet none of you would be in the world if it wasn't for your mothers. *This* is where your learning and your grey hairs come from!"; then turning her back on them she bent over and flipped up her skirts 'in the supreme gesture of contempt'. Most rule-breaking is less flamboyant and less risky than this.

In the 16th century, English, like many modern European languages, distinguished two second person singular pronouns, 'you' and 'thou'. It was customary for nobles to use 'you' reciprocally, to receive 'you' from their inferiors but to address them as 'thou'. If a speaker broke the 'rules', the rule-breaking was meaningful and thus Sir Edward Coke was able to insult Sir Walter Raleigh at his trial by addressing him as 'thou': 'All that he did at thy instigation, thou viper; for I thou thee, thou traitor.'

Ervin-Tripp (1972) presents a similar insult:

POLICEMAN: What's your name, boy?
DOCTOR: Doctor Poussaint. I'm a physician . . .
POLICEMAN: What's your first name, boy?
DOCTOR: Alvin.

and observes that the policeman insulted the doctor three times. Firstly, he employed a social selector for race, in addressing him as 'boy'; secondly, he treated the reply as a failure to answer, a non-name; thirdly, he repeated the term 'boy' emphasizing the irrelevance of the name Dr Poussaint. So, Ervin-Tripp points out, 'communication had been perfect in this interchange; both were familiar with an address system which contained a selector for race available to both blacks and whites for insult, condescension or deference, as needed. Only because they shared these norms could the policeman's act have its unequivocal impact.'

Norms of interaction

All communities have an underlying set of non-linguistic rules which governs when, how and how often speech occurs. Thus the Anang value speech highly and the young are trained in the arts of speech, while for the Wolof, speech, especially in quantity, is dangerous and demeaning. French children are encouraged to be silent when visitors are present at dinner, Russian children are encouraged to talk. Among the Arucanian there are different expectations of men and women, men being encouraged to talk on all occasions, women to be silent, indeed a new wife is not permitted to speak for several months.

Even within North-Western Europe there are surprising differences. One ethnographer reports how, when he was researching in Iceland, neighbouring Eskimos would visit once a day for an hour to check that all was well. During the hour there would be no more than half a dozen exchanges, and all the rest of the time was spent in silence. Another ethnographer describes staying with in-laws in Denmark and being joined by an American friend who, despite warnings, insisted on talking with American intensity until 'at 9 o'clock my in-laws retired to bed; they just couldn't stand it any more'.

Other norms govern the physical distance at which speech events, particularly conversations, take place. Watson and Graves (1966) report that compared with Americans, Arab students confront each other more directly when conversing, sit closer, are more likely to touch each other and speak more loudly, behaviour which is often interpreted as aggressive or over-friendly by Americans. There are differing norms for turn-taking; Tannen (1982) notes that whereas a typical feature of New York Jewish style is for speakers to overlap the utterances of others as 'a way of showing enthusiasm and interest', this same phenomenon is often interpreted by members of different groups as 'just the opposite: evidence of lack of attention'. Again, there are cultural differences in the ways in which speakers deal with encoding difficulties, occasions when they are forced to stop midway through a grammatical structure: Hymes (1972b) suggests that for white middle-class Americans the normal hesitation behaviour is to pause, and often fill the pause with 'um', 'er', and then to continue, while for many blacks, the normal pattern is to recycle to the beginning of the utterance (sometimes more than once). Recycling is a feature sometimes evident in children's speech but may be interpreted as a defect in adults, at least by whites.

The clashes of norms described so far may produce some personal discomfort, tension and even unjustified censure, but normally the norm-breaking is accepted as the performance of someone who doesn't share the same norms. Major problems can arise, however, when participants assume that they *do* share the same norms. Polgar (1960) discovered that Mesquaki Fox children interpreted the normal loudness of voice and directness of American English teachers as 'meanness' and 'getting mad', and even more serious has been the misinterpretation of the behaviour of thousands of Negro children in New York schools. These children were observed to be failing at school — on all standard tests of reading and verbal and non-verbal intelligence they were retarded while in individual interviews with educational psychologists they said very little and many of them appeared to be 'linguistically deprived'. Bereiter and Engelmann (1966) working with four-year-olds in Urbana claimed that they communicated by gestures, 'single words' and 'a series of badly-connected words or phrases' such as 'they mine' or 'me got juice'. They observed that the Negro children could not ask questions and 'without exaggerating . . . these four-year-olds could make no statements of any kind'. From observations like these Bereiter and Engelmann concluded that one must treat these children as if they had no language at all, and therefore they devised a pre-school programme using formal language drills to teach the children English. Even when the teaching was underway, they observed that some children, having been taught 'two plus one equals three . . . would continually lapse into amalgamations, "two pluh wunic'k three"'. It was claimed that having done this the children were no longer able to substitute other numbers for the "one", it having become fused with the beginning sound of "equals".

Labov (1969) counter-argues vehemently that the concept of 'verbal deprivation' has no basis in social reality — it is a nonsense created by educational psychologists who 'know very little about language and even less about Negro children'. He observes that to say the children have no language or even that they are linguistically deprived is a complete misunderstanding — they come from a culture where linguistic ability is highly valued, as is evident from the importance of 'sounding' and the fact that verbal skill is a prerequisite for peer group or gang leaders. The truth is that the children do not choose to display their abilities at school because they are not ones the school values and because the school is a hostile situation.

Negro children faced with a large, though friendly, coloured interviewer, let alone a white interviewer as used in Bereiter and Engelmann's tests, choose to produce monosyllabic, non-committal answers, whereas white middle-class children are willing to chatter away in the 'same' situation. It is because the situation or rather the speech event is assumed to be the same, with the same norms of interaction, that psychologists and sociologists alike feel able to compare the performance of different class and ethnic groups — only when one realizes that the norms are not the same can one perceive the uselessness of the exercise.

In a striking demonstration that the psychologists were wrongly inferring from what the children said to what they were able to say, Labov took a rabbit into a classroom where young Negro children were dutifully 'learning English':

T: This is a book. What is it?
P: It is a book.
T: What colour is the book?
P: It is a red book.

He explained to the children that he had a rabbit that was very shy
but if a few of them would take the rabbit into the next room and talk
to it, it would be quite happy — once there the children rapidly displayed grammatical sophistication far in excess of the structures being
drilled to their fellows next door.

4 Conversational analysis

Hymes (1972a) stresses that it is heuristically important for the ethnography of speaking 'to proceed as though all speech has formal
characteristics of some sort as manifestation of genres', though he
admits that the very notion of casual unmarked speech points to the
fact that there is a 'great range among genres in the number and explicitness of formal markers'. Perhaps for this reason those ethnographers of speaking who have provided detailed structural
descriptions have focused on well defined and often ritualized events
— greetings (Irvine 1974), ritual encounters (Salmond 1974), chanting (Sherzer 1974) — while those who have looked at conversation
have examined not its structure, but factors affecting the choice of
code or style (Blom and Gumperz 1972; Gumperz 1964; Geertz 1960).

Until very recently most of the advances in conversational analysis
had been made by three sociologists, Sacks, Schegloff and Jefferson,
who originally stressed that they worked with conversational materials
'not because of a special interest in language' but because they saw
conversational analysis as a first step towards achieving a 'naturalistic
observational discipline' to deal with details of social interaction in
'a rigorous, empirical and formal way'. Latterly, however, they and
those who follow in the tradition have seen their main concern as the
analysis of conversational structure and organization, and their findings are useful to and usable by anyone interested in the structure
of conversation.

Turn-taking

One of the basic facts of conversation is that the roles of speaker and
listener change, and this occurs with remarkably little overlapping
speech and remarkably few silences. Sacks (MS) suggests that there
is an underlying rule in American English conversation — 'at least
and not more than one party talks at a time'. This is not an empirical
fact, because there are obviously many instances of short pauses and
short overlaps, but rather a normative or 'observably oriented to' fea-

ture of conversation — in other words, it is a rule used by conversationalists themselves. If more than or less than one party is talking
it is 'noticeable' and participants set out to 'remedy' the situation and
return to a state of one and only one speaker. If the problem is more
than one speaker one of the participants usually yields the floor
quickly:

LORI: But that WZ — Then you wentuh Fre:ds
ELLEN: We⌐we left — we left —
BEN: ⌊No. That's the time we left *Fre:ds*   (Sacks MS)

while if the problem is silence other speakers begin speaking, or indicate their intention to speak by noises like 'er' or 'mm'. In other
words turns to speak typically occur successively without overlaps or
gaps between them. Overlapping is dealt with by one speaker ending
his turn quickly, gaps between turns by another speaker beginning
his turn or simply indicating that his turn has begun and incorporating
the silence into it.

A second feature of conversation is that speaker change recurs, and
this presents problems for the participants — how can they achieve
change of speaker while maintaining a situation in which at least, but
not more than, one speaker speaks at a time?

Sacks suggests that a current speaker can exercise three degrees
of control over the next turn. Firstly, he can select which participant
will speak next, either by naming him or by alluding to him with a
descriptive phrase, 'the Right Honorable Member for Bexley South'.
If the current speaker selects the next speaker, he usually also selects
the type of next utterance by producing the first part of an *adjacency
pair* (see below p. 69), for example a *question* or a *greeting* which constrains the selected speaker to produce an appropriate *answer* or *return
greeting*.

DOCTOR: Hello Mrs Jones
PATIENT: Hello Doctor
DOCTOR: Hello Catherine
CHILD: Hello

The current speaker's second option is simply to constrain the next
utterance, but not select the next speaker, while the third option is
to select neither and leave it to one of the other participants to continue the conversation by selecting himself.

Sacks emphasizes that these options are in an ordered relationship
— the first over-rides the second and the second over-rides the third.
If the current speaker selects the next speaker he alone should talk
next; Sacks notes that when an unselected speaker takes a turn al-

ready assigned to a selected one, the right of the selected speaker to speak next is usually preserved:

A (to C): Tell us about yourself so we can find something bad about you.
B: Yeah hurry up.

Importantly, these selection techniques operate only utterance by utterance: there is no mechanism in *conversation* by which the current speaker can select the next-but-one speaker — choice of the next speaker is always the prerogative of the current speaker if he chooses to exercise it. In more formal speech situations — classrooms, courtrooms, formal discussions — it is, of course, quite possible for one speaker, whose role assigns him extra authority, to select the speakers for several successive utterances.

While these speaker options explain how the next speaker comes to be selected, or to select himself, they do not explain how the next speaker knows when the current speaker has finished, and therefore when he can begin, although this is obviously essential if he is to avoid overlap or silence. Sacks suggests that in fact next speakers are not concerned and can never be concerned with actually completed utterances, because one can never be sure that an utterance is complete — it is always possible to add more to an apparently complete utterance, and speakers frequently do so. Therefore, next speakers are concerned with points of *possible completion.* In developing this idea, Sacks observes that turns consist of one or more *sentences*, with a sentence being defined as a unit which has

> its completion recognized on its completion, and that it is not complete recognizable by participants; also it can be monitored, from its beginning, to see from its beginning what it will take for its completion to be produced, in such a way that, on its completion, its completion may be recognized. (Sacks MS)

Speaker change takes place at the end of *sentences*: if the next speaker or next action has been selected, the next speaker will take over at the end of the sentence during which the selecting was done; if the current speaker has not selected, any participant may self-select at the end of any sentence. Thus, a speaker is vulnerable at every sentence completion whether he selects next speaker or action or not, and even if he gets past one sentence completion he is equally vulnerable at the end of the next sentence. Turns to speak are valued and sought and thus the majority of turns in any conversation consist of only a single sentence, unless permission has been sought for a longer turn, perhaps to tell a story or a joke.

The argument so far is that conversation is made up of units which are recognizable as either incomplete or possibly complete and that next speakers can begin as soon as a current speaker has reached a possible completion. This fact, Sacks suggests, explains the low incidence of overlap and silence. However, the ability to come in as soon as a speaker has reached a possible completion requires a high degree of skill on the part of participants — they need to be able not only to analyse and understand an ongoing sentence in order to recognize when it is possibly complete, but also to produce immediately a relevant next utterance. Do speakers have this ability?

Jefferson (1973) argues that the recipient of an ongoing utterance 'has the technical capacity to select a precise spot to start his own talk "no later" than the exact appropriate moment'. She gives three kinds of example. First she shows that speakers can, without a pause, produce a completion to a prior speaker's otherwise complete utterance:

BEN: An' there — there wz at least ten mi:les of traffic *bumper* tuh bumper.
ETHEL: — because a'that.

Much more impressive are instances of recipients coming in at just the right moment with their own proposed completion of an as yet uncompleted sentence:

LOUISE: No a Soshe is someone who-⎡is a carbon copy of their friend.
ROGER: ⎣drinks Pepsi.

A variant of this is when the recipient is able to predict the ending of the sentence and attempts to say the same thing at the same time:

DAN: The guy who doesn't run the race doesn't win it, but 'e
        doesn⎡'t lose it. ⎤
ROGER: ⎣B't lose it.⎦

Thus speakers demonstrably do have the ability to place their entries with great precision. Nevertheless, unintentional overlaps still occur, frequently caused by self-selection. If the current speaker has not selected a next speaker, a self-selecting speaker, beginning at a possible completion, may well overlap with the current speaker who has decided to continue, or with a second self-selecting speaker. The problem is usually 'remedied' quickly by one of the speakers yielding the floor; when the overlap is the result of two self-selecting speakers there appears to be a rule that the 'first starter' has the right to continue.

On occasions when both speakers cease speaking simultaneously, as in the last example above, there is the question of who has next turn; if one speaker was producing a completion of the other's utterance, as Roger is, the speaker whose turn was completed takes the next turn. If, in other circumstances, an overlap is ended by one speaker stopping first, if only by a syllable, he takes the next turn:

AGNES: ⌈That's about a:ll,
GUY: ⌊What else.
GUY: The hat,
           (0.5)
AGNES: En the hat,

Silence between turns similarly creates a problem and participants feel that a silence is attributable, usually to some intended next speaker. Schegloff and Sacks (1973) quote a report of a silence:

> He hadtuh come out tuh San Francisco. So he called hhh from their place, out here to the professors, en set up, the, time, and hh asked him to hh — if they'd make a reservation for him which they did cuz they paid for hiz room en etcetera en he asked them tuh:: make a reservation for iz parents. En there was a deep silence, she said, at the other end 'e sez Oh well they'll pay for their own uh-hh- room and accommodations.

They observe that the silence was noted by the speaker as not his, but that he then transformed it into a pause by continuing his turn.

There is a very low tolerance of silence between turns and if the intended next speaker does not begin almost at once the previous speaker is likely to produce a *post completor*, which is either a question, noticing the silence such as 'Didn't you hear me', or a marked repeat of his utterance. To avoid this, speakers who have not yet formulated what they want to say tend to indicate their intention to speak by 'erm', 'um', 'mm', or an audible intake of breath and thereby incorporate the silence into their turn.

We have seen that the basis of conversation is that at least and not more than one party speaks at a time, and that the system for allotting turns works only one turn at a time. Sacks *et al.* (1974) distinguish different *speech exchange systems* according to the organization of turn-taking. They observe that whereas in conversation turns are allocated singly, in some systems, debates or law suits for example, there is a high degree of pre-allocation of turns. The most extreme form is the system governing public discussion among the Burundi, where 'the order in which individuals speak in a group is strictly determined by seniority of rank' (Albert 1972). Turns come in a fixed order and only when everyone has had a turn and the cycle has recommenced can the first speaker speak again.

Sacks *et al.* (ibid.) suggest that different turn-taking systems produce differently structured turns. In a pre-allocated system there are no interruption pressures, turns tend to be longer and for these reasons consist of a series of linked sentences. In a turn-by-turn allocation system there are strong pressures from other participants wanting to speak, and the turn is typically only one sentence long.

There are several techniques open to the speaker who wishes to continue speaking past a particular 'possible completion'. The simplest technique is to employ what Sacks calls an *utterance incompletor* — these are items such as 'but', 'and', 'however' and other clause connectors, whose importance in conversation is that they turn a potentially complete sentence into an incomplete one. This, of course, is not a particularly sophisticated technique, because a self-selecting speaker, waiting for the first 'possible completion', may have already planned or even begun his turn — Ferguson (1975), in an examination of eleven hours of conversation, noted that 28% of interruptions occurred after conjunctions. Therefore the successful floorholder produces utterances which, 'while they could perfectly well be composed of talk that, in terms of "possible sentence completion", would have one, or more than one, such occurrence within them, are built in such a way as to not have possible completions within them' (Sacks MS).

One technique is to begin with an *incompletion marker*, 'if', 'since', or any other subordinator, which informs the other participants that there will be at least two clauses before the first possible completion. A speaker can also pre-structure a fairly large unit of speech by such devices as 'I'd like to make two points' or simply 'firstly', which explicitly indicate that there is more to come after what could otherwise have been regarded as a possible completion point. In the following extract a skilled politician operates the system beautifully to guarantee himself time to answer the question fully:

> Now I think one can see *several* major areas ... there's *first* the question ... now the *second* big area of course is the question of how you handle incomes and I myself very strongly believe that we have to establish in Britain *two* fundamental principles. *First of all* ...
>
> (Denis Healey: *Analysis*, BBC Radio 4)

None of these devices can guarantee that the speaker keeps the floor but they do force the other speaker into a position where he must interrupt and be seen to be interrupting. Speakers reject interruptions, if they choose not to yield the floor, by speaking more loudly, more quickly and in a higher pitch; often the surface grammar or phonology breaks down, and frequently there is a reference to the interruption.

ATHA: they have at their disposal enormous assets ┌and their policy
PITMAN: └ look can I just
          come in on that last year
ATHA: YES IN A MOMENT IF YOU MAY AND WHEN I'VE
          FINISHED ┌then you'll know what the point is
PITMAN: └ yes I'M SO SORRY

(Money at Work, BBC 2)

A non-speaker who wishes to speak, but is unable to find a suitable entry spot has the option of simply breaking in, though this is frequently heard as rudeness.

PITMAN: but there aren't enough people who need that service at two thirty
          at night ┌down to my particular sta
WIDLAKE: └ you talk like the chairman of British Rail

or of indicating by repeated short, single-tonic, utterances his desire for the floor. This is a technique which children master early as the following example of a two-year-old shows.

MOTHER: ┌ not sure what she's been saying
FATHER: not at all today dar┌ling
TOM: └ ah   ah   ah   ah   └ ah

MOTHER: oh┌ well at least well I'll need to know when she comes┌in for
FATHER: │   │
TOM: └ ah   ah   ah   ah   └ sto

MOTHER: my con   sorry darling.
FATHER:
TOM: stop talking

At the other extreme a non-speaker who is offered the floor but doesn't want it may simply remain silent until the speaker continues (Kendon 1967; de Long 1974) or produce a minimal response to confirm, agree or express interest, or use the whole of his turn to produce a *possible pre-closing* 'alright', 'okay', 'so', 'well', (see below p. 90), and thereby indicate that he has nothing further to add and is willing to close the topic.

The evidence adduced so far to describe and explain speaker change has been almost entirely grammatical and semantic. We have seen how grammatical markers and considerations of meaning turn certain points in utterances into 'possible completions' and it has been suggested that at each 'possible completion' a speaker is vulnerable. There is, however, evidence to suggest that speakers signal paralinguistically and kinesically to the other participants at which possible completions they are actually willing to relinquish the floor.

De Long (1974) reports a detailed analysis of a series of conversations between four- and five-year-old pre-school children, which shows a marked correlation between certain body movements and change of speaker. The transcription noted eight basic movements, including 'up', 'down', 'left', 'right', 'forward' and 'backward', for eight parts of the body, the head, the trunk and the left and right arms, hands, and fingers. Analysis showed that two movements co-occurred, either simultaneously or in rapid succession to signal a termination. The first was a leftward movement of the head, the second a downward movement by the head, arms or hands individually or in any combination.

However, we must evaluate this evidence with great care, because as Levinson (1983, p. 302) points out such signals can only be supportive and not the basis of the turn-taking system, as turn-taking can be managed perfectly well in telephone conversations with no visual cues at all, with 'less gap and shorter overlap' and apparently no compensatory 'special prosodic or intonational patterns'.

De Long stresses that 'to say that the intention to terminate verbalization, willingness to yield the floor, is signalled by downward and leftward movements does not mean that every time a left in the head is accompanied by a down in the head or in other parts of the body the speaker intends to terminate'. In fact it is only when such signalling occurs at possible completions that termination is signalled. To support his analysis de Long describes two apparent exceptions: a long gap between two utterances, and the only recorded interruption.

The gap occurred when one child ended 'I'll show you what's brown', tilting his head to the left but not making any downward signals. During the next few seconds he made intermittent downward and leftward movements while the other child remained silent; then 'after no less than an eight second delay we find left and downward successive signalling in the head'. Immediately, the other child began speaking. As confirmation of the significance of this signal, the only interruption is found to occur immediately following a series of downward movements by several parts of the body and a succession of downs and lefts in the head which the interrupter apparently took as speaker change signals.

Kendon (1967) suggests that one important factor enabling the smooth change-over of speaker is *gaze*. He notes that, while listening, A typically looks at B with fairly long gazes broken by very brief away gazes, but while speaking A looks at and away from B for more equal periods. Focusing on the ends of utterances of more than five seconds,

Kendon notes that 'usually the person who is bringing a long utterance to an end does so by assuming a characteristic head posture and
by looking steadily at the auditor before he actually finishes speaking'.
The auditor, who spends most of his time looking at the speaker, is
able to pick up these signals and tends to respond by looking away
just before or just as he begins to talk. By this time of course the initial
speaker is looking at the auditor and can pick up the signal that he
has accepted the offer of the floor. 'Such changes in behaviour which
precede the utterance itself clearly make it possible for each participant to anticipate how the other is going to deal with the actual point
of change of speaker role, perhaps facilitating the achievement of
smoother ... change overs.' Kendon notes that fewer than a third
of the utterances which ended with an extended gaze were followed
by silence or delayed response, as compared with almost three-
quarters of those that ended *without* the speaker looking up. In larger
groups the situation is more complicated, but Weisbrod (1965), studying a seven person discussion group, found that the person whom the
current speaker last looked at before ending was most likely to speak
next.

Most conversations, particularly two-party ones, have periods when
there is no talking; Goodwin (1981, p. 106) has interesting observations on how participants organize withdrawal from conversation.
He notes that the 'boundary between full engagement and mutual
disengagement is not structured as a sharp clear break'; rather, 'participants are afforded a space within which they can reorganize their
bodies'. He gives an example of a listener withdrawing gaze just as
the speaker was concluding and then holding her head 'facing just
to the side of the speaker' who was thus put in the position of being
able but not obliged to continue. In other words, in this position one
participant is able to monitor the other through peripheral vision and
re-attend if there is a resumption. This observation rings true and
most people will acknowledge having used it in embarrassing situations
when conversation had dried up and direct eye-contact was too
stressful. When there are three or more participants the 'gazing past'
posture can lead smoothly to complete disengagement as skilled cock-
tail party circulators know.

As we observed above, turns to speak are valued and speakers compete for them. One of the points at which a speaker is vulnerable is
when he pauses within a phrase — Ferguson (1975) discovered that
almost a third of interruptions occur following 'fillers' such as 'um',
'er', and 'y'know'. Kendon observed that speakers tend to avoid gazing during hesitant speech — they spend only 20% of the time gazing

during hesitant speech as compared with 50% of the time during fluent speech — probably as a defence against interruption. In Kendon's data interruptions were rare but in those cases where a small battle for the turn occurred both speakers stared fully until the conflict had been resolved.

Duncan (1973, 1974) suggests that the cues for speaker change can be grammatical, paralinguistic or kinesic or any combination of all three. A listener may claim the speaking turn when the current speaker gives a *turn signal*, defined as the display, at the end of a phonemic clause, of at least one of a set of six cues. The cues are

1. Intonation: the use of any pitch level/terminal juncture combination, other than 22.
2. Paralanguage: drawl on the final syllable or on the stressed syllable of the phonemic clause.
3. Body motion: the termination of any hand gesticulation or the relaxation of a tensed hand position.
4. Sociocentric sequences: the appearance of one of several stereotyped expressions, such as 'but uh', 'or something', 'you know', labelled sociocentric by Bernstein (1962).
5. Paralanguage: a drop in paralinguistic pitch and/or loudness, in conjunction with a sociocentric sequence.
6. Syntax: the completion of a grammatical clause involving a subject-predicate combination.

Duncan (1974) observes that the occurrence of a speaker turn signal does not necessarily condition a change of speaker; the listener always has the right to decline but the more cues displayed simultaneously the greater the likelihood that the listener will take over the floor. Duncan emphasizes the importance of the speaker turn signal by showing that in his data every smooth exchange of the speaker role followed a speaker turn signal, while every attempt by an auditor to claim the turn while no cues were being displayed resulted in simultaneous turns.

Duncan (1973) suggests that the speaker turn signal can be overridden by a claim-suppressing signal, which consists of hand gesticulations, and is apparently almost totally effective — 'of 88 auditor turn claims in response to turn signals, only two such claims were made when the suppression signal was additionally being displayed'. Once the auditor takes over the speaking role he typically displays a *speaker-state signal*, which consists of at least one of four cues: the averting of gaze noted by Kendon; the initiation of gesticulation;

sharp audible intake of breath; and paralinguistic overloudness.

In any description of turn-taking there is the problem of what constitutes a turn, and while most analysts accept that nods of agreement and murmurs of assent do not count, there are some important differences of opinion. Duncan uses the term *back channel* behaviour to cover contributions which do not constitute a turn but which provide the speaker with useful information as his turn progresses. Under this heading Duncan includes 'sentence completions', 'requests for clarification' and 'brief restatements', all of which for Sacks would be complete turns — indeed Duncan and Niederehe (1974) express some disquiet that 'for some of the longer back channels, particularly the brief restatements, the boundary between back channels and speaking turns became uncertain. On an intuitive basis, some of these longer back channels appeared to take on the quality of a turn.'

Duncan's main concern is to describe speaker change, and for this purpose it may be sufficient to categorize all utterances as either 'back channels' or 'turns'; for those interested in describing the structural relations between utterances, however, this is not sufficient — the options open following a 'request for clarification' are very different from those following a 'brief restatement'.

Conversational structure

Sacks (MS) observes that a conversation is a string of at least two turns. Some turns are more closely related than others and he isolates a class of sequences of turns called *adjacency pairs* which have the following features: they are two utterances long; the utterances are produced successively by different speakers; the utterances are ordered — the first must belong to the class of *first pair parts*, the second to the class of *second pair parts*; the utterances are related, not any second pair can follow any first pair part, but only an appropriate one; the first pair part often selects next speaker and always selects next action — it thus sets up a *transition relevance* and expectation which the next speaker fulfils, in other words the first part of a pair predicts the occurrence of the second: 'Given a question, regularly enough an answer will follow' (Sacks 1967).

There is a class of first pair parts which includes Questions, Greetings, Challenges, Offers, Requests, Complaints, Invitations, Announcements; for some first pair parts the second pair part is reciprocal (Greeting-Greeting), for some there is only one appropriate second (Question-Answer), for some more than one (Complaint-Apology/Justification).

Adjacency pairs are the basic structural units in conversation. They are used for opening and closing conversations,

{ Hi there
{ Hello

{ Bye then
{ Bye

and are very important during conversations both for operating the turn-taking system by enabling a speaker to select next action and next speaker, and also for enabling the next speaker to avoid both gap and overlap.

It is, however, no difficult matter to discover a question not followed by an answer and this raises a question about the status of the pair. Sacks argues that, whereas the absence of a particular item in conversation has initially no importance because there are any number of things that are similarly absent, in the case of an adjacency pair the first part provides specifically for the second and therefore the absence of the second is noticeable and noticed. He observes that people regularly complain 'You didn't answer my question' or 'I said hello, and she just walked past'.

Preference organization*

Work by Pomerantz (1978, 1984), Atkinson and Drew (1979) and Levinson (1983) has developed the notion of adjacency pair into a very powerful concept. As we saw, some first pair parts allowed for alternative seconds; however, we can now demonstrate that some options are *preferred* and some *dispreferred* — a distinction which may have a psychological basis and explanation but also has linguistic realizations: 'preferred seconds are *unmarked* — they occur as structurally simpler turns; in contrast dispreferred seconds are marked by various kinds of structural complexity' (Levinson ibid., p. 307). Invitations naturally prefer acceptances and we can see the differences in realization between the preferred acceptance and the dispreferred rejection in these two examples from Atkinson and Drew (ibid., p. 58):

A: Why don't you come up and *see* me some // times
B: I would like to

---

* This section draws heavily on Levinson's (1983) 30-page discussion which readers are recommended to consult.

C: Uh if you'd care to come and visit a little while this morning I'll give you a cup of *co*ffee

D: hehh   Well   that's awfully sweet of you
(DELAY) (MARKER)   (APPRECIATION)
I don't think I can make it this morning   hh uhm I'm running
(REFUSAL OF DECLINATION)
an ad in the paper and uh I have to stay near the phone (ACCOUNT)

Levinson observes that dispreferred seconds are distinguished by incorporating a 'substantial number of the following features':

a) *delays*: (i) by pause before delivery; (ii) by the use of a preface (see b); (iii) by displacement over a number of turns via use of *repair initiators* or insertion sequences

b) *prefaces*: (i) the use of markers or announcers of dispreferreds like *Uh* and *Well*; (ii) the production of token agreements before disagreements; (iii) the use of appreciations if relevant (for offers, invitations, suggestions, advice); (iv) the use of apologies if relevant (for requests, invitations, etc.); (v) the use of qualifiers (e.g. *I don't know for sure, but* . . .); (iv) hesitation in various forms, including self-editing

c) *accounts*: carefully formulated explanations for why the dispreferred act is being done

d) *declination component*: of a form suited to the nature of the first part of the pair, but characteristically indirect or mitigated   (pp. 334–5)

Preference is a very powerful concept and once it has been established with examples like those above it can be used to explain the occurrence of quite a number of other conversational phenomena as the results of speakers trying to avoid having to perform dispreferred seconds. Thus Schegloff *et al.* (1977) argue that conversationalists prefer the speaker to correct his own mistakes rather than to have to correct them for him and that they therefore use a series of *repair initiator* devices ranging from pausing, to return question, to actual, frequently mitigated, correction:

L: But y'know single beds'r awfully thin to sleep on.
S: What?
L: Single beds. // They're–
E: Y'mean narrow?
L: They're awfully narrow yeah

We can also now see a general explanation for *pre-invitations, pre-requests* and *pre-arrangements* — they are psychologically motivated structures to avoid loss of face for one or both participants resulting from a dispreferred second having to be performed:

Pre-invitation   JACK: Say what ya doin?
                     JUDY: Well, we're going out. Why?
                     JACK: Oh, I was just gonna say come out and come over here and talk to the people.

Participants can recognize pre-sequences fairly easily and indicate in their replies whether the invitation is likely to be accepted:

A: Say what you doin' tonight?
B: Oh, I'm just . . .

The very recognizability of the first part of a pre-sequence sometimes results in 'collapsing', in which the next speaker produces what is really an answer to the first part of an anticipated next sequence. In the following example utterance 1 was produced by a five-year-old and the actual reply was utterance 4: utterances 2 and 3 represent one form Sacks suggests an uncollapsed version might have taken:

Pre-request   1. Can you fix this needle?
               2. Sure.

Request   3. Will you?
               4. I'm busy.

The ellipsis in fact allowed the five-year-old to protest that an intended question had been misanalysed as a pre-request and to respond:

5. I just wanted to know if you can fix it.

Of course, an alternative analysis is that utterance 1 is an indirect request (see pp. 29–30) which refers to the second pre-condition on requests, B's ability; B's reply, 'I'm busy' is then heard as a refusal because it denies the third pre-condition, his willingness. However, Levinson persuasively argues that to think in terms of indirect requests is misguided — he suggests that one of the advantages of a pre-request is that, being transparent, it may save the speaker having to risk his face by making the request at all. In some instances the addressee may respond with an *offer*:

C: Do you have any pecan Danish today?
S: Yes we do. Would you like one of those?
C: Yes please.   (Merritt 1976)

or even proceed directly to the action:

S: Have you got Embassy Gold please?
H: Yes dear. (*provides*)   (A. Sinclair 1976)

Initially, of course, the indirect speech act analyst would argue that the first utterance in the above example is an indirect request, but then, asks Levinson, what does one do with the example below — surely one can't classify one as a question and the other as an indirect request:

A: Hi. Do you have uh size C flashlight batteries?   *(Pre-request)*
B: Yes sir.   *(Go ahead)*
A: I'll have four please.   *(Request)*
B: *(Turns to get)*   *(Response)*
    (Merritt 1976)

Inserted sequences

The structures described so far have been linear, one pair followed by another; there are also cases of embedding, of one pair occurring inside another. Schegloff (1972) calls these embedded pairs *insertion sequences*. Sometimes, either because he doesn't understand, or because he doesn't want to commit himself until he knows more, or because he's simply stalling, a next speaker produces not a second pair part but another first pair part. The suggestion is 'if you answer this one, I will answer yours'.

Insertion sequence	A: I don't know where the — wh — this address // is.	Q
	B: Well where do — which part of town do *you* live?	Qi
	A: I live four ten East Lowden.	Ai
	B: Well you don't live very far from me.	A

One question which immediately arises is in what sense is the pair QiAi inserted into the pair QA; surely this is treating conversation as an accomplished product rather than a developing process, because A may never occur. Schegloff, however, argues that

> the Q utterance makes an A utterance conditionally relevant. The action the Q does (here, direction asking) makes some other action sequentially relevant (here, giving directions by answering the Q). Which is to say, after the Q, the next speaker has that action specifically chosen for him to do and can show attention to, and grasp of, the preceding utterance by doing the chosen action then and there. If he does not, that will be a notable omission.

In other words, during the inserted sequence the original question retains its transition relevance, and if the second speaker does not then produce an answer it is noticeably absent in exactly the same way as it would be if there were no intervening sequence, and the questioner can complain about the lack of answer in exactly the same way. Adjacency pairs are normative structures, the second part ought to occur, and thus the other sequences are inserted between the first pair part that has occurred and the second pair part that is anticipated.

Methodological considerations

It is appropriate at this point to discuss the nature of the statements being made by the conversational analysts and their descriptive aims in making them. Schenkein (1978a), in his introduction to a collection of conversational analyses, observes that 'the descriptions presented here offer promising movement towards an empirically based grammar of natural conversation'. For readers with a linguistic perspective this is slightly misleading because, as Levinson points out, the aim of conversational analysts is not simply to show that 'some aspect of conversation *can* be viewed' as being structured in a particular way, but also 'that it actually is so conceived by the participants producing it' (pp. 318–19). In other words, the turn-taking mechanisms, the transition relevance set up by first pair parts and the existence of preferred and dispreferred second pair parts are significant because they are demonstrably 'oriented to' by conversationalists.

Paradoxically, the evidence showing that the structures are not just an artefact of the analysis comes from points where structures break down — then we can observe that participants 'either try to repair the hitch or . . . draw strong inferences of a quite specific kind from the absence of the expected behaviour' (p. 319). Thus in the following example there is a two-second pause between two contributions by participant c:

> c: So I was wondering would you be in your office on Monday (.) by any chance?
>
> (pause 2.0)
>
> c: Probably not.   (ibid., p. 320)

and the addressee's silence is obviously interpreted as a negative response to the question.

The strength of the conversational analysts' approach is that the structures they have isolated do not, like Grice's maxims, predict simply that inferencing will take place but also predict the *result* of the inferencing. Thus to spell out the steps in an interpretation of the example above: by the rules of the turn-taking system c has validly selected the next speaker and thus the pause is assigned to the addressee; the adjacency pair system makes a yes/no answer transitionally relevant and the preference system isolates delay as one of the markers of dispreferred seconds, in this case 'no'. Thus the system predicts, rather than simply accounts for, the fact that silence will be interpreted as implicating 'no'.

It is examples like this which justify Levinson's observation that the research methods of conversational analysis are to be recommended because they 'offer us a way of avoiding the indefinitely extendable and unverifiable categorization and speculation about actors' intents so typical of Discourse Analysis-style analysis' (p. 319). However, not all conversational analyses are so rigorous. If the aim is, as Schenkein suggests, to produce a grammar of conversation we must bear in mind that grammars are devices which use a small set of categories to generate a large number of structures. Within conversational analysis, however, too often categories are devised to cope with each new piece of data and, as we shall see, there are dangers inherent in using initially attractive 'transparent' categories like 'misapprehension sequence', 'clarification' and 'puzzle'. We need to exemplify the problem in some detail.

Jefferson (1972) proposes an embedded sequence different from Schegloff's insertion sequence and labelled *side sequence*. She observes that the general drift of a conversation is sometimes halted at an unpredictable point by a request for clarification and then the conversation picks up again where it left off. The following example is children preparing for a game of 'tag':

1. STEVEN: one, two, three, (pause) four, five, six, (pause) eleven, eight, nine, ten.
   SUSAN: Eleven? — eight, nine, ten.
   STEVEN: Eleven, eight, nine, ten.
   NANCY: Eleven?
   STEVEN: Seven, eight, nine, ten.
   SUSAN: That's better.

Whereupon the game resumes. The side sequence begins with a *questioning repeat* — an interrogative item indicating that there is a problem in what has just been said, 'and its work is to generate further talk directed to remedying the problem'. Questioning repeats occur typically after the questioned utterance has been completed, because only then can one be sure that the speaker is not going to correct himself or explain the unclear item; an interrupting questioning repeat is liable to attract not a clarification but a complaint, 'if you'd just let me finish'.

Jefferson suggests initially that the *misapprehension sequence* has a three-part structure, consisting of 'a statement of sorts, a misapprehension of sorts, and a clarification of sorts'. The example above is in fact more complex consisting of a statement followed by two misapprehension and clarification pairs. So far the side sequence looks rather like Schegloff's insertion sequence. There are, however, two major differences: firstly, the first item, the statement, is not a first pair part, the other items are in no sense inserted and there is no expectation of who should speak at the end of the sequence or of what type of utterance should follow; secondly, while the sequence misapprehension-clarification looks like a pair, there is actually a compulsory third element in the sequence, an indication by the misapprehender that he now understands and that the sequence is now terminated — 'That's better' in the example above, or 'yeah' in the example below.

2. Statement: If Percy goes with — Nixon I'd sure like that.
  Misapprehension: Who?
  Clarification: Percy. That young fella that uh — his daughter was murdered. (1.0)
  Terminator: Oh yea:h. Yeah.

Because the first item, the statement, is not a first pair part, the conversation cannot resume with the second pair part as after an insertion sequence, and there remains the problem of a *return*. Jefferson observes that 'it is not merely that there *occurs* a return to the on-going sequence, but that to return to the on-going sequence . . . is a task performed by participants'. She suggests that the return can be effected either as a *resumption* or as a *continuation* — a resumption is achieved by *attention getters* such as 'listen' or 'hey you know', which mark that there is a problem in accomplishing a return, while continuations, attempted by 'so' or 'and', are directed to 'covering-up' the problem, to proposing that there is no trouble, sometimes where that may not be the case. Thus the full system is:

3.
      statement: A: And a goodlooking girl comes to you
              and *asks* you, y'know,
Side { misapprehension: B: Gi (hh) rl asks you to — . . .
sequence clarification   C: Wella its happened a lotta times.
      termination   B: Okay okay go ahead.
      continuation: B: So he says 'no' . . .

In trying to understand and use the descriptive categories outlined above, the intending analyst has all sorts of problems. *Pair* is the only technical term which is defined; *sequence* appears to be a structurally coherent collection of not necessarily successive utterances or utterance parts, up to four in number, and pairs are also referred to as sequences; *misapprehension sequence* is apparently a subclass of *side sequence*, but we have no idea what other types of side sequence there are.

From the way the authors describe and exemplify their categories it would appear that the real difference between Schegloff's insertion sequence and Jefferson's side sequence is that the former has a ready-made *return*, the second pair part of the question-answer pair, while for the latter it has to be 'worked at'. However, one could surely insert a misapprehension sequence inside Schegloff's Question/Answer pair; would it, could it, then be classified as an insertion sequence?

A: I don't know where the — wh — this address // is.   Q
B: Which one?   Misapprehension
A: The one you just gave me.   Clarification
B: Oh yeah, yeah.   Termination
B: Well you don't live very far from me.   A

Perhaps it is a mistake to assume that insertion and side sequences necessarily have different distributions; perhaps the main difference between them is the fact that they have different internal structures. As it is difficult to see how misapprehension and clarification differ in any fundamental way from question and answer respectively, one must assume any structural difference lies in the *termination* element which completes the side sequence. However, there seems to be no reason why Schegloff's insertion sequence couldn't also have a termination.

A: I don't know where the — wh — this address // is.   Q
B: Which part of town do *you* live.   Qi
A: I live four ten East Lowden.   Ai
B: Ah yeah.   Termination
   Well you don't live very far from me.   A

Thus it appears that in fact these two sequences have different labels only because they have been labelled from different viewpoints — *insertion sequence* is a structural label, *misapprehension sequence* a semantic label attempting to capture the relationship between the first item in the sequence and the preceding utterance.

There is a similar confusion in the labelling of the constituent units of the misapprehension sequence. Following an item labelled clarification one might expect an item which indicates that the addressee now understands, the apparent function of 'oh yeah, yeah' in example 2 above, and therefore labelled something like *acknowledgement*. In fact it is labelled *termination*, a structural not a semantic label and one which leads the reader to question why the first item is not labelled *opener* or *initiation*.

In setting out to look for misapprehension sequences in his own data the reader has only the observation that they begin with a 'misapprehension of sorts' and the three examples to work from. Yet while it is possible to accept 'who' in example 2 as a misapprehension, the items in examples 1 and 3 look as if they would be more satisfactorily labelled as *challenges*, followed by a *correction* and a *justification* respectively. Confusion is increased by the data and analyses presented in Jefferson and Schenkein (1978):

PATTY:	Oh I'd say he's about what five three enna half =	C1
PATTY:	= Aren'tchu Ronald	C2
RONALD:	Five *four*.	C3
PATTY:	Five four,	C4
PATTY:	En 'e weighs about a hunnerd'n thirty five	C5
	pounds =	C6
RONALD:	= Aauggh! Whadda-l-lie	C7
PATTY:	Well how — =	C8
PATTY:	= Owright? How much d'you weigh	C9
RONALD:	One *twenty* five	C10
PATTY:	Oh one *twenny* five	C11

They comment:

Relying on Ronald's overhearing of her exchange with Gene (C1), Patty initiates an encounter with Ronald by soliciting a correction from him on her estimate of his weight [sic] (C2); Ronald offers the correction (C3), Patty acknowledges the correction (C4), and returns at once to her exchange with Gene (C5).

Thus the proposed analysis is

Correction Solicitor	(C2)
Correction	(C3)
Acknowledgement	(C4)

This seems perverse because, to this outsider at least, it appears that the last thing Patty is looking for is a correction; rather she is looking for confirmation or support. However, this labelling allows Jefferson and Schenkein to treat C5–C11 in the same terms, when this time we can agree that in C9 Patty certainly is looking for a correction following Ronald's outburst in C7. However, Ronald's C7 utterance is also labelled correction solicitor which wrongly implies that the utterances are similar — they differ crucially in terms of who holds the information and *therefore* in terms of what can occur in the third slot following the correction — if, as in this case, the person supplying the correction 'knows', i.e. it is in Labov's terms a B-event, the third slot will typically be filled by acknowledging items like C4 and C11; however, had Patty responded to Ronald's C7 the third slot would typically have included something like 'that's better', at which point we realize it would have been a sequence remarkably similar to that analysed in example 1, p. 75 as a misapprehension sequence.

The situation is further complicated by Schenkein (1978b), who presents examples of another type of four-part sequence which he labels Puzzle, Pass, Solution, Comment:

ELLEN: Fine just fine thank you 'cept for this fucking infection
PATTY: Infection?
ELLEN: I can't seem to get rid of this fucking, uh urinary track infection
PATTY: They're impossible I know all about it deary believe me . . .

in which the second and third utterances have more than a passing similarity to a Schegloff QA sequence and a Jefferson misapprehension-clarification.

Topic

Sacks (1968) observes that initially he did not attempt to describe 'topic' because it seemed to be 'the sort of thing in which direct content considerations were necessary and . . . [he] couldn't proceed in [his] usual fashion . . . to extract relatively formal procedures'. Now he considers structure to be massively present.

An initial question is what sorts of thing can and do form topics in conversation? Some topics are not relevant to particular conversations because 'it is a general rule about conversation that it is your business not to tell people what you can suppose they know' (1971), and the suitability of other topics depends on the person one is talking to.

We experience, see, hear about events all the time: some are 'tellable', some aren't, and of those that are tellable some are tellable to everyone, some have a restricted audience, some must be told immediately, some can wait and still retain their interest. For instance, if one's sister becomes engaged, some relatives must be told immediately, others on a first meeting after the event, whereas some of one's friends might not know the sister or even that one has a sister, and for them the event has no importance or even interest.

This concept of tellability or *newsworthiness* is difficult to apply to a particular item in a particular conversation, but it is used by conversationalists all the time. They constantly analyse what is said for its newsworthiness ,'why that now and to me', and someone who consistently produces talk which is not newsworthy is regarded as a bore.

The pressures on people to transmit relevant news are increased by the existence of the telephone — one no longer needs to wait until one meets friends or relatives nor does one need to make special or difficult journeys to pass on information. Sacks has a good example of this in a tape of a series of telephone conversations. A and B are friends; B works at a local department store; A was driving past the store in the morning when she noticed an incident outside involving police cars (part of the transcript is reproduced on p. 88); knowing it was B's day off she rings up to tell her the news, thus fulfilling her obligations of monitoring the world for her friend and reporting relevant events. However, B has a second friend, who also works at the store, who didn't ring up to tell her about it and whom she then rings to discover what all the commotion was about. This puts C in a difficult position; she has been caught out failing to keep her friend informed and she takes the only possible way out, that of denying that what happened was newsworthy:

C: It was nothing, uh — in fact I dn't even say anything to Willy about it.

In other words, if she didn't consider it worth telling her husband to whom virtually everything is newsworthy, it must have been an insignificant event.

Thus we see there are certain things which one *must* say to particular people and certain things which are tellable if one happens to meet them. This leads on to the idea of *reason for a call or visit* — it is a basic assumption of all except chance encounters that the person who initiates the encounter has some reason for so doing, and if there is no such reason people regularly feel the need to state this, 'I was just passing', 'I just felt like giving you a call'. Conversations tend to begin with the topic which is the reason for the encounter and then move on to other topics; though, of course, the association of 'reason for call' with 'first topic' can be exploited by producing a false reason for the call and introducing the real reason as just another topic later in the conversation.

Topic change

Sacks (1971) observes that in a conversation which is progressing well talk drifts imperceptibly from one topic to another, and suggests that the relative frequency of marked topic introduction is some measure of the quality of a conversation. Turns must display 'why that now', and 'speakers specifically place almost all their utterances', and the most usual way of doing this is by tying grammatically and topically to what has gone before.

However, as Sacks (1968) stresses, talking topically and talking about some topic chosen by another speaker is not the same thing at all. One can perfectly well have a sequence in which successive speakers talk in a way topically coherent with the last utterance, but in which each speaker talks on a different topic.

That is to say, 'talking topically' doesn't consist of blocks of talk about 'a topic'. And when one presents a topic, except under rather special circumstances, one may be assured that others will try to talk topically with what you've talked about, but you can't be assured that the topic you intended was the topic they will talk to.

Speakers are aware of this as a problem and have ways of formulating a topic to make it more likely that other speakers will talk to it. Sacks exemplifies with a hypothetical speaker who wants to talk about surfing. He could introduce the topic by saying 'I went surfing yesterday', but that allows topically coherent utterances of the form 'I did X yesterday'; that is, 'surfing' has been presented as one of a class of activities and a topically coherent next utterance can focus on another of that class. A better opening he suggests would be 'I went to Malibu yesterday'. Malibu is also one of a class, this time a class of places, but it is a known feature of the place that people surf there, and predisposes the next speaker to at least begin with a reference to surfing, if only to say that they don't like it. Thus a possible sequence would be

A: I was at Malibu yesterday
B: Yeah? I was at County Line
A: How was it?
B: Too low tide   (Sacks MS)

Topic conflict

The phenomenon of topic drift can be frustrating at times for conversationalists. Everyone has had the experience of failing to get in at the right time with a good story or experience, and then seeing it wasted because the opportunity never recurs. At times, within conversations, there is competitive talk when two speakers want to develop the topic in different ways; both fight because they know there will be no further opportunity to say what they want to say. In the following example Roger wants 'New Pike' to be the topic, Jim, 'P.O.P.':

ROGER: Isn't the New Pike depressing?
KEN: Hh. The Pike?
ROGER: Yeah! Oh the place is disgusting⌈Any day of the week
JIM: ⌊I think that P.O.P. is
       ⌈depressing it's just —
ROGER: ⌊But you go — you go — take —
JIM: Those guys are losing money.
ROGER: But you go down — dow . down to the New Pike there's a buncha
       people oh :: and they're old and they're pretending they're having
       fun . but they're really not.
KEN: How c'n you tell? Mm?

ROGER: They're — they're trying make a living, but the place is on the decline, 's like a de⌐generate place
JIM: ⌊so's P.O.P.
ROGER: Y'know?
JIM: P.O.P. is just —
ROGER: Yeah it's one of those pier joints y'know?
JIM: It's a flop! hehh.   (Sacks 1967)

As we saw earlier, utterances normally relate back to the previous utterance — here Roger and Jim compete by *skip-connecting*, relating back to the last-but-one utterance, their own. Each time one of them gets a turn he declines to talk about the previous speaker's topic and reasserts his own. Skip-connecting is not an uncommon phenomenon, but apparently speakers only skip-connect over one utterance and thus, Ken's entry with what is a challenging question 'How c'n you tell' in fact preserves Roger's topic. Jim in his next turn is forced to produce a normally connected utterance, but still is able to use it to assert P.O.P. as a possible topic, 'So's P.O.P.':

> it appears that Jim, seeing he loses out, making a gesture of acquiescence while holding onto P.O.P. gets from Roger an acquiescence in including P.O.P. in the talk, that is, in Roger's next 'Yeah it's one of those pier joints' he connects to Jim's last.
>
> (Sacks 1971)

Once this competition has been resolved the conversation moves forward again.

Stories

For Sacks a story is any report of an event — it may be only one sentence long, but is usually longer, and therefore presents a problem for any intending teller because, as we noted earlier, other speakers are likely to self-select at the first possible completion point. The intending story-teller therefore needs to seek a suspension of the usual turn-taking machinery and one way of achieving this is by a floor-seeker or *story-preface*, 'Wanna hear a joke?' or 'I was at the police station this morning'. The function of such utterances is to select not next speaker as is usual in the turn-taking system, but next speaker but one, and to guarantee this speaker a stretch of uninterrupted talk in which to accomplish the story. Usually anything but a direct refusal is sufficient to allow the speaker to begin:

A: I was at the *police* station this morning.
B: Big deal.
A: 'Big deal', yeah, somebody stole all my radio equipment outta my car.
                                                                       (Sacks 1967)

Jefferson (1978) looks at how stories are fitted into conversation. She notes that one problem facing storytellers is 'to display a relationship between the story and prior talk' — in the following extract we can see one of the ways in which this is done:

KEN: ... there's a place up in Mulholland where they've — where they're building those hous⌐ing projects
ROGER: ⌊oh have you ever taken them Mulhollan time trials?

Here we see 'two discrete devices'; there is a *disjunct marker*, 'Oh', which shows that what is to come isn't directly related to what has just been said, and then an *embedded repetition*, 'Mulholland', which marks 'the element of prior talk which triggered the story'; here they do, but 'the two devices need not occur in combination'.

Labov and Waletsky (1966), in an analysis of oral narratives, note that the stories themselves typically begin with an *abstract*, an item which carries 'the general proposition the narrative is intended to illustrate', and thus enables the listener to see the relevance of individual narrative events:

1. Now, I think I did the right thing   (Labov and Fanshel 1977, p. 105)
2. I talked a man out of — Old Doc Simon, I talked him out of pulling the trigger   (Labov 1972b, p. 363)

As they point out, 'one of the most important problems to solve in delivering a narrative is how to finish it' (p. 109) — the listener needs to know when the account is over and when it is appropriate for him to respond; the abstract sometimes gives the listener some idea of what is required for the story to be complete, but also speakers have a series of ways in which they can bring the listener 'back to the present time and so let him know that the narrative is completed':

and I see that man now and again ...
when they see me now they say ...
and ever since that time ...   (Labov and Waletsky 1967, p. 109)

There is also the option of an explicit return to the abstract; the speaker who began with utterance 1 above concluded fourteen utterances later, 'Now I think I did the right thing'.

Once a story ends the normal turn-taking mechanism resumes, normally. Jefferson (1978) focuses on an instance when no one appears to want to take over the speaking role, citing a speaker who produced five possible completions before solving the problem by producing half an idiom, 'through circumstances ...', which manages to re-engage two of the participants:

ROGER: through circumstances (*laughter*)
AL: beyond their con⌈trol
DAN: ·   ⌊beyond their c'ntrol

'While re-engagement of turn-by-turn talk may be the primary issue upon a story's completion' there are, as Jefferson points out, 'other matters to which a story-teller may be oriented' — specifically what other participants have made of the story, what its significance is taken to be. Obviously the preferred reception is listener agreement with the proposed significance — in Labov and Fanshel's example the therapist responds to the patient's evaluation with 'yes I think you did too' — but as Ryave (1978) points out participants can disagree about what the real significance of a story is.

Ryave confronts the question 'how do conversational participants go about orienting to a present story in such a way as to transform the results of that orientation into the work of constructing their own succeeding story, so as to assure the constitution of a series of stories?' His data is two closely-linked stories. He notes, first of all, the obvious similarities of content and specifications: both are concerned with the 'faulty operation of . . . amusement park rides', both have the 'storyteller . . . implicated as a principal character' and both are constructed in such a manner as to make 'a moral point' (p. 121). In other words the second story can be seen as parallel to the first. However, it is not merely similarity of content that participants are sensitive to when constructing a series of stories: story-tellers concern themselves not simply with telling their stories but also with expressing the 'import, relevance, significance of the recounting' and then

> a general procedure employable by a succeeding story-teller for construct-
> ing a story that observably displays a series-of-stories relationship with a
> preceding story is to organize the story in terms of a significance statement
> which also serves to formulate a preceding story. (p. 127)

Typically, second stories accept the first speaker's assessment of, or *significance statement* about, his story and show 'that and how they understand, support, sympathize and agree with the preceding story' with their own supportive one. Whereas first stories typically have an overt significance statement, second stories typically don't and are rather seen as further supportive exemplifications of the first significance statement. However, second speakers can propose alternative interpretations of previous stories because significance is not inherent in a story but is a 'participants' phenomenon', and in the example Ryave discusses the second speaker's story and significance statement are concerned with 'altering and undermining the implications' as-

serted by the first speaker — in other words he ends with a significance statement which fits his story and subtly re-interprets the first
story, thereby supplying other participants with a 'new sense of what
the preceding story is actually about'.

It is not, of course, only stories that are vulnerable to mis- or re-
interpretation. Sharrock and Turner (1978) look at the ways in which
people make 'complaints' to the police. They observe that complainants are often aware that '"complaints" can undergo ... a shift, so
as to yield a story focused on the complainant and complained-
againsts can correspondingly appear in *this* version as victims'. They
produce interesting evidence of complainants making the point that
they haven't complained at the first opportunity, haven't specifically
looked for the evidence or incident about which they are complaining
and don't necessarily want to implicate people by name — all of these
devices to ensure that the police accept that 'their complaints *are* what
they seem to be'.

Topical coherence

The referential and descriptive items within any story are related in
highly complex ways, and each occurrence serves to reinforce and re-
emphasize the topic. Sacks (1972a) presents some techniques for analysing topical coherence by focusing on the 'story'

> The baby cried. The mommy picked it up.

Initially he suggests that most people will 'hear' the story in the same
way and will agree with the following 'facts'. Firstly, although there
is no genitive in the story, the mommy who picks up the baby is the
baby's mommy; secondly, that the two events occur sequentially; and
thirdly, that the second event occurs because of the first event. He
sets out to produce a descriptive apparatus that will account for these
facts, and, because it is 'overbuilt', for similar facts in other stories.

Sacks introduces the concept of *membership categorization device* to
handle a descriptive category, for example 'sex', which comprises one
or more subordinate concepts or *categories*, for example 'male' and
'female', and a set of rules which enables one to pair population members with a category. There are a large number of membership categorization devices and, because some words have more than one
meaning, some categories will be members of more than one device.
Thus, while 'baby' along with 'mommy' and 'daddy' is a member of the
device 'family', it is also a member of the device 'stage of life' along
with 'adult' and 'adolescent'.

Sacks then introduces two rules, the *economy* rule and the *consistency* rule. The economy rule states that 'if a member uses a single category from any device then he can be recognized to be doing *adequate reference* to a person'; the consistency rule states that once one member of a device has been used 'other categories of the same collection *may* be used to categorize further members of the population'. From the consistency rule he derives a corollary, which he calls a *hearer's maxim*: 'If two or more categories are used to categorize two or more members of some population and those categories can be heard as categories from the same collection then: Hear them that way.' Thus 'mommy' and 'baby' are heard as being co-members of the device 'family', but how do we hear that this particular mommy and baby are related? Sacks further notes that many devices are duplicatively organized, that is, the population is seen to consist of a series of such devices and is analysed as such — the population consists of a large number of *families*, not a large number of unrelated mothers, fathers, children, babies, and each device has a number of each. It is for this reason that the mommy is heard as the mommy of the baby, and for exactly the same reason the story

The first baseman looked round, the third baseman scratched himself.

will be heard as implying that the basemen are in the same team.

Sacks next introduces the concept of *category-bound activities*. He suggests that some activities are appropriate to, or done by, members of certain devices — thus 'crying' is an activity bound to the category 'baby' when it is a member of the 'stage of life' device. Some devices he notes, incidentally, are organized in a positional way, that is there is an ordered relationship like baby, child, adolescent, adult, and in this case category-bound activities can be instanced to praise or degrade. For babies and young children, crying, in certain circumstances, may be the norm and an absence of crying is a cause for praise, 'what a big boy you are', while alternatively an older child who cries may be told not to 'be a baby'. Because, in this story, the baby is crying and this is an activity bound to the category 'baby' in the 'stage of life' device, both meanings of baby are simultaneously present.

The idea of membership outlined in this article is developed in Schegloff (1972). Schegloff points out that any speaker wishing to refer to a place or location has a relatively large number of possible formulations — as he writes he could describe the location of his notes as 'right in front of me, next to the telephone, on the desk, in my office, in the office . . . in Manhattan, in New York City . . .' While all these 'correctly' describe the location of the notes, on any occasion of actual use not all of them are 'correct'. The problem Schegloff poses is 'how is it that on a particular occasion of use some term from the set is selected and other terms rejected?' The answer depends partly on whom one is talking to and partly on the topic.

Whatever the topic of the conversation, the speaker must *membership* his listener, put him into one of two or more mutually exclusive boxes. Each time a topic changes the listener must be re-membershipped, and during a conversation the same person may be membershipped as a doctor, a rugby player, a liberal, a gardener, a bridge player. Speakers usually membership their friends correctly but may make mistakes with strangers, and shoppers membershipped as shop-assistants can become very annoyed. Sacks (1968) reports an exchange on an aeroplane:

PASSENGER: Do you have a cigarette?
STEWARDESS: No we don't. They don't provide that service any more.

The stewardess assumes quite naturally that she has been membershipped as a stewardess and that the question is addressed to her in that role. She indicates this in her use of 'we', and replies, on behalf of the organization, that cigarettes aren't available any more. Had she taken it that the passenger was membershipping her as a stranger not a stewardess, Sacks argues, she might have offered him one of her own cigarettes.

Thus membershipping is not simply a feature recoverable from what is said, it is also a vitally necessary determiner of what one says. As Schegloff points out, before a speaker can produce even a location term he must membership his hearer, and if he gets it wrong one gets sequences like:

A: I just came back from Irzuapa.
B: Where's that?

When in doubt about how to membership someone speakers play safe and use a pre-sequence:

A: D'you know where the Triboro Bridge is?
B: Yeah.
A: Well you make a right there.

The fact that there is a diversity of possible formulations for the same person, place or event allows for much greater topical coherence because the speaker can choose categories from the same device. Sacks (1968) and Schegloff (1972) quote the following piece of a telephone conversation:

ESTELLE: Well, I just thought I'd — re — better report to you what's happen' at Bullocks today. Well I-v-got outta my car at five-thirty. I drove aroun' an' at first I had t'go by the *front door a' the store,*

JEANETTE: Eyeah.

ESTELLE: An' there was two p'leece cars *across the street,* andeh — colored lady wan'tuh go *in the main entrance* there *where the silver is an all the gifts an' things,*

JEANETTE: Yeah,

ESTELLE: And they, wouldn' let 'er go in and he hadda gun he was holding a gun in 'is hand a great big long gun

JEANETTE: Yeh.

ESTELLE: An'nen *over on the other side,* I mean *to the right of there, where the employees come out* there was a whole oh musta been tenuh eight'r ten employees stanning there.

It is immediately obvious that once Estelle has given the name of the store where the incident happened, all other places are described in relation to it. The police cars were 'across the street'; the coloured lady wanted to go 'in the main entrance', 'where the silver is'; the eight or ten employees were standing 'over on the other side', 'to the right of there'. Bullocks is the topic and all the locations are formulated to emphasize this. Had the teller, for instance, been coming out of the store across the road, the police cars would have been parked in front of the store and the incident would have been 'across the street'. The choice of location terms follows the consistency rule, Bullocks is the topic and the way in which the places are formulated emphasizes its centrality. As Sacks observes, 'the phenomenon of being "parked across the street from" is obviously one sort of characterization which turns on not only where you are but what it is that is being talked about, and where *that* is'.

The analysis of conversation

The techniques described above are designed to handle parts of conversations, short sequences, topics, stories. Sacks (MS) asks whether one can use *conversation* as an analytic unit. The basic question is whether there are some universal features which all conversations share, or whether conversations consist of a random collection of smaller units in no fixed sequence. He suggests that *greetings* are close to being universal in conversation and although they sometimes don't occur, on some of these occasions their absence is noticeable, which suggests that conversationalists feel they are an almost invariant feature.

There are two important features about greetings: firstly, they occur at the very beginning of a conversation, and cannot be done anywhere else in the conversation; secondly they allow all the speakers a turn, right at the beginning of the conversation:

> Hello there you two
> Hi
> Hi there

There are two major types of occasion on which a conversation does not open with a greeting. Firstly, conversations between people who do not consider themselves co-conversationalists, for example strangers. They are not on greeting terms and therefore do not exchange a greeting. The speaker who opens must demonstrate in his first utterance why he is beginning the conversation:

> Excuse me. Can you tell me the way to . . .

or:

> Hey. You've dropped your book.

The other conversations which typically don't open with a greeting are telephone conversations. Schegloff (1968) argues that although the person who answers the telephone may say 'hello' this is not a greeting, it is an *answer* to the *summons* from the caller embodied in the ringing of the telephone. Following this indication that the channel is open there is often a greetings sequence to begin the conversation proper, although sometimes, if the answerer simply answers with 'hello', there is first a checking sequence to make sure the caller is talking to the right person.

> *Summons*   Telephone rings.
> *Answer*   A: Hello.
> *Greeting* ⎰ B: Goodmorning.
> *sequence* ⎱ A: Oh hi.

Following the opening sequence the conversation consists of a series of one or more topics, though occasionally, as Schegloff and Sacks (1973) observe, the conversation may be closed before speakers reach the first topic:

> Am I taking you away from your dinner?
> Are you busy?

It is a general rule that the caller or visitor introduces the first topic, and as we noted earlier if there is no specific reason for the call or visit this is often explicitly stated — 'I was just dropping by'. There are of course exceptions, most notably when the caller has been asked to call and wants to be told why, and also when the called (wants to give the impression that he) has been trying to contact the caller, and uses his second turn not simply to reply to the greeting but to initiate the first topic:

Where you been all day, I've been trying to get hold of you?

Even if the called doesn't initiate, the first topic may still not be the 'reason for the call'. We mentioned above that sometimes a caller may not want the real reason to occur in the distinctive first topic slot and may therefore substitute another. At other times conversationalists may not feel they have anything sufficiently important to be preserved as the 'reason for the conversation' and there are ways of talking past the first topic slot.

A: Hello there.
B: Hello.
A: What's new with you?
B: Not much, and you?
A: Nothing.   (Sacks MS)

The endings of conversations are also things that have to be achieved — speakers don't just stop speaking. Conversations virtually always end with a *closing* pair, composed of 'goodbye', 'goodnight', 'see you', and so on. However, the closing sequence can only occur when a topic has been ended and other speakers have agreed not to introduce any new topics. Arriving at a point where a closing sequence can begin requires a certain amount of work.

As we noted earlier, topics frequently merge one into another. There are, however, ways of *bounding* topics to produce a clean ending. One way involves one party producing a proverbial or aphoristic summary or comment on the topic which the other party can agree with.

DORINNE: Uh — you know, it's just like bringin the — blood up.
THERESA: Yeah well. THINGS UH ALWAYS WORK OUT FOR
         THE ⌈ BEST.
DORINNE: ⌊ Oh certainly.   (Schegloff and Sacks 1973)

Another technique is for the speaker to indicate that he has nothing further to add to the topic by using his turn to produce simply 'alright', 'okay', 'so', 'well', often lengthened and with a falling intonation contour. In doing this the speaker 'passes'. This allows the next speaker the choice of either introducing an entirely new topic, because the constraints of topical coherence have been lifted, or of also passing and turning the first speaker's offered *possible pre-closing* into a pre-closing sequence. Then, as neither speaker has raised a new topic they can move into a closing sequence and end the conversation:

Topic *bounding* *sequence*	THERESA:	Yeah well. Things uh always work out for the ⌈ best.
	DORINNE:	⌊ Oh certainly.
Pre-closing *sequence*	DORINNE:	Alright Tess.
	THERESA:	uh huh. Okay.
Closing *sequence*	DORINNE:	G'bye.
	THERESA:	Goodnight. (ibid.)

In this example both participants agreed that the conversation had gone on long enough; however, sometimes one speaker wants to end but for some reason is unable to achieve a topic bounding sequence and is then forced into a different type of pre-closing: either a statement which presents a reason for stopping:

I gotta go, baby's crying.

or an offer to allow the other speaker to stop:

Well, I'll letchu go. I don't wanna tie up your phone.
This is costing you a lot of money.
Okay I'll letcha go back to watch your Daktari.   (ibid.)

Again, these are only possible pre-closings and especially the latter kind may not be accepted; the other speaker may deny that he wants to get away, though if he does accept they can then move straight into the closing sequence:

(B has called to invite C, but has been told C is going out to dinner)

Pre-closing *sequence*	B:	Yeah. Well get on your clothes and get out and collect some of that free food and we'll make it some other time Judy then.
	C:	Okay Jack.
Closing *sequence*	B:	Bye bye.
	C:	Bye bye. (Schegloff and Sacks 1973)

These examples contain only the essentials of a closing, an achieved pre-closing sequence and closing pair, but pre-closings may include making arrangements, re-emphasizing arrangements made earlier, re-stating the reason for the call, as well as many repetitions, and may continue for many utterances: Schegloff and Sacks quote a 'modest' example of a closing containing twelve utterances.

The slot after the 'possible pre-closing' is the one provided for introducing any topic which has not yet received mention, but new topics can be introduced after a pre-closing or even after a closing, provided they are marked as being misplaced.

CALLER: Okay, thank you.
CRANDALL: Okay dear.
CALLER: OH BY THE WAY I'd just like to . . .   (ibid.)

Any items inserted during the closing after earlier opportunities have been passed up have the status of after-thoughts and this position can be exploited in order to take away the importance of a piece of news — one doesn't normally forget really important items.

Schegloff and Sacks (ibid.) quote the following example which occurs, at the end of a fairly long telephone conversation, following the pre-closing, when both speakers have apparently indicated they have no more topics.

A: I — uh ;;; I *did* wanna tell you an I didn' wanna tell you uh;; last night. Uh because you had entert — uh, company. I-I-I had something — terrible t'tell you. So⌈uh
B: ⌊how terrible is it?
A: Uh, tuh . as worse it could be.
                                    (0.8)
B: W-y' mean Ada?
A: Uh yah.
B: What'she do, die?
A: Mm;:hm.

Stylistic features of conversation

In a fascinating series of lectures given during 1971 Sacks suggested that conversation has much of the additional phonological, grammatical and thematic patterning which is usually thought to typify works of literature.

In a discussion of an extended version of the 'skip-connecting' passage (this volume pp. 81–2) he points out marked phonological patterning. There is a series of words, 'depressing', 'disgusting', 'degenerate', 'decline', 'decrepit', in which the first two phonemes are identical, displaying 'reverse rhyme'. There are also words and phrases which echo each other because they share phonemes — 'degenerate', and 'pier joint'; 'walkin aroun drunk', and 'all kindsa fun'; 'alcoholics' and 'all kindsa things'.

Sacks argues that features such as these cannot be rejected as chance because they occur too frequently and any rejection on the grounds of implausibility ignores the fact that speakers are all the time achieving effects of similar sophistication and complexity. These phonological echoes are evidence of how closely attentive speakers are to each other — a speaker's choice of one formulation rather than another is partly determined by the phonological patterning of the previous text and the alternative formulations.

Texts also display marked lexical patterning. This same fragment has a large number of marked contrast terms, for example, 'these' and 'those'; 'go to' and 'come from'; 'in' and 'out'; 'you' and 'they'; 'men' and 'ladies'; 'new' and 'old'; 'ever' and 'never'; 'pretending' and 'really'; 'depressing' and 'fun'. The use of such contrasting terms is particularly appropriate at this point in the conversation because of the topic conflict which we discussed above.

In the following example from a group therapy session Roger is complaining about the way in which he has to describe his preferred occupation — he wants to describe it as life-pervasive:

ROGER: When I say I wanna be something, it's not just that I wanna be this, it's just I-I-I just — that's the only thing I *tell* people that I wanna be an artist. It's really a whole way of life ...

⋮

You visualise yourself uh living a certain way

⋮

I see it as a whole picture

⋮

I don't see it that way at all

⋮

I — How am I gonna live, what am I gonna do for a living, and the whole scene

⋮

And uh since most people don't think along these lines ...

(Sacks 1971)

One must remember that this is unplanned conversation and that while there is a vast number of ways to describe his problem he consistently uses specifically visual, artist-appropriate, terms. 'You visualise yourself'; 'I see it as a whole picture'; 'I don't see'; 'the whole scheme'; 'along these lines'.

This topic-appropriate choice of terms applies to many metaphorical uses of language. Sacks presents another extract from a group therapy session where the patients have been talking round the subject of 'sex' without actually mentioning it. The therapist observes, 'Well so far, all of you skirted around the subject. That see(hh)ms to b(h)e predominantly uh on your *minds* at any rate'. The problem facing the therapist in producing this utterance is to indicate that he knows the topic they have been talking around, without actually introducing it himself. He does this by choosing an expression, 'skirt around', which both means 'to allude to' and also itself alludes, by a pun on 'skirt', to the hidden topic.

Stories in conversation tend to be created anew for each retelling;

jokes usually have a fixed form and can be ruined by slight alterations. Sacks focuses on the structural complexities of the following 'dirty joke':

> KEN: You wanna hear muh — eh my sister told me a story last night . . . There — There was these three *girls*. And they were all *sisters*. And they'd just got married to three brothers . . . So, first of all, that night, theya're — on their honeymoon the — uh mother-in-law, says — (to 'em) well ,why don'tcha all spend the night here an' then you cn go on yer honeymoon in the *mor*ning. First night, th' mother walks up t' the first door an' she hears this uuuuuuuuuuhh! Second door is HHOOOHH! Third door there is *no*thin. She stands there fer about *tw*unny five minutes waitin fer sumpna happen — nuthin. Next morning she talks t' the first daughter an she sz — wh how come ya — how come y'went YEEEEEEAAHAGGHH last night, 'n daughter sez well, it *tick*led mommy, 'n second girl how come ya screamed. O mommy it *hu*rts. hh third girl, walks up t' her — why didn' ya *say* anything last night. W'*you* told me it was always impolite t' talk with my mouth full.   (Sacks 1978)

Sacks points out that the joke has a simple temporal ordering — the events are told in the order in which they are said to have happened. There is also a more complex *sequential* organization by which each of the events depends for its significance on its position with relation to other events — 'next morning' has its relevance because there was a 'last night' and in order to understand what is being implied by the reference to a 'second door' one uses that there was a 'first door'. The joke has two major units, the 'first night' and the 'next morning'; the 'first night' poses a problem which is solved the 'next morning', and the solution is nicely placed as the punch line which closes the second sequence and the joke itself.

The mother in the joke acts as a guide — the listener sees the events through her eyes. The fact that she moves from first door to second and second door to third as soon as she hears a noise shows that it is noise which is important and enables the listener to see that lack of noise is the important event at the third door. Her questions next morning elicit explanations of why the noises were different and the meaning of the silence.

As Sacks notes, the economy and organization of the events in each sequence is admirable. The joke depends on the fact that silence in the third room is unexpected, but the joke doesn't actually say the mother was surprised. In order to show that something is not normal one needs at least but not more than three instances, two normal and one non-normal. The events could be presented in any order, but then it would be necessary to comment on the unexpectedness of one of them. The joke presents two 'normal' events first and reinforces this by the fact that the mother moves from one door to the next; the third event is seen as different from the first two and the mother waits. The second sequence, 'next morning' preserves the sequence and allows the explanation of the unexpected event to occur last, after two 'normal' explanations can predispose the listener to hear the punning response in its intended meaning.

The punch-line to this joke has an extra dimension to it. The joke was told to Ken by his 12-year-old sister, and it embodies adolescent girls' objections to parental rules and interference. The cleverness of the punch-line is that it uses one rule to explain the breach of another and incidentally complains that sometimes it is impossible to satisfy one's parents.

5 Intonation

It is surprising if not startling to realize that although all the work reported in the preceding chapters has been concerned with the analysis of speech, there has been virtually no attempt to account for the significance of variations in the major channel-specific phenomena of supra-segmentals: *paralinguistic* features of voice quality and *prosodic* features such as pitch, pitch movement, loudness and length. Voice quality, embracing such characteristics as 'whisper', 'breathy', 'husky', 'creaky', 'falsetto', 'resonant', 'giggle', 'sob' (Crystal 1969, p. 135), is a phenomenon speakers and analysts are very much aware of but, although Crystal (ibid.) and Laver (1980) offer detailed descriptions, it is difficult to attach specific meanings to the choices beyond the observation that 'their function might well be to give additional emphasis or pointing to an attitude already present in an utterance' (Crystal ibid., p. 137).

Austin (1962) refers on several occasions to the importance of 'tone of voice, cadence, emphasis' and 'intonation' but in fact his analysis takes no account of these features; Searle (1965) includes 'intonation contour' among his 'function indicating devices', but never expands; while of the 'ethnography of speaking' investigations reported above, only Irvine's (1974) discussion of Wolof greetings makes use of prosodic features — 'stress' and 'tempo/quantity' — to distinguish speech styles. Even the major work of Sacks, Schegloff and of Jefferson herself (1974) takes virtually no account of the available prosodic and para-linguistic information, though much of the conversational analysts' data is quoted in the detailed Jefferson transcription which shows hesitation phenomena, length, stress and some information about pitch and pitch movement. In fact all the analyses discussed so far can be applied very successfully to ordinary orthographic transcripts with no accompanying tape, which confirms that appeal to intonation is spasmodic, if not haphazard, and occurs when differences are perceived for which there can be no other explanation.

Intonation, the systematic patterning of prosodic features, is of course also a problem area — whereas native speakers have no difficulty using the system communicatively, they find it very difficult to introspect about the significance of the choices they make, and even to produce citation forms reliably and correctly. Sadly, when discourse analysts coming from varying backgrounds look to linguistics for help, they find very little — in the main American linguists have ignored intonation; Trager and Smith (1951) produced a simple partial description, while Transformational Grammar saw intonation as a feature to be added later, once all the major grammatical decisions and lexical insertions had been made. Thus all the work reported here will be on British English.

Theoretical preliminaries

Discourse analysts need to be able to describe the meaning of suprasegmental choices and this requires a two-stage process, first assigning the data to categories, and then assigning meaning to the categories. For the first stage, we need to draw on three traditional principles of phonetic and linguistic description. First, features that are acoustically on a continuum must be analysed as realizations of a small number of discrete units that 'form a closed set, defined by their mutual oppositions' (Labov and Fanshel 1977, p. 42) — just as we accept that a given phoneme conflates a large number of acoustically distinct sounds, so a falling tone, for example, will as a category include large variations in length and steepness of the fall.

The second principle is that there is no *constant* relationship between particular acoustic phenomena and particular analytic categories; it is contrasts and not absolute values which are important. This principle is not novel and creates no problems theoretically or practically, as analysts of tone languages discovered long ago:

> tone languages have a major characteristic in common: it is the relative height of their tonemes, not their actual pitch which is pertinent to their linguistic analysis ... the important feature is the relative height of a syllable in relation to preceding and following syllables. A toneme is 'high' only if it is higher than its neighbours in the sentence, not if its frequency of vibrations is high.
>
> (Pike 1948, p. 4)

A third principle is that there is no necessary one-to-one relationship between a given suprasegmental choice and a meaning: on the one hand, as Bolinger's (1964) 'wave' and 'swell' metaphor suggests, a given pitch choice can at the very least be *simultaneously* carrying both general information about emotional state and a specific local meaning of the kind described in detail below, pp. 104–110; on the other hand, certain interactionally significant signals, like for instance a request for back-channel support, may be carried by the co-occurrence of a particular pitch choice and a particular kinesic one, each of which singly has a different significance (Gosling, in preparation).

Descriptions of intonation

There is in fact a large measure of agreement about the basic facts of English intonation, though descriptions differ markedly in the significance they attach to choices. O'Connor and Arnold (1959) suggested that 'the contribution that intonation makes is to express in addition to and beyond the bare words and grammatical constructions used, the speaker's attitude to the situation in which he is placed' (p. 2). However, their attempts to provide valid generalizations about the attitudinal meanings of the tunes they isolated serve only to demonstrate the difficulties. For instance, they suggested that a speaker uses a low falling intonation with a statement to indicate that it is definite and complete in the sense that it is a 'separate item of interest'; but that in addition the intonation conveys a 'cool, calm, phlegmatic, detached, reserved, dispassionate, dull, possibly grim or surly attitude on the part of the speaker'. Their own examples demonstrate the problems admirably:

You've got ,lipstick on your collar again.
It's getting ,late.

It is difficult to hear the first utterance as 'cool', 'calm' or 'detached', and the second as 'grim' or 'surly'. In fact, even though O'Connor and Arnold offer a hundred different 'meanings' including such fine distinctions as 'mild surprise but acceptance of the listener's premises', 'critical surprise' and 'affronted surprise', these meanings seem to depend, as Brazil (1975) observes, far too much on 'the co-occurrence of particular lexical items'.

Could it be that O'Connor and Arnold's intuition that intonation carries attitudinal meaning is correct but that the attitudinal labels they assign are badly selected? Apparently not; Crystal (1969) reports an experiment which demonstrated that native speakers find it virtually impossible to agree when matching attitudinal labels with intonation contours, and this confirms feelings that individual intonation choices do not in fact carry specific attitudinal information. Crystal himself proposed a very detailed analysis of the intonation choices available in English, which has met with general agreement, but while accepting that 'statements of the meaning of the prosodic contrasts . . . must indeed be the dominant aim of the linguist' (p. 282), he confessed himself unable to make any valid generalizations — and by 1975 he was arguing that 'the vast majority of tones in connected speech carry no meaning', although accepting that a few carry attitudinal options like 'absence of emotional involvement'.

By contrast, Halliday (1970) asserts that 'the importance of intonation is . . . that it is a means of saying different things. If you change the intonation of a sentence you change its meaning'. He suggests that intonation choices carry two kinds of information: firstly, the relative importance of different parts of the message determines and therefore is conveyed by decisions about when and where to make major pitch movements; secondly, the choice of one pitch contour rather than another relates to grammatical 'mood (kinds of statement, question, etc.), modality (assessment of the possibility, probability, validity, relevance, etc. of what is being said) and key (speaker's attitude of politeness, assertiveness, indifference, etc.)' (p. 22).

Halliday (1967) suggests that the number of significant choices is only five (Table 5.1). When he comes to attach meanings to intonation choices he suggests an even more powerful generalization, that there is a major binary distinction between rising and falling tones which indicates whether polarity is certain or uncertain (polarity is the choice between positive and negative):

> if polarity is certain, the pitch of the tonic falls; if uncertain, it rises. Thus tone 1 is an assertion or a query not involving polarity; and tone 4, which falls and then rises is an assertion which involves or entails some query. Tone 2 is a query . . . and tone 5 which rises and then falls is a dismissed query, one countered by an assertion. Tone 3 avoids a decision, as an assertion, it is at best confirmatory, contingent or immaterial. ·

TABLE 5.1   Significant intonation choices

Tone	Symbol	Tonic movement	Terminal pitch tendency
1	`	falling	low
2	{ˊ ˇ	rising falling-rising	high high
3	–ˊ	rising	mid
4	~	(rising)-falling-rising	mid
5	◝	(falling)-rising-falling	low

(Halliday 1967)

We can exemplify the way these general meanings are given specific, even attitudinal, significance by examining a declarative utterance. For declaratives with certain polarity, tone 1 is the neutral or unmarked choice; all other tones are meaningful as marked choices. The double lines // indicate the boundaries of the tone group, the number at the beginning the tone, while the syllable underlined is the one on which the tonic movement begins:

// 1. I saw him <u>yes</u>terday //	neutral
// 2. I saw him <u>yes</u>terday //	contradictory ('challenging', 'oppressive', 'defensive', 'indignant', etc.)
// 3. I saw him <u>yes</u>terday //	non-committal ('disengaged', 'uncon- cerned', 'discouraging')
// 4. I saw him <u>yes</u>terday //	reservation ('there's a "but" about it')
// 5. I saw him <u>yes</u>terday //	committed ('involved', 'assertive', 'super- ior', 'encouraging')

Thus, the speaker is seen as having four major options which allow him to indicate his degree of involvement with the information and his interlocutor.

It is evident that this kind of analysis has great potential for discourse analysis — it has a small and therefore powerful set of categories and a linked set of general meanings which, combined with individual clauses, generate a more delicate meaning in context. Sinclair *et al.* (1972) is one early attempt to employ this system, which also showed up some problems.

Brazil

In a series of publications Brazil (1973, 1975, 1978, 1985) has modified, refined and gradually diverged from the original Hallidayan model, adapting it to fit with the model of discourse structure presented in Sinclair and Coulthard (1975). Brazil's model keeps the major distinction between rising and falling tones, though he attributes different significance to the opposition, but radically moves away from tying the description to the grammatical clause, arguing that the intonational divisions speakers make in their utterances are motivated by the need to add moment-by-moment situationally-specific meanings to particular words or groups of words. It is to the still developing description, available in a more detailed form in Brazil *et al.* (1980) and Brazil (1985), that the rest of this chapter will be devoted.*

* This discussion draws heavily on Brazil's contribution to Brazil, Coulthard and Johns (1980) and Coulthard and Brazil (1982).

Like the other descriptions already discussed, Brazil's is expressed in terms of pitch choices, though this is almost certainly a simplification. Intensity and durational features regularly co-occur with the pitch choices and it may well turn out that the choices described as being realized by pitch phenomena are being identified by hearers at least some of the time through associated intensity and durational phenomena — Lieberman's (1960) experiments on stress urge caution in this area.

Brazil suggests that there are four sets of options associated with the tone unit — *prominence, tone, key,* and *termination* — each of which adds a different kind of information. The tone unit itself has the following structure.

(Proclitic segment)   Tonic segment   (Enclitic segment)

As this structure implies, tone units may consist simply of a *tonic segment*, and many do; indeed a considerable number consist of no more than a tonic *syllable*, i.e. the syllable on which there is a major pitch movement:

// GOOD //, // YES //, // ME //, // JOHN //

Most tone units, of course, do consist of more than the tonic segment, and here the question of segmentation arises. With the syllables following the tonic there is in fact no analytic problem: even though the pitch *movement* of the tone may be continued over succeeding syllables, for reasons which will be explained later the *tonic segment* is considered to end with the *tonic syllable*. Thus:

Tonic segment	Enclitic segment
// GOOD	ness knows //
// YES	sir //
// WE	did //
// JOHN	ny's coming //

However, while the *final* boundary of the tonic segment is by definition unproblematic, recognizing where the tonic segment *begins* is a more difficult matter and depends on an understanding of the concept of *prominent syllable*, which will necessitate a short digression.

It is not always easy to be sure what significance writers attach to such terms as 'stress', 'accent' and 'prominence'. For Brazil, *accent* means the attribute which invariably distinguishes the marked from the unmarked syllables in words like '*cur* tain, con'*tain*, re'*la* tion, and distinguishes the lexical items from the others in a sentence like '*Tom is the best boy* in the *class*'. Thus, when we say 'Tom *is* the best boy in the class' we are not *accenting* 'is', we are making it *pitch prominent**. (Readers will notice, when performing the example, that 'is' is highlighted by having a higher pitch than 'Tom'.) Prominence is thus the name given to a property that is not inherent, like accent, but only associated with a word by virtue of its function as a constituent part of a tone unit.

To return, it is now possible to define the scope of the tonic segment: it begins with the first prominent syllable, henceforth called the *onset*, and ends with the last prominent syllable, the *tonic*, which has the additional feature of *tone* or pitch movement, whose significance will be discussed at length below. There are thus, by definition, no prominent syllables in the proclitic and enclitic segments. All prominent syllables will now be distinguished by capitals and tonic syllables will in addition be underlined.

Proclitic segment	Tonic segment	Enclitic segment
he was	GOing to GO	
that's a	VERy TALL STOR	y
it was a	WED	nesday

If we expand the first example to

   // he was GOing to GO again //

we now have four classes of syllable: unaccented, 'he', 'was', '-ing', 'to', 'a-'; accented, '-gain'; prominent, 'GO'; and tonic 'GO'. It is interesting to speculate how far these are in fact the four degrees of stress which Trager and Smith (1951) proposed, and which others have had great difficulty in recognizing.

Prominence, then, is a linguistic choice available to the speaker independent both of the grammatical structure of his utterance and of word-accent. What then is its significance?

Let us begin with the following question/response pairs:

1. Q: Which card did you play?
   R: // the QUEEN of HEARTS //

2. Q: Which queen did you play?
   R: // the queen of HEARTS //

3. Q: Which heart did you play?
   R: // the QUEEN of hearts //

---

* A full discussion of the fundamental frequency characteristics of prominent syllables will be found in Brazil 1978 and a briefer but more accessible discussion in Brazil, Coulthard and Johns 1980.

The three responses differ only in terms of the assignment of prominence and we can see already that prominence has something to do with informativeness. In exploring this concept further let us begin with the word 'of'. It is easy to see that 'of' is totally predictable: it is the only word that could occupy the place between 'queen' and 'hearts'. If we think of each word in the phrase as representing a selection from a set or paradigm of words available, then at the place filled by 'of' there is a set of one. In this respect it can be compared with the places filled by 'queen' and 'hearts' where the options are greater:

	ace		hearts
	two		clubs
the	:	of	diamonds
	queen		spades
	king		

In the context of the question 'which card did you play?' the speaker has a choice of thirteen possibilities at the first place and of four at the second, but this time the limitation has nothing to do with the working of the language system: as Brazil points out, there is no *linguistic* reason why the response should not have been 'the prince of forks' or 'the seventeen of rubies', or any of an enormous number of combinations. What imposes the limitation this time is an extralinguistic factor, the conventional composition of the pack of playing cards.

This is a *crucial* distinction and it makes clear the need to distinguish the *existential paradigm*, that set of possibilities that a speaker can regard as actually available in a given situation, from the *general paradigm* which is inherent in the language system. Obviously at the place occupied by 'of' the two paradigms coincide: there can be no possibility of selection in the existential paradigm because there is none in the general paradigm, whereas at the place occupied by 'queen' the general paradigm of thousands of nouns has been reduced to an existential paradigm of thirteen. We can now explain the prominences in pairs 1 and 3 as marking a selection from an existential paradigm — when 'queen' occurs in the question as in 2 there is no choice in the response, i.e. no existential paradigm at the position occupied by 'queen', and the word is therefore non-prominent. We can support this assertion by imagining a context in which 'of' can be seen as a choice from an existential paradigm — for example, when a foreigner makes a mistake in his choice of preposition then the correction contains a prominent 'of':

Q: Which card did you play?
R: // QUEEN in HEARTS //
C: // the queen OF hearts //

The examples used so far suggest that the non-prominent/prominent distinction is a realization of the *textually given/textually new* distinction, but this is misleading; rather, it is concerned with the *interactionally* given.

Thus one can imagine a situation in which items are contextually given, as in a game of cards when one player has, without saying anything, put down the jack of hearts and a next player verbalizes as he plays

// QUEEN of hearts //

or another situation when an addressee known to drink only coffee is asked

// CUP of coffee //

where the question implies choice from an existential paradigm consisting of 'cup' and 'mug'.

We can already see that far from being a system that 'adds virtually nothing', intonation is crucially concerned with marking situationally informative items; it is no accident that young children repeat selectively, as Brown and Bellugi (1964) report they do — the words they select are the ones that adults have marked as significant by prominence.

Tone

Like Halliday, Brazil sees speakers as having a basic choice between falling and rising tones, though he sees the fundamental choice being between a falling tone and a falling-rising tone, Halliday's tones 1 and 4.

1. // when I've finished Middlemarch // I shall read Adam Bede //

2. // when I've finished Middlemarch // I shall read Adam Bede //

Whatever additional implications these intonation choices may have, the first utterance is certainly addressed to someone who is expected to know already that the speaker is reading *Middlemarch*, but to whom the speaker's future intentions are an item of news; whereas in the second example, the question of the speaker's reading *Adam Bede* has already arisen in some way and he is offering information about when he will read it. Significantly the same interpretation holds when the order of the *grammatical* constituents is reversed:

3. // I shall read Adam Bede // when I've finished Middlemarch //

4. // I shall read Adam Bede // when I've finished Middlemarch //

Obviously, created contrasting examples demonstrate points more clearly, but we can see exactly the same opposition in the following extracts from a lesson on 'energy':

5. // when you strike a match // it is a rubbing movement //

6. // when we rub our hands together // we are causing friction //

The context makes it clear that in (5) the teacher is providing some commonplace instances of 'rubbing movements' — this notion has just been introduced in an experiment involving rubbing a pencil on 'something woollen' to create static electricity, and the teacher is now amplifying it by mentioning a series of familiar events like 'sliding' and 'rubbing out in your books'. Later in the lesson when he produces (6) the teacher is taking one of these events and presenting it as an instance of 'causing friction'. Thus in (5) the informational content of the second tone unit is treated as being conversationally in play: 'rubbing movement' is referred to as the area of common concern to which the class and the teacher are currently addressing themselves; by contrast the content of the first tone unit is presented as news. In (6), on the other hand, it is the content of the first tone unit that is treated as part of the shared universe of reference: the 'rubbing of hands' has already been mentioned and is now reinvoked, while the new information, namely the appropriate terminology, occurs in the second tone unit.

We can generalize from these examples and see that a basic function of the fall-rise tone is to mark the experiential content of the tone unit, the *matter*, as part of the shared, already negotiated, common ground, occupied by the participants at a particular moment in an ongoing interaction. By contrast, falling tone marks the matter as new.

All interaction proceeds, and can only proceed, on the basis of the existence of a great deal of *common ground* between the participants. In fact a major difference between interactions between strangers and those between friends lies in the degree of uncertainty about the boundaries of common ground and in the amount of time spent exploring these boundaries. Common ground is not *restricted* to shared experience of a particular linguistic interaction up to the moment of utterance; rather it is a product of the interpenetrating biographies of the participants, of which common involvement in a particular ongoing interaction constitutes only a part. Brazil suggests that it is useful to think of the speaker seeing his world and the hearer's as overlapping,

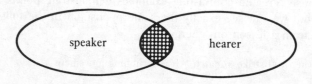

and of him being faced, as he composes, with moment-by-moment decisions as to whether what he says can be assumed to be shared or not.

Brazil argues that in choosing the fall-rise tone, hereafter called *referring* tone (symbol *r*), for a particular part of his message the speaker is marking it as part of the existing common ground, whereas by choosing the falling proclaiming tone (symbol *p*) he is indicating his expectation that the area of common ground will be enlarged, as a result of the listener being told something he didn't already know.

In the following examples we can see the effect of altering the tone selections:

7. // *r* he'll be TWENty // *p* in AUgust //

8. // *p* he'll be TWENty // *r* in AUgust //

In lay terms, it may be said that in (7) a potential hearer is 'told' when a mutual acquaintance will have his twentieth birthday, while in (8) he is 'told' how old the acquaintance is (or will be). In either case, the tone unit having referring tone serves to match the assertion with an assumed focus of interest, perhaps, though not necessarily, made explicit in the preceding dialogue either by a question from another participant or by being mentioned by the speaker himself.

Decisions about what information to proclaim and what to refer to are a speaker's constant concern and are made in the light of his moment-by-moment assessment of the state of play. In the more extended example below, taken from a doctor/patient interview, we can see some of the factors which influence such decisions:

// *r* i've come to <u>SEE</u> you // *p* with the <u>RASH</u> // *r* i've got on my <u>CHIN</u> // *p* and under<u>NEATH</u> // *r* which has de<u>VEL</u>oped // *p* in the past three <u>DAYS</u> // *r* i <u>FIND</u> it's <u>IR</u>ritating // *r* and at <u>WORK</u> // *r* with the <u>DUST</u> // *r* us being a <u>CLOTH</u>ing factory // *r* well i find it's <u>IR</u>ritating // *p* makes me want to <u>SCRATCH</u> it //.

The only items of information the patient feels it necessary to *proclaim* are that his problem is the rash, that it is also underneath his chin and that he feels the need to scratch it. The facts that the patient has come to see the doctor, that his rash (once it has been identified as the reason for the visit) is on his chin, and that it has 'developed', are all visibly evident, while the fact that the rash is 'irritating' is scarcely something one would need to point out to a doctor. The doctor could also reasonably be expected to know that the patient goes to work. All these items are therefore *referred* to.

The explanation for the patient's choice of referring tone when mentioning the 'dust' and the fact that he works at a 'clothing factory' may be more complex. It may well be that the doctor does know the conditions and place of his employment, but equally it may be that the patient has tactically chosen, for politeness perhaps, to present new information as if it were already shared. For we must remember that the *r/p* opposition, like all other linguistic options, is available for exploitation. Indeed, if tone choices were simply predictable on the basis of what could be ascertained about the context, they would be of very little interest. Ultimately, it is the speaker's choice whether to present information as already shared or new.

So far we have distinguished proclaiming and referring tones using the concept of *common ground*. Thus the choice of the second tone in an example like:

// *p* we <u>GAVE</u> it to our <u>NEIGH</u>bours // the <u>ROB</u>insons //

is seen to depend on the speaker's assessment of whether or not the matter of the tone unit was already known to the listener. In other words, we have been implicitly equating common ground with shared knowledge, but this is too simple a view — choice of tone can also carry the more general social meanings of convergence/divergence, or solidarity/separateness.

As we have already noticed, quite a lot of what speakers say is not in any real sense informing and is usually marked as not informing by not being made prominent. But there are times when such items are not simply prominent but even tonic. If we take examples like:

// r to <u>TELL</u> you the <u>TRUTH</u> //
// r <u>FRANK</u>ly //
// r <u>AC</u>tually //
// r <u>HON</u>estly //

we can see that their matter is usually non-informing, since truth-telling and frankness, as Grice (1975) reminds us, are generally taken as conversational norms and as such not remarked upon. However, while their communicative value derives little or nothing from their matter, it does have a social component, and such items serve to insinuate intimacy or solidarity.

On this argument, by choosing proclaiming tone with an apparently superfluous item the speaker places himself outside the area of convergence: he is heard to be reserving his position in some general way or perhaps staking a proprietory claim to the view expressed in the ensuing discourse, or simply emphasizing the likely lack of agreement on a point. Thus the item //r <u>SURE</u>ly// is used very frequently in persuasive argument precisely to evoke existing solidarity, convergence or agreement, in support of a particular point, though, as the following example from an argument where a speaker wants to emphasize his *disagreement* shows, it can be used with *p*-tone to stress the divergence:

// r but a <u>TY</u>rant // p <u>SURE</u>ly // p IS a form of <u>LEAD</u>ership //

As the matter of the tone unit can vary along a line from highly informing to virtually non-informing, so the meaning of *r* tone varies along a continuum from 'this is shared matter' to 'we are in some unspecified sense at one with each other'. The extreme social pole is probably represented when the patient, quoted earlier, says:

// p <u>WELL</u> // r i've COME to <u>SEE</u> you // ...

There is little doubt that his assertion is uninforming, and he seems to be doing little more than insinuate a state of unfocused 'togetherness' preliminary to describing his ailment.

r+ tone

Brazil treats the *rise* as a marked version of the fall-rise and labels it *r+*. He suggests that references to common ground can be either

1. vividly present background, (*r* tone), or
2. matter which, while deemed to be present in the area of convergence, has need of reactivation, (*r+* tone).

So if we imagine replies to the question 'Where's the typewriter?', we might hear:

a) // r in the CUPboard // (where it always is), or
b) // r+ in the CUPboard // (why don't you ever remember . . .?)

In order to expand on the function of choices in the more delicate r/r+ system, it is necessary to focus upon another aspect of the context of interaction: *role-relationships*.

In all situations there are social rules which determine who speaks when and to whom, and in many situations speaking rights are distributed differentially. For instance, it is part of a teacher's function to follow up and evaluate pupils' answers; pupils are not expected to reciprocate. This is not to say that pupils can't, it is just that it is unusual and if they do so they are seen as doing something different from the teacher, usually they are 'being cheeky'. Brazil uses the term *dominant* in a technical sense to indicate the person who has the greater freedom in making linguistic choices, and then argues that the freedom to make choices in the r/r+ system is available only to a dominant speaker, or to one who is using the system to *claim* dominance.

To begin elaborating this idea, we may compare the consistent use of r tone for reference to common ground in the patient's statement on p. 107 with the teacher's use of r+ tone in:

p NOW // p beFORE i came to SCHOOL // r THIS MORNing // p i HAD my BREAKfast // r i had some CEReal // r+ and i had some TOAST // r+ and i had an EGG // r+ and i had a cup of TEA // r+ and i had a BIScuit // p and then i came to SCHOOL //

Both teacher and patient are evoking common experience, but it is part of the point of what the teacher is doing that the experience is not, so far, conversationally present. To use the term introduced earlier, he is 'reactivating' the pupils' incipient awareness of the variety of things that go to make up the received notion of 'breakfast'. But over and above these considerations, there is a sense in which both speakers' choices reflect a relationship holding between them and their fellow-interactants. This is in line with a general observation that, in some circumstances, speakers do not feel themselves in a position to 'remind', in the sense of making the formal choice represented by r+ tone; and as a predictable corollary to this, to choose r+ tone in certain circumstances is, in itself, to assert dominance. We can consider the possibility of the patient beginning:

r+ i've COME to SEE you // p with the RASH // r+ i've GOT on my CHIN //

This would almost certainly be heard as an aggressive opening, because it is inappropriate to the patient's role. The intonation choice fits much more easily with an utterance like:

// p <u>WELL</u> // r+ i've COME to <u>SEE</u> you // p about the <u>CAR</u>
// r+ you SOLD me <u>YES</u>terday // . . .

Tones *r* and *r*+, then, have values which are distinguished most generally, exactly like those of the primary referring/proclaiming choice, by reference to their social implications. And in their case, the relevant aspect of the context of interaction is the role-attribute that has been described here as dominance. Both choices make reference to an area of presumed convergence, but the *r*+ option represents a kind of intervention, in that the speaker takes a positive initiative in invoking common ground. A dominant speaker is one who is for the time being privileged to intervene in this way; or, alternatively, intervention implies dominance.

There is a similarly marked proclaiming option *p*+ realized by a rise-fall pitch movement. The intonation manuals usually gloss this choice as 'surprise' or 'horror' which in certain circumstances is true. The explanation Brazil offers is that by choosing the *p*+ tone the speaker signals that he is simultaneously adding information both to the common ground and to his *own* store of knowledge. In other words, the information is marked as doubly new — 'I also didn't know' and hence in the context 'I am surprised, disappointed, delighted'. For this reason, the *p*+ tone is common when one person is reading out interesting information from a newspaper or book:

// r it says <u>GAM</u>ay // p+ is the GRAPE that makes <u>BEAU</u>jolais //

This meaning of *p*+ is even more evident in responses to unexpected news such as:

// p+ <u>REAL</u>ly //
// p+ <u>AR</u>thur //

or almost anything blasphemous or obscene. Their matter contributes nothing to their information value, so we must attribute whatever communicative function they have to co-occurring intonation choices. Extended paraphrases like 'That's a surprise!', 'I can't believe it!', or 'How could you say (or do) such a thing!' help to bring out their common meaning which is the equivalent of something like 'That alters my world view!'. This option, like the *r*+ option, tends to be exploited by a dominant speaker.

Key

In addition to making choices in the prominence and tone systems, a speaker must also for each tone unit select relative pitch or *key* from a three-term system, *high, mid,* and *low.* Key choices are made and recognized with reference to the key of the immediately preceding tone unit; in other words there are no absolute values for high, mid and low key, even for a particular speaker; in fact a given high key tone unit may well be lower than an earlier mid key one, but as we stressed above the continually varying reference point is already well attested in analyses of tone languages.

The key choice is realized on the first prominent syllable of the tonic segment and adds a meaning that can be glossed at the most general level as:

high key   contrastive
mid key   additive
low key   equative

The way in which these intonational meanings combine with lexico-grammatical ones is discussed in detail in Brazil *et al.* (1980) but can be simply illustrated in the following invented examples where only key is varied. (In all subsequent examples // marks the *mid* line; items that are high or low key will be printed above or below this notional line.)

// *p* he GAMbled // *p* and $\overline{\text{LOST}}$ // CONTRASTIVE (contrary to expecta-
                                            tions; i.e. there is an interaction-bound
                                            opposition between the two)
// *p* he GAMbled // *p* and LOST // ADDITIVE (he did both)
// *p* he GAMbled // *p* and $\underset{\text{LOST}}{}$ // EQUATIVE (as you would expect,
                                            i.e. there is an interaction-bound
                                            equivalence between them)

Here we see key being used to indicate particular relationships between successive tone units in a single utterance, but the same relationships can occur between successive utterances. If we begin with the polar options 'yes' and 'no' we quickly realize that only when they co-occur with high key are they in opposition. In other words, if he wishes to convey 'yes not no' or 'no not yes' a speaker must select high key:

// *p* well you $\overset{\text{WON'T be}}{}$ $\underline{\text{HOME}}$ } (i) // *p* $\overset{\text{YES}}{}$ i will //

// *p* before SEVen //   (ii) // *p* $\overset{\text{NO}}{}$ i won't //

In (i) the speaker chooses contrastive high key to mark the choice of opposite polarity in his response; in (ii) he chooses to highlight an agreed polarity and this apparently unnecessary action is usually interpreted as emphatic and then in a particular context as 'surprised', 'delighted', 'annoyed', and so on. Much more usual than (ii) is (iii):

// p well you ^{WON'T be} <u>HOME</u> ⎫   (iii) // p <u>NO</u> i won't //

// p before <u>SEV</u>en // ⎭   *(iv) // p <u>YES</u> i will //

(iv) sounds odd because the speaker is heard as simultaneously agreeing and contradicting, or perhaps rather agreeing with something that hasn't been said, and the normal interpretation would be that he had misheard. The contradiction is in fact only made *evident* by the repeated auxiliary, which carries the polarity, because interestingly 'yes' is the unmarked term of the pair and as a result, if the speaker does not repeat the auxiliary, he can choose either 'yes' or 'no', an option which at times causes confusion even for native speakers:

// p well you ^{WON'T be} <u>HOME</u> ⎫   (v) // p <u>NO</u> // (I agree I won't)

// p before <u>SEV</u>en // ⎭   (vi) // p <u>YES</u> // (I agree with your assessment)

When the polarity is positive, of course, there is only one choice:

// p well you'll be <u>HOME</u> ⎫   (vii) // p <u>YES</u> // (I agree I will/I

// p before <u>SEV</u>en // ⎭   agree with your assessment)

         *(viii) // p <u>NO</u> // (I agree I won't)

'Right' can often be used instead of 'yes' or 'no' — in (iii), (v), (vi) and (vii) it could equally well occur with mid key to express agreement, whereas with high key 'right' asserts 'right not wrong' and this is the use in this example from Labov and Fanshel (1977, pp. 146–7):

RHODA: then nobody else knows an' everybody thinks everything is fine, and good

THERAPIST: mhm

RHODA: and I end up — hurting myself

THERAPIST: // p ^{RIGHT} //

Here and in Figure 5.1 the therapist is seen using high key to mark 'right' as evaluative, and thus to let Rhoda know that she is 'restating one of the most important lessons she had learned in treatment' (p. 148).

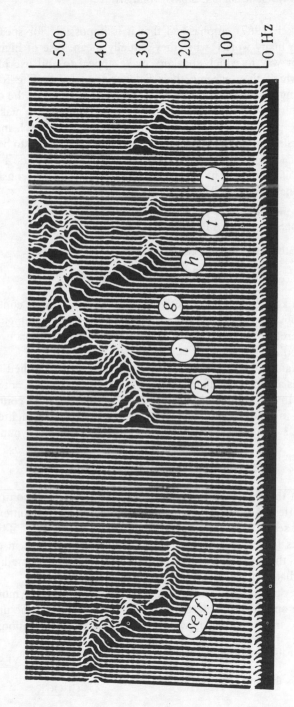

FIGURE 5.1

(Labov and Fanshel 1977, p. 147)

Garfinkel (1967) emphasized that it is impossible for speakers to 'say in so many words' what they actually mean. Use of high key is one major way in which speakers make appeal to and use of information which they assume their listener(s) to have. The following 'misreading' from a BBC newscast is amusing because of the contrast which listeners were forced to derive from the utterance to make sense of it. The previous day Mrs Thatcher had made a speech including comments on immigration and the newscast was supposed to be saying that *in addition* to other things she was going to do Mrs Thatcher would make a statement on immigration that would be 'considered', i.e. reasonable and well presented:

> . . . and tomorrow Mrs Thatcher will make
> // p a conSIDered STATEment on immiGRAtion //

However the final phrase came out:

> // p a con$\underline{\text{SIDered statement}}$ // r on immiGRAtion //

The high key choice for 'considered' marked this item as contrastive, and the obvious contrast was with the previous day's statement which must therefore be, by implication, not 'considered' or even 'ill-considered'.

Our examples of high key contrastivity have so far implied that the contrast is a binary one between polar opposites but this is not necessarily so. In the following example 'wife' could in some contexts be heard as in contrast with the only other possibility, 'daughter', and therefore a flattering introduction, i.e. 'doesn't she look young':

> // p $\overset{\text{MEET el}}{}$IZabeth // p john's $\underline{\text{WIFE}}$ //

but given the right context, 'wife' could be heard as in contrast to a whole series of other relationships one might, in the context, have assumed: secretary, sister, sister-in-law, friend, mistress . . . Thus high key marks for the listener that an item is to be heard as in contrast with something but leaves him to fill out the existential paradigm, i.e. decide what in the context are possible contrastive items.

Low key marks an item as *equative*, as contextually synonymous; thus when the option is co-selected with 'yes' or a repetition the utterance does little more than acknowledge receipt of the information:

> D: whereabouts in your chest?   P: on the heart side.   D: // p $\underline{\text{YES}}$ //

> A: what's the time?   B: ten o'clock   A: // p ten o'$\underline{\text{CLOCK}}$ //

If a speaker reformulates in low key he is indicating that he doesn't feel he is adding any new information, but simply verbalizing an agreement that the two versions are situationally equivalent in meaning:

A: what's the time? B: ten o'clock A: // p BEDtime //

// p HE'S DEAD // p and BURied //

The third option, mid-key, marks the matter of the tone unit as *additionally* informing and thus its selection with this example sounds slightly odd:

// p HE'S DEAD // p and BURied //

as does the following, from a newscast reporting how a Palestinian terrorist organization had tried to invade Israel by balloon, but had met disaster when the balloon

// p CRASHED // p and BURNED //

This listener, at least, expected a low key for 'burned', indicating 'as you would have expected'.

Pitch concord: key and termination

It has long been accepted that some polar questions seem to expect or even predict a particular answer, like (9) below, while others, like (10), appear to allow for either:

9. You'll come, won't you?
10. Will you come?

In fact *all* utterances set up expectations at a very general level about what will follow; in order to demonstrate this we need to discuss the fourth option, *termination*. Brazil argues that for each tonic syllable, as well as choosing a pitch movement, the speaker chooses to begin, in the case of falling tones, or end, in the case of rising tones, with high, mid or low pitch; this choice he labels *termination*.

When we look at transcribed texts we discover a remarkable tendency for concord between the *termination* choice of the final tone unit of one utterance and the *initial key* choice of the next; in other words it appears that with his termination choice a speaker predicts or asks for a particular key choice and therefore by implication a particular meaning from the next speaker. This is easiest to exemplify with questions. In example (9) above the speaker is looking for agreement, i.e. a mid key 'yes', and his utterance is likely therefore to end with mid termination, as in (9a) below, to constrain the required response (remember that key and termination can be realized in the same syllable),

9a. A: $//$ p you'll $\underline{\text{COME}}$ $//$ p $\underline{\text{WON'T}}$ you $//$

   B: $//$ p $\underline{\text{YES}}$ $//$ (I agree I will)

Choice of high termination for 'won't you' needs some ingenuity to contextualize, because the conflict between the lexico-grammatical markers of a search for agreement and the intonational indication that there is a 'yes/no' choice makes it sound like either a threat or a plea:

9b. $//$ p you'll COME $//$ p $\overline{\text{WON'T}}$ you $//$

Example (10), by contrast, naturally takes a high termination, looking for a 'yes/no' contrastive answer:

10a. A: $//$ p will you $\underline{\text{COME}}$ $//$ B: $\begin{cases} // \ p \ \overline{\text{YES}} \ // \\ // \ p \ \overline{\text{NO}} \ // \end{cases}$

although the persuasiveness of 10b can be explained simply as the intonation choice converting an apparently open request into one looking for agreement.

10b. A: $//$ p $\overline{\text{WILL}}$ ^{you} $\underline{\text{COME}}$ $//$ B: $//$ p $\underline{\text{YES}}$ of course $//$

We can see this pitch concord working in the two examples below, both from the same doctor/patient interview:

11. D: $//$ p it's $\overline{\text{DRY}}$ ^{skin} $//$ p $\underline{\text{IS}}$n't it $//$ P: $//$ p $\overline{\text{MM}}$ $//$

12. D: $//$ p VERy $\overline{\text{IR}}$ritating $^{you\ say}$ $//$ P: $//$ p $\overline{\text{VER}}$y irritating $//$

The initial key choices in the responses have the meanings we have discussed above, and in both examples we can see the doctor asking for or constraining a response of a particular kind by his final termination choice. Thus in (11) he ends with mid termination because he wants the patient to *agree* with his observation, while in (12) he wants the patient to exploit the contrastive 'yes not no' meaning of high key to *confirm* what he has said. Had the doctor stopped at 'skin', in (11), his question would have had a very different force, and he would again have been heard as asking for confirmation of a fact in doubt, but both the key and the lexical realization of the rest of the utterance show that what is required is agreement with a proposed shared opinion.

The pressure towards pitch concord can of course be disregarded; the patient could have responded to the doctor's mid key 'isn't it' with a high key 'yes' or 'mm', but telling the doctor he was right would, in these circumstances, sound like non-compliant behaviour, suggesting perhaps annoyance at an unnecessary question. In the following example the patient solves his dilemma by selecting the predicted agreeing mid key but lexicalizing the correctness just to be sure:

D: // p ^{FIVE tiller} <u>ROAD</u> // r+ <u>IS</u>n't it //
P: // p THAT'S cor<u>RECT</u> // p <u>YES</u> //

While high and mid termination place concord constraints on what follows, low termination does not; it marks, in fact, the point at which prospective constraints stop. The following is unremarkable:

13. A: // p ^{have you GOT the} <u>TIME</u> // B: // p it's THREE o'<u>CLOCK</u> //

In choosing low termination the second speaker doesn't preclude the first from making a follow-up move, but he certainly doesn't constrain him to do so as he could have done by choice of high termination. If the first speaker chooses to continue, one option is a low key 'thanks', which one might expect if the exchange occurred between strangers in the street in Britain, in which case the item would serve simultaneously to acknowledge receipt of the information and to terminate the encounter. (In the USA one would expect a mid or even high termination 'thanks' allowing for or constraining respectively the 'you're welcome', 'sure', 'OK', which almost invariably follows.) If the exchange had occurred during a longish interaction, the acknowledging function could equally well have been realized by an 'mm', a repetition, or an equative reformulation:

// p <u>MM</u> //; // p THREE o'<u>CLOCK</u> //; // p TIME to <u>GO</u> //

Form and function

We can now use these observations on the significance of pitch concord to attack one of the major problems in discourse analysis — why some items which are declarative or moodless in form are taken to be questioning in function. In the above example we cited some of the possible next utterances following the question about the time; options we did not discuss were those in which the speaker ends with mid or high termination, rather than low. A possible sequence is:

13a. A: have you got the time?
     B: it's three o'clock
     A: // p _{TIME to} <u>GO</u> //

with a meaning of 'I take "three o'clock" as equivalent in this context to "time to go" (indicated by choice of low key), *and* I assume you will agree' (mid termination predicting mid key 'yes I agree'). Another alternative would be:

13b. // p TIME to $\overline{\text{GO}}$ //

and this time the speaker will be heard as both adding the information that he considers 'three o'clock' to be 'time to go' and asking for positive confirmation in the form of a 'yes/no' response.

We can see the significance of termination choice in these two extracts from a doctor/patient interview: in (14) the repetition with low termination is heard as closing; in (15) the repeated item with high termination is heard as questioning:

14. D: How long have you had these for?
     P: Well I had them a week last Wednesday
     D: // p a WEEK last $_{\text{WEDnesday}}$ //
     D: // p HOW many atTACKS have you $\underline{\text{HAD}}$ //

15. D: What were you doing at the time?
     P: Coming home in the car. I felt a tight pain in the middle of the chest.

     D: // p ^{TIGHT} pain //
     P: // r ^{YOU} KNOW // like a — // p DULL $_{\text{ACHE}}$ //

There are two significant points about these observations: firstly, although the items with mid or high termination in examples (13a), (13b) and (15) are initiating and in some sense questioning, the pitch movement on the tonic is *falling*, not rising, as is often claimed in the intonation manuals — in other words, it is definitely *termination* and not *tone* choice which carries the eliciting function; secondly, we are now able to identify the function of these items through the phonological criteria which realize them and do not need to draw on assumptions about speaker's and hearer's knowledge or A-events and B-events as suggested by Labov (1972a).

As we discussed in Chapter 2, above, philosophers have frequently pointed out that the two major assumptions underlying directives are that the speaker has the right to tell the listener to do X and that the listener is, in the most general sense, willing or agreeable to doing X. From what has been said above about termination choices, pitch concord and the meanings of choices in the key system, one would expect orders to end with a mid termination choice, looking for a mid key agreeing // <u>YES</u> //, // <u>SURE</u>ly //, // <u>CER</u>tainly //. It is thus quite fascinating to discover that most classroom instructions, even those in a series and to the whole class, when no acknowledgement is possible or expected, also end with mid termination, symbolically predicting the absent agreement:

FOLD your _{<u>ARMS</u>} // LOOK at the_{<u>WIN</u>dow} // LOOK at the_{<u>CEIL</u>ing} //

LOOK at the _{<u>FLOOR</u>} // LOOK at the _{<u>DOOR</u>} //

It is also instructive, if not worrying, to realize that when parents and teachers get cross because their instructions are being ignored they typically switch to high termination which paradoxically allows for the high key contrastive refusal:

PARENT: // *p* PUT it ^{<u>DOWN</u>} // CHILD: // *p* ^{<u>NO</u>} //

Concluding remarks

Although it has not been possible to do full justice to Brazil's description, it is evident that discourse analysts ignore intonation at their peril — a description which can incorporate a systematic treatment of intonation will obviously handle more of the interactive meaning of utterances. Brazil's description has so far not attracted a great deal of criticism, though Stubbs (1984) warns that it 'must remain very provisional until corroborated by much more data and study'. Certainly neither Stubbs (1981, 1983) nor Berry (1981), although working on data and problems raised in Coulthard and Brazil (1979) and partly explained through an appeal to intonation, feel the need to either adopt or refute Brazil's proposals.

It has always seemed likely that if there were any linguistic universals they would be phonological ones, and early results (Mansfield 1983) suggest that key, prominence, termination and perhaps even tone work in similar ways in at least European languages.

6 A linguistic approach

This chapter will concentrate on the model of discourse analysis developed collectively by members of English Language Research during the past fifteen years. Though the analytic system first outlined in Sinclair *et al.* (1972) and Sinclair and Coulthard (1975) has undergone many modifications, the underlying theoretical assumptions remain basically unaltered so the chapter will first present the original model and then the significant modifications.

The work began in 1970 as a research project to investigate the structure of verbal interaction in classrooms, and from the beginning the aim was to anchor this study within the discipline of linguistics and to use tried linguistic techniques on new data. The intellectual climate was not initially sympathetic. Within American linguistics the conflict between generative and interpretive semantics was at its height and Robin Lakoff's paper arguing for the importance of context was two years away, while in England, despite the Firthian tradition, the SSRC linguistics panel was soon to define suprasentential studies as outside linguistics. Also, all the articles which are now considered seminal were yet to come: Hymes was arguing for a broader definition of the scope of linguistics but the 1972 paper outlining the concept of 'communicative competence' had not been published; the work of Labov on sequencing and A-B events and the Sacks lecture notes were unknown; the now considerable body of work in conversational analysis was not yet written; the work by Grice and Gordon and Lakoff on conversational inferencing would not be widely available for another five years. Only the work by Austin and Searle, offering the powerful idea that people do things with words, was available then in much the same form as it is now.

The Birmingham description is located within the major British linguistic framework of the time which derived its theoretical basis from Halliday's classic article 'Categories of the theory of grammar' — there was no existing linguistic description of interaction, let alone a linguistic *theory* of interaction, and the procedure adopted was to analogize from existing grammatical theory.

A first assumption of a 'categories' description is that the analytic units can be arranged on a *rank-scale* which implies that units are related in a 'consists-of' relationship with smaller units combining with other units of the same size to form larger ones. Thus a sentence consists of one or more clauses, each of which in turn consists of one or more groups, and so on. The *structure* of each unit is expressed in terms of permissible combinations of units from the rank below, the structure of a clause for example being described in terms of nominal, verbal, adverbial and prepositional groups.

By definition the unit at the lowest rank has no structure — for example, *morpheme* is the smallest meaningful unit and cannot be divided into smaller meaningful units — but there is obviously a sense in which morphemes are made up of sounds. Certainly it is sounds which the listener hears, and from which he reconstructs the morphemes, but the meaning of a morpheme has nothing to do with the sounds of which it is composed and restrictions on combinations of sounds are not described in terms of morpheme boundaries — the sound system of the language has its own rank scale with structure described in terms of phonemes, syllables, feet and tone units. There are thus two separate areas or *levels* of organization, and the level of sound is said to *realize* units from the level of grammar.

The unit at the highest rank in a particular level is one which has a structure that can be expressed in terms of smaller units but which does not itself form part of the structure of any larger unit. Any attempt to describe structure assumes implicitly that there are certain combinations of units which either do not occur, or if they do occur are unacceptable — within grammar such structures are classified as ungrammatical. The corollary is that a potential unit upon whose structure one can discover no constraints in terms of combinations of the unit next below has no structure and is therefore not a unit in the rank scale. It is for this reason that sentence must in fact be regarded as the highest unit of grammar, for despite many attempts to describe paragraph structure, and despite the obvious cohesive links between sentences, it is impossible to characterize paragraphs in terms of permissible and non-permissible combinations of classes of sentence — all combinations are possible and the actual sequence of sentence types within a paragraph depends on content and stylistic decisions, not grammatical ones. Similarly, in interaction a given interrogative places no grammatical constraints on a next item:

	Int.	Is it in the cupboard?
Where's the typewriter?	Decl.	It's in the cupboard
	Imp.	Look in the cupboard
	Moodless	In the cupboard

Sinclair *et al.* therefore proposed a new level, *discourse*, with its own rank scale, to cope with the structure of classroom interaction, and suggested that the units were *realized* by items at the level of grammar. In commenting on the separateness of the levels of grammar and phonology as *form* and *substance*, Halliday had observed that whereas '*all* formal distinctions presuppose *some* distinction in substance . . . no relation whatsoever is presupposed between the *categories* required to state the distinction in form (grammar and lexis) and the *categories* required to state phonologically the distinction in substance which carries it'. A simple example of this principle is the plural morpheme which even in regular cases may be realized at the level of phonology by the unit 'syllable' or the unit 'phoneme', horse:hors*es* but cat:cat*s*; there are, of course, much more complex cases. It is a similar lack of fit between units that provides strong support for the existence of the level of discourse. For example, not only can the act *directive* (see below) be realized by all four clause types — imperative, interrogative, declarative and moodless — but also in many cases, as the following examples illustrate, the 'directiveness' appears in some way to derive from the occurrence of the base form of the verb irrespective of whatever other grammatical items precede it. The function of the preceding items seems to be in part to carry as yet unclassifiable degrees of 'politeness':

> shut the door
> can you shut the door
> I wonder if you could shut the door
> I want you to shut the door
> please shut the door
> let's shut the door

This set of examples suggests that just as categories at the level of grammar, like the plural morphemes discussed above, cut across phonological units, so in discourse there are categories whose nature we cannot fully envisage which cut right through traditional grammatical units like verbal groups. The following examples from a five-year-old suggest that he was learning to construct discourse acts on exactly this principle:

> please may you { fasten my shoe
>   open the door
>   give me a drink

Discourse structure

Sinclair *et al.* proposed five ranks to handle the structure of classroom interaction:

lesson
transaction
exchange
move
act

but in fact postulating the largest unit, *lesson*, was an act of faith since they were unable to provide any structural statement in terms of transactions. As no structure has been discovered since, it looks as if in fact lesson has the same status as paragraph in grammar.

Transactions do have a structure, expressed in terms of exchanges, and Sinclair *et al.* note that the boundaries of transactions are typically marked by *frames* whose realization at the level of form is largely limited to five words — 'OK', 'well', 'right', 'now', 'good' — uttered with strong stress, high falling intonation and followed by a short pause. It was also observed that teachers frequently follow a frame, indicating the beginning of the transaction, with a *focus*, a metastatement *about* the transaction.

frame: well
focus: today I thought we'd do three quizzes

and often end the transaction with another focus summarizing what the transaction was about or has achieved:

focus: what we've just done, what we've just done is given some energy
to this pen
frame: now

It is instructive to compare these findings for the classroom with those of Sacks and Schegloff for conversation. The teacher, because his role involves choosing topic, is able to indicate in advance what a chunk of discourse will be about, while the following example would be anomalous in conversation just because conversationalists do not have this degree of control:

well
today I thought we'd talk about my holidays in France

However, as we saw in Chapter 4, conversationalists can 'close down' a topic by using items identical to those isolated as frames in classroom discourse, and while they cannot produce metastatements about the future content of the discourse they can and certainly do produce retrospective metastatements, as transaction boundaries.

Incorporating the later work of Brazil on intonation allows us now to produce a more general explanation of the phenomenon of framing, and the significance of the associated high falling intonation. Speakers can be observed to use pitch to structure their messages and low termination, to which we made only a passing reference on page 117, is in fact a speaker's signal that he has reached a point of semantic completeness. The next tone unit can then begin either with mid key marking what follows as additively related, a fact often emphasized by the use of 'and', or with high key which marks what follows as contrastively separate. It now seems reasonable to regard this pitch contrast, evident in the example below, as in fact marking the transaction boundary:

T: so we get energy from petrol and we get energy from food
// *p* TWO kinds of $_{ENergy}$ /// *p* $\overline{NOW}$ then // . . .

Here the pitch contrast is reinforced by the item 'now', but we can see the boundary carried by pitch alone in the following example:

T: we use, we're using energy, we're using
// *p* $_{ENergy}$ /// *r* when a $\underline{CAR}$ // . . .

Transactions have a structure expressed in terms of exchanges — they begin and often end with a *boundary exchange*, which consists of a frame and/or focus, followed by a succession of *informing, directing*, or *eliciting* exchanges. Informing, directing and eliciting exchanges are concerned with what is more commonly known as 'stating', 'commanding' and 'questioning' behaviour, though these terms are not used, for reasons explained below.

The structure of exchanges is expressed in terms of *moves* and for illustrative purposes we will concentrate on eliciting exchanges. Remembering Sacks' work on Question-Answer sequences one might have expected the eliciting exchange to consist typically of a teacher question followed by a pupil answer and a series of eliciting exchanges to produce the pattern T–P, T–P, T–P, but this in fact is not the case; the structure is rather T–P–T, T–P–T, T–P–T. In other words, the teacher almost always has the last word and two turns to speak for every pupil turn. This, incidentally, goes some way to explaining the consistent finding that teachers talk on average for two-thirds of talking time. The teacher asks a question, the pupil answers it and the teacher provides an evaluative follow-up before asking another question:

T: Those letters have special names. Do you know what it is? What is one name that we give to these letters?
P: Vowels.
T: They're vowels, aren't they?
T: Do you think you could say that sentence without having the vowels in it?

A three-move structure was proposed for exchanges — Initiation, Response, Follow-up — and it was suggested that the three-move eliciting structure is the normal form inside the classroom, for two reasons: firstly, answers directed to the teacher are difficult for others to hear and thus the repetition, when it occurs, may be the first chance some children have to hear what their colleague said; secondly, and more importantly, a distinguishing feature of classroom discourse is that many of the questions asked are ones to which the teacher-questioner already knows the answer, the intention being to discover whether the pupils also know. Often answers which are 'correct' in terms of the question are not the ones the teacher is seeking and therefore it is essential for him to provide feedback to indicate whether a particular answer was the one he was looking for.

T: (elicit)   What does the food give you?
P: (reply)   Strength.
T: (feedback)   Not only strength we have another word for it.
P: (reply)   Energy.
T: (feedback)   Good girl, energy, yes.

This three-part structure is so powerful that if the third move does not occur it is, in Sacks' terms, 'noticeably absent', and this is often a covert clue that the answer is wrong.

T: (elicit)   Can you think why I changed 'mat' to 'rug'?
P: (reply)   Mat's got two vowels in it.
T: (feedback)

T: (elicit)   Which are they? What are they?
P: (reply)   'a' and 't'.
T: (feedback)

T: (elicit)   Is 't' a vowel?
P: (reply)   No.
T: (feedback)   No.

Moves combine to form exchanges; moves themselves consist of one or more *acts*. The status and relationship of moves and acts in discourse is very similar to that of words and morphemes in grammar. Just as the word is the minimal free form, so the move is the minimal contribution a speaker can make to an exchange; just as some words consist of a single morpheme, so some moves consist of a single act; just as some morphemes are bound while some are free and can occur alone as words, so some acts are bound and do not normally occur as the sole item in a move.

The category *act* is very different from Austin's illocutionary acts and Searle's speech acts. Acts are defined principally by their interactive function. The definitions of the acts are very general; *elicitation* for instance has as its function 'to request a linguistic response', *informative* 'to provide information'. The analysis thus does not attempt to distinguish, for example, between 'request', 'ask', 'entreat', 'beg', 'enquire'. However, as a descriptive system within the Hallidayan framework it allows the concept of *delicacy* — initially crude or general classifications can at a secondary stage be more finely distinguished. Thus, if it is possible to show that moves containing an act 'request' are followed by a different class of items from those containing an act 'entreat', this distinction can be built in at secondary delicacy — Straker-Cook (1975) demonstrates how this can be done in an adaptation of the system to handle lectures, and Stenström (1984) offers a very detailed subcategorization of elicitations and responses.

Sinclair *et al.* proposed twenty-two acts; with hindsight it is evident that some of these were subvarieties distinguished in terms of content, not discourse function, and thus we can present the system here without oversimplification in terms of seventeen acts, which can be grouped into three major categories — meta-interactive, interactive, and those concerned specifically with turn-taking; the seventeenth act, *aside*, was proposed to handle occasions in the classroom when the teacher withdrew from interaction and produced utterances like 'Where did I put my chalk?'.

Meta-interactive	*Interactive*		*Turn-taking*
marker	informative	acknowledge	cue
metastatement	directive	react	bid
loop	elicitation	reply	nomination
	starter	comment	
	accept	evaluate	

Taking the meta-interactive acts first, *marker* is the act which realizes framing moves, 'now', 'right', etc.; *metastatement*, talks about the discourse, realizes focusing moves; and *loop*, realized by such terms as 'pardon', 'again', 'what did you say', which can occur following any move, puts the discourse back to where it was before the preceding move.

The interactive acts themselves consist of the initiation options, *informative*, *directive*, and *elicitation*, their appropriate responses, *acknowledge*, *react* and *reply*, and the follow-up options, *accept*, *evaluate* and *comment*, which will be discussed further below.

Initiation	*Response*	*Follow-up*
informative	acknowledge	—
directive	(acknowledge) react	⎰ accept
elicitation	reply	⎱ evaluate comment

In addition, there are three acts concerned with turn-taking in the classroom. Sometimes teachers *nominate* a child:

Joan, do you know who these people were?

sometimes children are required to *bid* by raising their hand or shouting 'sir' or 'miss' and the teacher then nominates one of those who have bid:

T:	(elicit)	Anyone think they know what it says?
P:	(bid)	HANDS RAISED
T:	(nomination)	Let's see what you think, Martin.
P:	(reply)	Heeroglyphs.
T:	(evaluation)	Yes, you're pronouncing it almost right.

At times with a new or difficult class a teacher may find he needs to insist on the speaker-selection process. The following example comes from a lesson given by an experienced teacher to a class he hasn't taught before, when he felt it necessary to provide *cues* to the children to raise their hands and bid:

T:	(cue)	Hands up.
	(elicit)	What's that?
P:	(bid)	RAISED HAND
T:	(nomination)	Janet.
P:	(reply)	A nail.
T:	(evaluation)	A nail, well done, a nail.

Figure 6.1 shows an illustrative analysis of part of a lesson. This extract was chosen because there is a detailed intonation transcript available in Brazil *et al.* (1980, pp. 159–61) and the recording is available on the tape that accompanies that book. It is always difficult to represent structural analyses in two dimensions; here the following conventions have been adopted: a horizontal line across the page

FIGURE 6.1   Sample analysis

Exchange type	Initiation	Act	Response	Act	Follow-up	Act
directing	Put it near your tissue paper	dir				
eliciting	Tell me what happens when you put your pen near your tissue paper	el	Sir the pen er picks it up	rep	Yes	ev
eliciting	Would you say the pen is doing some work	el	Yes sir	rep	Yes	ev
eliciting	Would you say the pen was using something	el	i) Yes sir ii) Energy sir	rep rep	i) Yes ii) It's using energy Yes	ev ev acc
eliciting	Where did you get the energy from	el	Sir, sir From your arm	bid rep	From the rubbing yes	ev acc
boundary	Right FRAME	mark				
directing	Put your pens down	dir				
directing	All eyes on me	dir				
informing	Now. What we've just done what we've just done is given some energy to this pen	mark inf				
eliciting	Now. Where've we got the energy from	mark el				

marks an exchange boundary, and a bold line a transaction boundary; the initiating, responding and follow-up moves are then presented sequentially across the page.

Form and function

Just as in the level of form there are closed and open classes of items, so some of the discourse acts like 'bid', 'nomination', 'cue', 'frame', 'focus', 'loop' and to a lesser extent 'acknowledge', 'accept' and 'evaluate' can have their realizations closely specified, while other acts are open class and therefore can present interpretive problems.

Sinclair *et al.* observe that while their categories of *elicitation*, *directive* and *informative* are frequently realized by interrogative, imperative and declarative structures respectively, there are many occasions when this is not so. The opportunity for variety arises from the relationship between grammar (in the broad sense) and discourse. The *unmarked* form of a directive may be imperative — 'Shut the door' — but there are many *marked* versions, using interrogative, declarative and moodless structures.

> Can you shut the door?
> Would you mind shutting the door?
> I wonder if you could shut the door?
> The door is still open.
> The door.

To handle this lack of fit between grammar and discourse, which Searle (1975) was to approach through indirect speech acts and Grice (1975) with conversational postulates, Sinclair *et al.* suggested a two-stage interpretive process involving information first about *situation* and then about *tactics*. Situation refers to all relevant factors in the environment, social conventions and the shared experience of the participants, while tactics handles the syntagmatic patterns of discourse, the way in which items precede, follow and are related to each other. 'It is place in the structure of the discourse which determines ultimately which act a particular grammatical item is interpreted as realising, though classification can only be made of items already tagged with features from grammar and situation.' (Sinclair and Coulthard 1975, p. 29)

As a first step, knowledge about schools, classrooms, one particular moment in a lesson, is used to reclassify items already labelled by the grammar. Often the grammatical types declarative, interrogative and imperative realize the situational categories *statement*, *question* and *command* respectively, but this is by no means always so, and of the nine possibilities, declarative question, interrogative question and so on, only imperative statement is difficult to instance.

Grammatical categories	Situational categories
declarative	statement
interrogative	question
imperative	command

The interrogative 'what are you laughing at', for example, is interpretable either as a question, or as a command to stop laughing. Inside the classroom it is usually the latter, so in the following example, where the teacher has just played the children a tape of a man with a 'funny' accent in order to discuss reactions to accents with them, he still has to work quite hard to convince the pupil that he is asking a question and not issuing a command requiring the cessation of the activity and a conventionalized acknowledgement/apology.

TEACHER: What kind of person do you think he is? Do you — what are you laughing at?
PUPIL: Nothing.
TEACHER: Pardon?
PUPIL: Nothing.
TEACHER: You're laughing at nothing, nothing at all?
PUPIL: No. . . It's funny really 'cos they don't think as though they were there they might not like it and it sounds rather a pompous attitude.

The pupil's mistake lies in misinterpreting the *situation*, and the example demonstrates the crucial role of situational information in the analysis and interpretation of discourse.

Classification using situational information can be exemplified by looking at interrogatives. Sinclair *et al.* suggest that there are four questions to be asked of an interrogative clause:

1. Is the addressee also the subject?
2. What actions or activities have been *pre*scribed up to the time of utterance?
3. What actions or activities are physically possible at the time of utterance?
4. What actions or activities are *pro*scribed at the time of utterance?

Using answers to these questions they formulate three rules to predict when a teacher's interrogative is realizing a command.

Rule 1 Any interrogative is to be interpreted as a *command to do* if it refers to an action or activity which teacher and pupil(s) know ought to have been performed or completed and hasn't been.

1. Did you shut the door.	command
2. Did you shut the door?	question

Example 1 is apparently a question to which all participants know the answer but it draws attention to what hasn't been done in order to cause someone to do it. Example 2 is a question only when the teacher does *not* know whether the action has been performed.

> **Rule 2** An interrogative clause is to be interpreted as a *command to do* if it fulfils all the following conditions:
> a) it contains one of the modals can, could, will, would, (and sometimes going to);
> b) if the subject of the clause is also the addressee;
> c) the predicate describes an action which is physically possible at the time of the utterance.

1. Can you play the piano, John.	command
2. Can John play the piano?	question
3. Can you swim a length, John?	question

The first example is a command because it fulfils the three conditions — assuming there is a piano in the room. The second is a question because the subject and addressee are not the same person. The third is also heard as a question if the children are in the classroom, and the activity is not therefore possible at the time of the utterance. However, Sinclair *et al.* predict that if the class were at the swimming baths example 3 would be interpreted as a command and followed by a splash.

Some speakers in fact mark the distinction between question and command intonationally — not, as one might think, by a different tone choice but by whether or not 'can' is made prominent,

> a) // CAN you SWIM a LENGTH john //
> b) // can you SWIM a <u>LENGTH</u> john //

where 'can' in (a) is prominent because it is being questioned, but in (b) is non-prominent because non-informing — it would make no difference if 'can' were substituted by 'will', 'would', 'could', because it is just part of a mitigation or negative politeness formula.

> **Rule 3** Any interrogative is to be interpreted as a *command to stop* if it refers to an action or activity which is proscribed at the time of the utterance.

1. Is someone laughing.	command
2. What are you laughing at.	command
3. What are you laughing at?	question

Examples 1 and 2 work by drawing attention to the laughter, and example 3 is interpreted as a question only when laughter is not forbidden, as in the extract above. Figure 6.2 summarizes these choices.

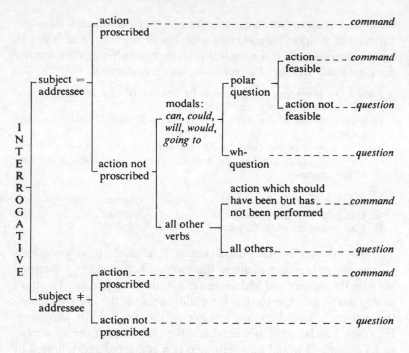

FIGURE 6.2   The classification of an interrogative using situational information

Obviously some of these rules are very similar to those proposed in Labov (1970, 1972a) and Labov and Fanshel (1977), and depend like Grice's maxims both on assuming inferencing by listeners and on an appeal to shared world knowledge. Many linguists object that one cannot appeal to participants' knowledge of the world, or even of the situation, because it is not available to the analyst. Bever and Ross (1966), discussing the example 'Everyone should read the Bible. Deuteronomy is one of the great books of the world', argued that in order to handle this the descriptive apparatus would need to include such information as the fact that Deuteronomy is one of the books of the Bible. In other words, it would be necessary to build speaker's knowledge into the grammar, which is obviously impossible. However, rules such as those proposed by Labov and by Sinclair *et al.* manage to explain interpretation of utterances by *appealing* to speakers' knowledge without *characterizing* it. In this way they reflect what speakers do all the time; they continuously 'membership' their co-conversationalists, and if they make wrong assumptions their utterances are misinterpreted. Successful discourse rules must predict and cope with such ambiguities; those of Labov and Sinclair *et al.* certainly handle some of them.

We have so far seen how one can use situational information to reclassify declarative, interrogative and imperative items as statements, questions and commands. However, the *discourse value* of an item depends also on what linguistic items have preceded it, what are expected to follow and what do follow. Such sequence relationships are handled in *tactics* where items are relabelled. The definitions of *informative, elicitation* and *directive* make them sound very similar to statement, question and command but there is a crucial difference which can perhaps best be described as potential as opposed to actual. Statements, questions and commands realize informatives, elicitations and directives only when they are in initiating position: thus an elicitation is an initiating question, a directive an initiating command, and an inform an initiating statement — statements in particular frequently occur realizing *replies* and *comments*.

Spoken discourse is produced in real time and speakers inevitably make mistakes. In the 'what are you laughing at' example discussed above the teacher abruptly changes course in the middle of an intended elicitation, and this signals to the class that they should ignore what has just been said. More frequently, as in the example below, a teacher may produce an item which he fully intends to be initiating and then, realizing he could have expressed his intention better, follow the potential informative, directive or elicitation with another, usually more explicit one, signalling paralinguistically — by intonation, absence of pausing, speeding up of speech rate — that what he has just said must be regarded as a *starter*, a bound act devoid of any initiating force:

T:	(starter)	What about this one
	(starter)	This I think this is a super one
	(nomination)	Isobel
	(elicit)	Can you think what it means?

The teacher begins with a question which appears to have been intended as an elicitation. She changes her mind and relegates it to a starter and the relegating statement is in turn relegated by a second question which then does stand as an elicitation. Thus whenever there is a succession of statements, questions and commands a pupil can usually be safe in assuming that it is the last one that has the status of initiation. This 'rule' can, of course, lead to an incorrect response if the pupil doesn't fully hear or understand what the teacher is saying. In the following example a quoted question is heard as an elicitation.

PUPIL: Well, he should take some look at what the man's point of view is.
TEACHER: Yes, yes.
          But he wasn't asked that question don't forget. He was merely asked the question 'Why, why are they reacting like this?'
PUPIL: Well, maybe it's the way they've been brought up.

All descriptive systems have strengths and weaknesses, and any attempt to use this system quickly reveals one major inadequacy — at the simplest level there is the question of whether a two-minute lecture by the teacher is one *inform* or a series; a more difficult problem comes in the third part in an exchange if the teacher produces a *comment* on the pupil's utterance which appears to drift into an *inform* beginning a new exchange — in the example below it is difficult to know where or indeed whether to draw the line:

T: (elicit)   See if you can see anything that you think is rather peculiar.
P: (reply)   There's two aitches.
T: (evaluate)   Yes.
?   Some are are duplicated aren't they?
?   There are two symbols for one sound.
?   I haven't been able to find out why this is.
?   I've got some books that you can look at just now to see if you can find out just why it is.

Pearce (1973) argues that perhaps the best solution is to see longer contributions as a different type of discourse, not interactive in the same way and therefore not suitable for this type of analysis, which would then simply cope with the points of speaker change at the beginnings and ends. Montgomery (1977) follows this suggestion and offers an interesting analysis of lecture monologue drawing on ideas from Winter (1977), Halliday and Hasan (1976) and blending these with the insights offered by Brazil's description of intonation.

Exchange structure

Since the development of the original model, the major advances have been in the characterization of the exchange; the proposals by Coulthard and Brazil (1981) are presented below, and there are further modifications suggested in Stubbs (1981) and Berry (1981).

In the original description initiation and response were conceived of as complementary elements of structure; a given realization of initiation was seen as prospectively constraining the next move, while a given realization of response was thought of as retrospective in focus and an attempt to be 'appropriate . . . in the terms laid down' (Sinclair and Coulthard 1975, p. 45). The third element of structure was seen as an additional element in the exchange, not structurally required or predicted by the preceding move, but nevertheless related to it.

Only two criteria are necessary to distinguish these elements of exchange structure: (i) does the element generate constraints which amount to a prediction that a particular element will follow; and (ii) has a preceding element predicted its occurrence? An initiation is then seen to be an item which begins anew and sets up an expectation of a response; a response is predicted but itself sets up no expectations; a follow-up is neither predicted nor predicting in this particular sense. Thus:

		Predicting	Predicted
1.	Initiation	Yes	No
2.	Response	No	Yes
3.	Follow-up	No	No
4.	?	Yes	Yes

When we set out the criteria in the form of a matrix like this, we discover a gap, and this prompts us to ask whether there is not also a fourth element of exchange structure which is both predicted and predicting. It is not in fact difficult to find pupil responses which appear to be looking for an evaluatory follow-up from the teacher:

TEACHER: can anyone tell me what this means
PUPIL: does it mean danger men at work
TEACHER: yes. . .

We have here in the pupil's contribution an element which partakes of the predictive characteristics of both response and initiation: to put it another way, we may say that it functions as a response with respect to the preceding element and as an initiation with respect to the following element.

We are now in fact able to explain a paradox in the original description of classroom discourse. On the one hand the follow-up move is, as defined, optional, but on the other it is so important that 'if it does not occur we feel confident in saying that the teacher has deliberately withheld it for some strategic purpose' (Sinclair and Coulthard 1975, p. 51). One explanation of the paradox may lie in the peculiar nature of much classroom questioning — the teacher is not seeking information in the accepted sense, as he already knows the answer, but it is essential for the pupils to know whether their answer is the one the teacher was looking for, and hence there is a situational necessity for the follow-up move. There is, however, a more satisfactory explanation. When we look at examples like

T: // p ^{WHY would you want to be} <u>STRONG</u> //

P: // p to MAKE <u>MUSCLES</u> //

T: // p ^{to MAKE} <u>MUSCLES</u> // r+ <u>YES</u> //

We discover that very often pupils, by using the predictive concord implications of high termination discussed in Chapter 5, are in a very real sense requesting a high key evaluative 'yes not no' response from the teacher. Thus we have an example of a move which looks both ways, or which is, in the terms used above, both predicted like a response and also predicting like an initiation.

We can here point to an interesting analogy in grammar where phased predicators (Sinclair 1972) are frequently separated by an element of clause structure that 'faces both ways', standing as object to the first predicator and as subject to the second:

> Let him go

For much the same reason that 'him' in the example above is labelled O/S (object/subject) we shall use the label R/I (response/initiation) to capture a similar dual function. We are thus suggesting that many classroom eliciting exchanges have the structure I, R/I, R with the R/I move being distinguished from the R by high termination and/or interrogative syntax. This doesn't mean that there will be no IRF exchanges, there obviously will

I: // p <u>FIN</u>ished miri //
R: // p <u>YES</u> //
E: // p <u>GOOD</u> //

and there will also be occasions when a pupil selects low termination with a discourse implication that no further move is needed, and a social interpretation of truculence or insolence:

I: // p ^{what's the CAPital of} <u>FRANCE</u> //
R: // p <u>PAris</u> //

The structure proposed for exchanges is now

I (R/I) R (F) (F)

which conveys the information that an exchange is minimally a two-part structure but that it can consist of up to five moves, though such long exchanges are comparatively rare. It may seem strange to have the move R/I both optional and 'predicted', but this, in fact, copes with the ongoing interpretive process. In the example below, A can assume that B is fulfilling his predictions and producing a responding move but does not know whether or not it is an R/I to which he is expected in turn to respond until he hears the termination choice:

A: // p have you GOT the TIME //   B: // p it's THREE o'$\frac{\text{CLOCK}}{\text{CLOCK}}$ //

The obvious question at this point is whether R/I is recursive — it is not, in fact, for reasons connected to communicative content discussed below.

If we put directive exchanges on one side for the moment, all other exchanges are basically concerned with the transmission of information in its most general sense and thus must contain one informing move, which can occur in either the initiating or the responding slot. In some cases one participant initiates by offering a piece of information and then wants to know, minimally, that it has been understood and hopefully accepted and agreed with — in such cases, as the IR structure makes clear, the acknowledging move is socially required. In other cases information is elicited and then the reason for its occurrence and its interpretation should not be problematic, so an acknowledging move is not essential — a fact captured by the observation that in such cases it occupies the follow-up slot.

As soon as we conceptualize the exchange in these terms, with the initiating slot being used either to elicit or to provide information and the responding slot to provide an appropriate next contribution, we achieve the following differential relationship between slots and fillers:

I   eliciting move

     informing move

R

     acknowledging move

F

This represents a simplification because inform and reply, accept and acknowledge can now be recognized as pairs of identical acts which were distinguished in the original description because they occurred at different places in structure.

Prospective classification

The powerful structural relationship between I and R means that any move occurring in the I slot will be heard as setting up a prediction that there will be an appropriate move in the R slot. The result is that a speaker will make every effort to hear what follows his initiation as an appropriate response, and only in the last resort will he admit that it may be an unrelated new initiation. Thus, to take the simple case of an eliciting move in the I slot looking for information about polarity, it will classify whatever comes next as conveying polar information, if this is at all possible:

can you come round tonight $\begin{cases} \text{no. . .} \\ \text{I've got an essay to finish} \\ \text{thanks} \end{cases}$

The joke in the following example from Labov (1972a) derives from the fact that Linus does not accept Violet's utterance as a response meaning 'no', either because he is conversationally incompetent (!) or because he rejects the underlying assumption, and therefore asserts that she has begun a new unrelated exchange leaving his Initiation without a completing Response:

LINUS: do you want to play with me Violet
VIOLET: you're younger than me (*shuts door*)
LINUS: she didn't answer my question.

Wh-elicitations work in the same way:

where's the typewriter $\begin{cases} \text{it's in the cupboard} \\ \text{try the cupboard} \\ \text{isn't it in the cupboard?} \\ \text{in the cupboard?} \end{cases}$

Again all the items in the response slot are interpreted as attempts to provide the required information. However, these items are not necessarily informing moves; the third and fourth alternatives above, assuming a high termination, are in fact polar eliciting moves, an option available to a speaker to enable him both to comply with the constraints of the initiating move and to mark the potential unreliability of his information. The following is a perfectly normal exchange:

I: elicit: $//\,p$ WHERE's the $\frac{\text{TYPE}\text{writer}}{}\,//$
R/I: elicit: $//\,p$ IS it in the $\frac{\text{CUP}\text{board}}{}\,//$
R: inform: $//\,p\,\frac{\text{NO}}{}\,//$

The limits of the exchange

In the earlier version of exchange structure, each move class could only occur once; however, it has now been claimed that two eliciting moves can occur in the same exchange and it will soon be suggested that two informing moves can also co-occur. How, then, can one recognize an exchange boundary?

It has been argued earlier that the exchange is the unit concerned with negotiating the transmission of information and that it will contain an informing move at I or R; the exchange carries only one (potentially complex) piece of information and its polarity — truth or falseness realized through positive and negative choices in the clause — and the information and the polarity can be asserted only once. As just described it looks as if semantic and not structural criteria are being used, but in fact the claims can be supported and exemplified structurally, for the power of the exchange is that as it progresses the options decrease rapidly.

Before we go any further we need to subdivide both the eliciting and informing moves into two sub-classes:

e_1 eliciting moves which seek major information and polarity
e_2 eliciting moves which seek polarity information
i_1 informing moves which assert major information (and polarity)
i_2 informing moves which assert polarity information

Each of these moves can occur only once in an exchange in the sequence e_1, i_1 or e_2, i_2 and thus a second occurrence of any move marks a new exchange. This provides a strong structural criterion to account for intuitions about exchange boundaries which we recognize for instance between the following pairs of utterances, even though in each case the first exchange is structurally incomplete.

e_1 A: where are you going
e_1 B: why do you ask

i_1 A: well I've applied to fairly selective big biggish civil engineering contractors
i_1 B: most of the people I'm applying to aren't pre-selective

e_2 A: would you like to come round for coffee tonight
e_2 B: are you being serious

We must of course always be careful not to misinterpret a particular linguistic realization: in the example below each of the alternatives offered for B could in other contexts be realizing respectively e_1, i_1 and e_2 moves, but here they are all interpretable as paraphrases of the basic i_2 realization 'yes':

e_2 A: would you like to come round for coffee tonight

i_2 B: $\begin{cases} \text{who wouldn't} \\ \text{I'll be there by nine} \\ \text{are you kidding} \end{cases}$

Although the most frequent exchanges are the ones with the sequence e_1 i_1 or e_2 i_2, it is, as we mentioned above, possible to have the sequence i_1i_2 as in:

i_1 A: I think it's raining
i_2 B: // p $\underline{YES}$ // p it $\underline{IS}$ //

In this example A has marked the truth of his utterance as in doubt, but in some situations like classrooms, certain speakers are typically able to produce only i_1 informing moves without any assertion of polarity, because this is seen to be the prerogative of another speaker. More typical following i_1, of course, is a move indicating acceptance or understanding of the information:

i_1 A: It's raining
ack B: // p $\underline{YES}$ // p it $\underline{IS}$ //
ack A: // p $\underline{YEH}$ //

Whereas all the other moves can occur only once in a particular exchange, acknowledging can, though it rarely does, occur twice, but in such cases it is almost invariably lexicalized the second time as 'yes' and is used by a speaker to 'pass' when it is his turn to speak and thus allow the other speaker to select the next topic, as in this example from a native/non-native conversation.

A: e_2 to the foreman
B: i_2 yeah
A: ack   yeah
B: ack   yeah   (Aston MS)

Two further restrictions need to be noted: firstly, if e_2 is selected following e_1 as in:

e_1:   where's the typewriter
e_2:   is it in the cupboard

there are obviously massive content restrictions on the available realizations for the e_2; secondly, i_1 and e_2 cannot occur within the same exchange. As we said above, information and polarity can be asserted only once within an exchange, and thus to follow an i_1 with an e_2 is, in Burton's (1980) terms, to *challenge* and thereby to begin a new exchange — though one must never forget that acknowledging moves can have interrogative syntax:

i_1:   it's raining again
ack: is it really

The restrictions on co-occurrence — that each eliciting and informing move can occur only once and that e_2 and i_1 cannot both occur in the same exchange — now enable us to account both for the fact that the largest exchange consists of five moves:

```
  I:   e₁   where's the typewriter
R/I:   e₂   is it in the cupboard
  R:   i₂   no
  F:   ack  oh dear
  F:   ack  yeh
```

and for the fact that R/I is not recursive. R/I can be realized only by e_2 and it would be pointless for a second speaker to seek information about polarity from one who has just indicated he hasn't got that information:

```
A:      I:   e₁ where's the typewriter
B:    R/I:   e₂ is it in the cupboard
A:   *R/I:   e₂ is it or isn't it
```

In what has gone before we have assumed and indeed implied that the distinction between class 1 informing moves and class 2 eliciting moves is unproblematic. We certainly pointed out that while a class 1 eliciting move predicts a class 1 informing move and indeed gets one in response 1 below, it may be followed by a class 2 eliciting move as in response 2:

where's the typewriter $\left\{ \begin{array}{l} \text{1. it's in the cupboard} \\ \text{2. is it in the cupboard} \end{array} \right.$

However, there are times when it is difficult to decide which category an item belongs to because it is difficult to describe/delimit the boundary. A high-termination choice at the end of a move certainly constrains the other speaker to make a contribution as in (a) and (b):

a) // *r* and so <u>THEN</u> // *p* i went to the <u>MAR</u>ket // $\left\{ \begin{array}{l} // p \ \underline{\text{REA}}\text{lly} \ // \\ // p \ \underline{\text{GOSH}} \ // \end{array} \right.$

b) // *p* it's ALready <u>FREE</u>zing //

and it is instructive to compare (a) and (b) with (c) and (d):

c) // *r* and so <u>THEN</u> // *p* you went to the <u>MAR</u>ket //

d) // *p* you're ALready <u>FREE</u>zing // $\left\{ \begin{array}{l} // p \ \underline{\text{YEH}} \ // \end{array} \right.$

which are unproblematically heard as elicitations. We are obviously on the borderline here — is it better to see utterances like (a) and (b), which appear to constrain the next speaker to verbalize his reaction to the information, as the most extreme type of inform, or the mildest of elicit? As the class of items which follows high-termination items like (a) and (b) can also follow unproblematic informs but cannot follow class 2 elicits, it does appear more sensible to categorize (a) and (b) as informs, but there are still doubts.

Criticisms

The model outlined above has attracted considerable published and unpublished criticism. Mountford (1975) comments that the system proposed in Sinclair *et al.* 'sets out to analyse the products of . . . discourse activity' — that is, it begins with transcribed texts and then accounts for these in terms of 'a descriptive apparatus that is applied to the data *ex post facto*'. In other words, it is an analysis that is concerned with the *product* of communication rather than the *process* and that can say nothing useful about how 'participants understand discourse as a communicative activity'.

Willis (1983) observes that the implication of these observations is that 'the description is a post facto rationalisation of a particular discourse' (p. 214), and this is patently untrue. Indeed it suggests a misunderstanding of the nature of formal descriptions. Certainly, as Willis stresses, formal descriptions are used and useful to describe data 'after the event', but they also 'highlight choices' and 'a systemic grammar, for example, is expressly designed to show not only the paths which are taken but also those which are not but could have been' (p. 214). Just as a grammatical description of formal potentials enables us to explain how native speakers set about decoding *Jabberwocky*, so the notions of the structural frame and the derived concept of prospective classification enabled us on p. 138 above to describe how items of many different forms following yes/no questions came to be interpreted as versions of 'yes' or 'no' — this surely is a contribution to process analysis.

In developing his argument, Willis points out that whereas the model cannot and indeed as a linguistic description should not handle intention — why a given participant has chosen at a given point to produce an elicitation — there is in the interpretive and classificatory rules proposed for *situation* and *tactics* a genuine attempt to approach the process of utterance analysis — indeed, the act *starter* is a pure process act — and suggestions in Coulthard and Brazil (1981) and

Willis (ibid.) about the ways in which utterances can even be retro-spectively reclassified strengthen the process nature of the descrip-tion. For example, in the following extract the doctor doesn't mishear or misinterpret the patient's elicitation but he chooses not to respond to it as an elicitation and to mark, through his response, that he is in fact treating it as an inform about her worries:

P: Now tell me doctor, could it be my kidneys
D: I see

Thus, whereas no one would want to deny that the description could be 'greatly extended in scope and delicacy', or even that it may be possible to design 'a better motivated description using a radically different descriptive model' (ibid., p. 226), it is in fact a misunder-standing of the model to describe it as a static *product* description.

One problem that the presentation earlier in the chapter has played down is that it is not always easy to analyse text unambiguously. We have already seen that *comments* may shade into new *informs* and that long *informs* on their own create difficulties. Then there are examples like the following:

T: I don't know your name
P: Yeah I'm Theklitze   (Watson 1984)

A: Would you like another drink
B: Yes I would thank you but make it a small one
                                             (Levinson 1983, p. 290)

in which the second speaker responds, apparently, to two separate initiating potentials in the first utterance — at the moment the de-scription, having, as Levinson (1983) points out, an underlying as-sumption of only one interactive function per utterance unit, finds these something of an embarrassment. Further problems come with discontinuity — it is not uncommon for addressees to produce ac-knowledging items, verbal and non-verbal, during rather than follow-ing a speaker's turn, and indeed for a speaker specifically to request such reactions by a high termination intonation choice during his turn. Finally there is the problem of embedding. The Birmingham group has so far tried to see exchanges as not permitting embedding, arguing that once a new exchange has begun, even if the previous one was incomplete, it is impossible to return and complete it. However, ex-amples like the following from Levinson (pp. 304–5) are strong evi-dence for embedding:

A: May I have a bottle of milch (Q.1)
B: Are you 21   (Q.2)
A: No   (A.2)
B: No   (A.1)   (Merritt 1976, p. 333)

B: U:hm what's the price now eh with V.A.T. Do you know (Q.1)
A: Er I'll just work that out for you =   (HOLD)
B: = thanks   (ACCEPT)
    (10.0)
A: Three pounds nineteen a tube sir   (A.1)

Levinson goes on to argue that the whole enterprise of producing descriptions like that embodied in the structure of exchanges proposed above is in fact misconceived:

> the assumption embodies a strong claim about the 'syntactic' nature of sequential constraints in conversation, and essential to such a claim is that there should be clear cases of ill-formed sequences (like *XYX. . .) just as there are in sentence grammars (like *on cat the sat mat the). Yet cases of such *impossible* discourses are hard if not impossible to find.   (p. 292)

Such criticism is in fact based on a misunderstanding not simply of the nature of the description proposed for exchanges but also of the nature of grammatical structure. As we observed in Coulthard and Brazil (1981, pp. 83–4), it is all very well to say that 'cat the. . .' contravenes the rule that words of the class *determiner* must precede words of the class *noun*, but in the pair 'the cuddly black cat' and 'the black cuddly cat' the situation is somewhat different. 'Cuddly' is one of a large group of adjectives which can be either *quality* or *classifying* epithets (Sinclair 1972), and it is sequential position, before or after a colour adjective, which determines the classification. In other words, in instances like this it is the hearer/reader's knowledge of nominal group structure that enables him to interpret the item and on a larger scale to make sense of the e.e. cummings poem 'Anyone lived in a pretty how town'.

When we move from grammar to discourse we are concerned with an object created collaboratively by at least two speakers, and in these circumstances it is difficult to see how anything can be ruled out as 'undiscoursical' — there is no way in which one speaker can place absolute constraints upon another which are in any sense comparable to the grammatical rules which block the production of certain sequences within his own utterance. When 'mistakes' occur and are remarked upon they are usually of the type

A: so the meeting's on Friday
B: thanks
A: no, I'm asking you

where B wrongly classifies A's contribution and rectification requires help of a metalinguistic kind. However, there is no way in which B could have recognized the 'wrongness' of his response simply by reflecting on it, as he could with a grammatical mistake.

Thus we must accept that a speaker can do anything he likes at any time, but at the same time we must recognize that what he does do will be classified as a contribution to the discourse in the light of whatever structural predictions the previous contribution may have set up — in other words, the structure offered for exchanges is very much an interpretive template which makes predictions about what a speaker will do next *provided he chooses to stay within the same exchange*. In the following example, only A's knowledge of B's family relationships and his current state of mind will enable him to calculate whether B is staying within the exchange or not, and if so whether he is likely to be implicating 'yes' or 'no' — and even then he may be wrong:

A: will you come for a drink
B: my brother's just left for the States.

7 Discourse analysis and language teaching

Like other branches of linguistics, language teaching has until recently been concerned with grammatical rather than communicative competence. Wilkins (1972b) observes that although there have been major changes in the methodology of language teaching over the years the underlying principle has remained the same: 'it has been assumed that units of learning should be defined in grammatical terms, although the precise sequence in which they occurred would be influenced by pedagogic considerations'. Further, he suggests that even those courses which encourage dialogue and improvised drama are structured grammatically and the 'situations that are created are pedagogic, bearing little resemblance to natural language use'.

It is not, of course, that grammatical and communicative syllabuses have different goals, as Widdowson (1979) emphasizes: 'both types of syllabus recognise that the learner's goal should be the ability to communicate' (p. 248); rather, they differ in their premises about 'what needs to be actually taught for this ability to be acquired' (ibid.). It is one thing to omit something deliberately from a syllabus, and quite another to include items which are actually misleading or wrong, yet in their concentration on grammar, course books may use interactional structures for what are in reality grammar drills, and thus students may be taught to produce answers that are grammatically correct but unusual or even deviant in terms of discourse rules:

Q: What is this?
A: This ⎫
   It   ⎬ is a book.

Q: Where is the typewriter?
A: The typewriter is in the cupboard.

In a methodology that leaves students to deduce rules of use, the hidden curriculum can be dangerous.

Grammatical syllabuses can, of course, have great success in their own terms and those who have followed them conscientiously have usually managed to swim, eventually, when dropped into interactive situations — the crucial question is whether, with all our recently-acquired knowledge about the organization of interaction and about form-function relationships, we can produce syllabuses which make the task of becoming a successful non-native interactant easier. An immediate problem is that although Hymes (1972b) proposed the description of communicative competence as the real goal of linguistics, and although it is his work which has fuelled the discussion of communicatively oriented syllabuses, neither he nor his co-workers have, as we have seen, been able as yet to provide even a fragment of a description of communicative competence — thus whereas a grammatical syllabus can be based on a well developed description of a native speaker's grammar, a communicative syllabus can have no similarly firm foundation.

Following Canale (1983) we can usefully see communicative competence as being composed of four areas of knowledge and skill: *grammatical, sociolinguistic, discourse* and *strategic* competences. *Grammatical* competence is concerned with 'the knowledge and skill required to understand and express the literal meaning of utterances' and as such is the traditional concern of grammatical syllabuses. *Sociolinguistic* competence is concerned with appropriateness — 'both appropriateness of meaning and appropriateness of form' — and this includes not simply rules of address and questions of politeness but also selection and formulation of topic and the social significance of indirect speech acts. *Discourse* competence he sees as concerned with cohesion and coherence in the structure of texts; it therefore includes knowledge about the organization of different speech events and the interpretive rules for relating form to function. Finally, *strategic* competence is 'composed of verbal and non-verbal communication strategies' which enable speakers to handle breakdowns in communication and their own lexico-grammatical inadequacies and to enhance the effectiveness of their message.

Given this subdivision of communicative competence, we can imagine syllabuses that attempt to teach the component concurrently and others that are organized consecutively. Johns (1976) and Candlin *et al.* (1978) report interesting Special Purpose communicative courses which follow the second strategy. These courses were designed for specialists, teachers and doctors respectively, who already have grammatical competence and some sociolinguistic, discourse and strategic competence in the language and who need to be able to perform like native speakers in their professional roles. Given the narrow area of competence involved, it was possible to base these materials on a detailed analysis of the target speech event and both courses included teaching about the discourse structure of the event as well as instruction in how to perform in it.

Johns' course is based on the analysis of classroom interaction proposed in Sinclair *et al.* (1972) and outlined in Chapter 6, and comprises eight units with each unit consisting of

a) an explicit presentation of a simplified version of the descriptive model;
b) intensive listening to extracts from recordings of authentic lessons followed by analysis;
c) language laboratory simulation of the analysed features of classroom interaction, through imitation and drill-like exercises.

By the time the students reach unit 4 they have covered the three-part exchange structure, and are practising different ways of responding to pupil utterances and ways of controlling turn-taking. The following drill sequence comes after the student has listened to, and analysed, two 'authentic recordings of teachers getting pupils to name objects'. (A Hallidayan intonation transcription is used.)

Drill one

I want you to get your pupils to identify the objects shown in the pictures above

1. // 1 what's / *this* //   (a hacksaw)   // 1 + *yes* it's a // 1 *hack*saw //
2. // 1 what's / *this* //   (a fountain pen) // 1 + *yes* it's a
                                              // 1 *foun*tain pen // etc.

Drill two

This time I want you to get your pupils to identify the same objects, but this time you *cue* them to put their hands up: every time it is Arthur who makes the first *bid*: and so he is the one you *nominate*.

1. // 3 *hands* up what's // 1 *this* //
   // 2 *Ar*thur //   (a hacksaw) // 1 + *yes* it's a // 1 *hack*saw // etc.

Drill three

Here are some new pictures: this time Arthur does not get the answer right, so you have to ask the next pupil who bids, whose name is Brenda: if Brenda gets it wrong, the next is Charlie, and after Charlie, Diana.

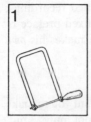   

1. // 3 *hands* up what's // 1 *this* //
   // 2 *Arthur* //   (a saucepan) // 3 *no* //
   // 2 *Brenda* //   (a motorcar) // 1+ *yes* it's a // 1 *mo*torcar //

2. // 3 *hands* up what's // 1 *this* //
   // 2 *Arthur* //   (a spoon)   // 3 *no* //
   // 2 *Brenda* //   (a hammer) // 3 *no* //
   // 2 *Charlie* //   (a screwdriver) // 1+ *yes* it's a // 1 *scre*wdriver //

   etc.

Like Johns, Candlin *et al.* focus on a particular Special Purpose, this time the language needs of foreign doctors working in casualty departments. Again like Johns, their materials are based on a detailed functional description of native speaker interaction, and attempt to teach single functions not simply showing the doctors how to open and close interviews, but how to participate in other types of exchange, how to build these exchanges into longer sequences and how to manipulate the turn-taking system. The doctors first learn *greeting*, then *eliciting*, then *interrogating*, and at this point they are able to participate in the following exercise generating the first few exchanges of a simulated interview:

> One learner as patient, other as doctor. Doctor uses a GREET and an ELICIT, after which the patient describes the nature, cause, etc. of his complaint. At an appropriate moment, the doctor inserts an INTERROGATE.

Johns (ibid.) reports another set of materials based on his own analysis of discussion strategies and designed for foreign social science postgraduates who frequently come from undergraduate courses taught entirely by lecture to postgraduate courses structured round participatory seminars; their major problems are in the area of strategic competence: turn-taking, handling discontinuity, linking, mitigation, and repair work. There are ten units in this course; the following extracts come from one on '*prefaces* and *suppletion*'. By this stage the students have been introduced to six ways of responding to previous informatives: *amplification, contradiction, counter, restriction, explanation, consequence*. Now the student is first given practice in identifying prefaces in authentic texts and in imitating them on gapped recordings; next he practises producing suppleted moves after a fixed preface of the form 'I'd like to come in here if I may'; finally he makes his *own* amplification on hearing a signal.

Drill one — Preface + Amplification
You will hear an amplification made in a *short* form. I want you to make the same amplification in a *long* form using the 'not only...but' construction.

   1. 'Mary's very pretty.'   'I'D LIKE TO COME IN HERE IF I MAY.
      'Intelligent too.'   NOT ONLY IS MARY VERY PRETTY,
                            BUT SHE'S INTELLIGENT, TOO.'
   2. 'The theory needs to 'I'D LIKE TO COME IN HERE IF I MAY.
      be discussed.'   NOT ONLY DOES THE THEORY NEED
      'And tested.'   TO BE DISCUSSED, BUT IT NEEDS TO
                            BE TESTED, TOO.'   (8 examples)

Drill four — Preface + Amplification
This time you will hear six extracts from the discussion: this time you must make your *own* amplification of the speaker's remark when you hear the signal.

   1. '... there are, however, many many more undergraduates today.'
   2. '... what it was always possible to do was to determine what class your
      children should belong to.'   (6 examples)

Johns observes that in these materials there is a triple progression from: (i) universal to restricted preface; (ii) idealized to authentic prompt; (iii) controlled to freer production. The suggested prefaces are formal if not stilted, but Johns suggests that it is the act of interrupting which causes the foreign students their problems — once they have a formula they are prepared to use it 'in a real discussion taking place in real time'. Success ultimately is the only criterion and these materials are rated enjoyable and successful by the students for whom they are designed.

Notional syllabuses

The courses we have discussed so far have been small scale and designed for optimal situations — based on a detailed analysis of, and intending to improve competence in, one speech event and presupposing a high level of grammatical competence and a supportive second language background. The question we must now face is how far is it possible to design a communicative syllabus for beginners or false beginners.

Wilkins (1972a, 1976) takes up the challenge, and the *notional* syllabus he proposes is designed to take communicative facts into account 'from the beginning without losing sight of grammatical and situational factors' (1976, p. 19). One obvious advantage of a communicative or *notional* syllabus is that it need not be language specific, but can be designed for a series of culturally related speech communities, that is, communities with a large degree of overlap in their norms of interaction. Wilkins, assuming that Western Europe is a fairly homogeneous speech area, asks what are the notions that the European learner will expect to be able to express through the target language (1972a) and sets out to describe them in some detail. Two sets of notions, the semantico-grammatical ones, concerned with 'time', 'space', 'quality', 'matter', 'deixis', and the modal notions of 'modality', 'certainty', 'commitment', are covered in some form by most structural syllabuses, but the categories of communicative function, designed to handle 'what speakers *do* with language', are 'the more original part of the framework' (ibid, p. 23).

He observes that 'language learning has concentrated . . . on the use of language to report and describe' but argues that these two functions 'are by no means the only ones that are important for the learner of a foreign language' (1972a), and he therefore sets out to classify the functions utterances can perform and also to suggest, for English, the realizations which should be taught first.

He proposes six types of communicative function, 'six kinds of thing that we do with language' (1976, p. 44), stressing that he has not restricted himself to 'what have come to be called speech acts' (ibid., p. 42) — *judgement and evaluation; suasion; argument; rational enquiry and exposition; personal emotions*; and *emotive relations*. Each function is subclassified, so for instance argument includes *information asserted, information sought, information denied, agreement, disagreement* and *concession*, and in the 1972 version each subdivision is followed on the left-hand side of the page by 'a list of vocabulary items falling within or closely related to its semantic field', while on the right-hand side of the page are suggested grammatical realizations for students at an early stage of learning. Thus:

Information sought:
— request
    question
    ask

'*Question*':
Information seeking is likely to be an important aspect of a learner's language use.
a) Interrogatives
b) Declaratives + question intonation
c) Question-word questions
   When
   Where
   What   How + { far
   Who   much
   What (time)   ?
'*Request*'
Would you shut the window, please
(Would you mind shutting . . .)

There are many criticisms one can make of Wilkins' framework: some of the categories overlap; some of the realizations sound stilted or odd; and it may not be an accident that there are no suggested realizations for the functions 'sympathy' and 'flattery', but he disarmingly admits the problems, and points out himself that it is an 'ad hoc' framework which he expects to be refined and modified in the light of further research. The question we must address is whether such a communicatively based syllabus is in principle to be preferred, because in solving one problem it may create another: if we accept a communicative syllabus in which students are taught at any one time only those grammar items, or even phrases, necessary for the realization of the particular function being taught, this raises, as Johns (ibid.) points out,

> the question of *structuralization*: how can the student be assisted to relate a particular structure 'to the overall framework of the language'. In other words instead of being presented with a coherent grammar of the language and having to construct for himself realization rules for particular functions, there is a danger that the student may be given little more than a series of guidebook phrases for greeting, apologizing or complaining and have to construct his own grammar.

Wilkins is very much aware of this — he notes that one of the problems that faces the syllabus constructor is to 'decide just how much weighting to give to grammatical criteria' (p. 65), but other than suggesting a cyclic approach in which students return at different stages of the course and thus with improving grammatical competence to the same function, he doesn't really confront the problem of teaching grammar. Obviously one solution would be to graft the communicative syllabus on to a grammatical one and teach functions as and when their realizations become possible. This is not in fact an unreasonable suggestion because as Wilkins himself points out there is no 'intrinsic ordering to the categories' of his syllabus nor any 'intrinsic way of linking one unit to the next', but it is not an option that he considers.

Wilkins himself has never published a communicatively structured course, but obviously those who do must make decisions about the sequencing of items and their grammatical realizations. Jakobovitz and Gordon (1974) offer a sketch of the first ten lessons of an inter-mediate course — interestingly, half of the lessons are concerned with 'describing' and 'reporting', one of the major faults of non-communicative courses according to Wilkins.

Lesson 1: Greeting and Leave-taking
Lesson 2: Making Requests: Part 1
Lesson 3: Making Requests: Part 2
Lesson 4: Extending Invitations
Lesson 5: Making Apologies
Lesson 6: Describing Events: Part 1
Lesson 7: Describing Events: Part 2
Lesson 8: Reporting Events: Part 1
Lesson 9: Reporting Events: Part 2
Lesson 10: Reporting Events: Part 3

For Lesson 2 they suggest three major categories of request:

A. Asking Informational Questions
   A1 — that take yes/no answers
   A2 — Other

B. Requesting Agreement
   B1 — for personal opinion or feeling
   B2   for proposed action

C. Asking for permission

and for 'Requesting Agreement', they offer the following grammatical structures, two of which sound odd to the British ear:

Bl. For personal opinion or feeling:
   1. S + don't you think so?
      (It's a beautiful day, don't you think so?)
   2. S + isn't it?
      (It's a beautiful day, isn't it?)
   3. S + wouldn't you agree?
      (We're much better off here, wouldn't you agree?)

From this outline it is apparent that although the lesson is communicatively labelled, 'making requests', it is in fact structurally organized as a lesson on *interrogation* — polar, wh- and tag-questions. The hidden curriculum is that the three grammatical forms are matched respectively with A1, A2 and B1, but tag-questions are only one of the ways to request agreement, others being:

Isn't it a beautiful day
What a beautiful day
It's a beautiful day

and tag questions can also be used to ask for information. In fact the generalization we proposed in Chapter 6 was that it is intonation choice and not grammatical form that marks whether it is information or agreement that is being requested.

Abbs *et al.* (1975), one of the earliest published courses to be functionally rather than grammatically structured, claim that

the learner is taught strategies for handling particular language functions such as identifying people and places, expressing personal tastes, emotions, moods and opinions, giving information, making suggestions, giving advice and so on. The structural contents have been selected as being appropriate to the particular function, rather than as an unrelated series of structures arranged in order of supposed linguistic difficulty.

The first few functions are introduced in the following order — with no apparent functionally-based ordering:

Identification
Invitations
Likes and dislikes (1)
Description: People
Description: Places
Impatience
Not knowing
The Past (1)
Surprise and disbelief

It will already be evident that there are major problems in realizing a communicative syllabus — it is not simply that there is no logical sequence in which to teach the functions — that, as we have seen, could be an advantage — it is rather that it is not at all clear what a function is, or how we recognize one. It is all very well to say that functions are concerned with language use, but as we saw in Chapter 2 speech act analysis suggests that it is possible to perform several speech acts simultaneously with an indirect utterance; is it possible to perform several functions simultaneously? Certainly Wilkins' cat-

egory of personal emotions, which 'express the speaker's emotional reaction to events and people', and Abbs' 'impatience' and 'surprise and
disbelief' look more like modalities on other functions.

Secondly, there appears to be some confusion between functions
like 'invite' and 'warn', which are in a general sense illocutionary and
therefore arguably teachable, and 'persuade' and 'incite', which are
perlocutionary and thus not really candidates for inclusion in a language course at all. Thirdly, the water is further muddied by Wilkins'
passing observation that it is 'possible for one function to be contained within another' (p. 49). Fourthly, the problem becomes more
acute when we look at the suggested realizations for functions; a large
number of Wilkins' examples contain explicit performative verbs —
'I suggest a visit to the zoo', 'I blame John', 'I assert, contend, swear
. . . that I was not responsible for the accident' — but we know that
the majority of speech acts are indirect, and if we take one of Wilkins'
examples for 'blame', 'That was completely unjustified', we realize it
could equally well occur realizing (part of) the functions 'valuation',
'verdiction', 'inducement', 'information asserted', 'disagreement',
'negative emotion' and 'hostility'.

It is not, of course, in the least surprising that there are these problems, because they are exactly the ones that, as we have seen in previous chapters, have been troubling those involved in the analysis of
interaction. However, what is now necessary is for the functional approach to react to and absorb some of the major findings: that there
is organization above the utterance and some structures like greetings,
closings and invitations can be described with some accuracy, that
context and position in sequence are vital determinants of functional
meaning, that intonation is of crucial significance and that inferencing
is an integral part of interpreting utterances.

Communicative teaching

So far we have concentrated on communicative syllabuses, which are
essentially lists of functional items, without considering methodology.
It is in fact possible to implement a communicative syllabus metalin-
guistically — Woolard (1984) reports a Malaysian school course
based on 88 functional categories and examined and therefore frequently taught in terms of labelling rather than performing. The following examples from a Malaysian textbook give some idea of the
problem.

GIRL: How can I ever trust you in future?
BOY: On my honour, darling, I won't ever lie to you again

    A. to claim   C. to promise
    B. to explain   D. to inform

FATHER: He's an ungrateful, selfish excuse for a son. He never cares whether we live or die.
MOTHER: Perhaps he's too busy to come. He's always so busy with his business deals.

    A. to disagree   C. to advise
    B. to defend   D. to claim

                                       (ibid., p. 218)

However, communicative syllabuses are not intended as a basis for courses on discourse analysis — their main aim is to facilitate and encourage communication in the classroom. The problem is that they tend to encourage a concentration on 'components of discourse' and not the 'process of its creation' (Widdowson 1979, p. 249). Paradoxically, one doesn't need to follow a Wilkins-type communicative syllabus to emphasize communication. Thus Brumfit (1979) argues that the lasting effect of the communicative movement may be more a shift in methodology than a change in syllabus specification. The traditional methodology, he suggests, was basically

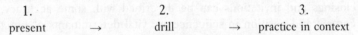

     1.   2.   3.

   present   →   drill   →   practice in context

and it was this that Wilkins (1972b) was reacting against when he talked about the interactive situations being 'pedagogic, bearing little resemblance to natural language use'. Brumfit (1978) sees the post-communicative model as

     1.   2.   3.

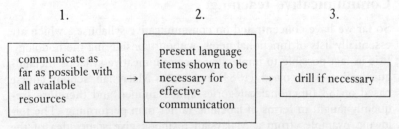

and comments that this is now a student-determined system with the advantage that 'what needs to be taught is defined by the failures to communicate at the first stage which thus operates as a diagnosis'.

Wilkins suggested that by following a communicative syllabus the learner would 'approximate more and more to the language use characteristic of the community whose language he is acquiring' (1976, p. 13), but Brumfit points out that this may be aiming too high, because the learner 'is not, usually, aiming to become a member of that community, but merely to be able to communicate with it' (1978, p. 103). In other words, the aim is not to produce someone who is communicatively competent but rather someone who is a competent communicator — and there is an enormous difference. Thus one of the skills communicative teaching tries to foster is how to cope with limited language resources, a problem which requires excessive use of non-verbal signalling, paraphrase, inferencing, circumlocution, repetition and checking.

It is important at this point to consider what is meant by communication because the label is used for activities which 'range from drills to simulations, from dialogues to communicative games' (Harmer 1982). Much of what goes on in the foreign language classroom is not genuinely communicative. Apart from those occasions when the teacher is organizing the classroom and the lesson, 'open the window/close your books', instructing, 'a noun is . . .', and socializing, 'hello Susan . . .', all the language used is more or less artificial because it arises not from a need to use the language but from a requirement by the teacher to produce language. There are, however, degrees of communicativeness and artificiality.

Willis (1983) suggests that all classroom language activities can be grouped into three kinds, *citation, simulation* and *replication*, with only the third being in any real sense communicative. *Citation* activities are formal exercises like repeating, combining and transforming and give rise to sequences like

T: What is this?   T: What is this?
P: It is a red pen.   P: It is a blue book.

Simulation, including such activities as discussion and role play, is often regarded as communicative (Sturtridge 1981) but is not genuinely so. As Willis points out, it is only when an activity has an outcome that it is truly communicative — 'one of the features of communication is that the communicative decisions we take carry rewards and penalties', whereas in 'role play' there are no penalties — as he observes, in a role-playing situation the 'shopkeeper' can treat his customers 'in a surly monosyllabic manner with no risk of his losing their custom' (p. 240), and it matters little to the customer if he pays 2p or £2 a dozen for his eggs; in simulation activities as in citation activities success is in fact measured linguistically.

Replication, Willis suggests, is the closest we can get to genuine communication in the classroom, and this is achieved by creating situations in which there is a real need for communication in order to achieve something else, usually to solve a problem or play a game. In this instance the only artificiality is that the foreign and not the native language is used. *Concept 7–9*, devised originally for an ESL situation, represents one of the earliest examples of such activities; there are now many more, and their advantage is that they involve the student intellectually and affectively, but their very genuineness can be a disadvantage — Fish (personal communication) tells of two Japanese students completing a tangram puzzle well ahead of other students, but the only English they used was 'yes' and 'no'. There is thus the danger of students creating a special problem-solving dialect and also of the involvement with the task generating not the intended motivation to learn more communicative strategies but rather a growing frustration at having to perform in the foreign language at all.

Brumfit's proposed sequence, attempts to communicate leading to necessary remedial teaching, conceals the very difficult link between the two stages. As Willis (ibid., p. 253) points out, 'many teachers will have great, possibly insurmountable difficulty in diagnosing quickly and effectively the problems students have in their communicative exercises' — as it stands, Brumfit's proposal has the claimed advantage of being student-centred, but the disadvantage of being almost impossible to implement. Willis suggests as a modification the sequence

1.		2.		3.
Replication	→	Citation	→	Simulation

This of course implies a course structured in terms of a careful presentation of activities designed to stimulate the need for certain items which can then be taught explicitly through citation and later practised in simulation situations. Willis conceives the activities in terms of 'illocutionary sequences and semantico-grammatical categories' and offers an interesting sketch of a course which takes *sequence* as the basic communicative unit and sets out to teach students to build up sequences from exchanges and exchanges from moves — different macro-functions can be slotted into this abstract framework; decisions about what functions to teach, their sequence and their grammatical realizations are based on insights derived from speech act theory, conversational analysis, discourse analysis and Willis's own research.

An attractive feature of the Willis-Brumfit proposal is that it doesn't require an out-and-out commitment to structural or communicative syllabuses. As Willis observes, a replication exercise concerned with distinguishing and matching shapes will naturally lead into citation exercises concerned with the specific lexis of size and shape and the grammar of nominal group structure. One should also note that whereas replication is a vital part of communicative teaching, certain essential aspects of communication, like greetings, closings, invitations and presequences, can in fact only be practised through simulation exercises.

It is still early days to make a final evaluation of the communicative syllabus but as we have seen there are many areas in which it can be improved. There is still a great deal of research to do but we can now see more clearly the areas where it is needed. Firstly, we need a detailed description of the skills of the competent non-native speaker — and even more importantly a ranking of these skills. How do some speakers with limited resources manage to understand and communicate with a great degree of success — in advance of research we can suggest that formulae for agreeing, checking, requesting clarification and repetition, and practice in inferring from context and partial understanding, are essential components of a communicative course.

Secondly, there is a great need for contrastive studies — as Schmidt and Richards (1980) point out, 'so far little attention has been given to the effect of transfer operating at the level of discourse rules'. Comparative studies would tell us what stylistic structures and linguistic and sociolinguistic formulations were comparable, and therefore less important from a teaching point of view, and which were very different. It would be useful to know if greetings and closings work in the same way, if kissing and handshaking is customary or forbidden, if pre-sequences are part of the system, whether the language is one in which the indirect formulae work in similar ways, whether the politeness system in terms of rules of address and situations requiring mitigation are comparable, what topics are usual and what are taboo in interactions between strangers.

Finally, and most importantly, we need some serious research into the teaching/learning process — a disturbingly large number of those who have successfully learned several foreign languages see the problem largely in terms of learning vocabulary and structures. Language teachers work in a real and not an ideal world and will always have too little time. Only when we have studies which compare the ultimate *communicative* performance of students who have followed structural, communicative and mixed syllabuses will we be able to say for sure whether the best way to teach students to communicate is to teach them communicatively.

8 The acquisition of discourse

The focus and success of research into child language acquisition is both conditioned and constrained by the linguistic framework within which the researcher works. As the major focus of linguistics moved from writing surface grammars to investigating the native speaker-hearer's grammatical competence to analysing semantic deep structure and now to a concern with pragmatics, speech acts, contextualized utterances and the structure of conversation, so there were parallel changes in the focus of child language research.

For fifteen years child language researchers concentrated on the child's early grammar and therefore began at the two-word stage — the major research in the early 1960s concentrated on surface structure and attempted to write rules to account for the regularities in children's utterances in exactly the same way a linguist would for a newly discovered language. Three independent investigations produced very similar descriptions in terms of two major word classes called *pivot* and *open* by Braine (1963), *modifier* and *noun* by Brown and Bellugi (1964) and *operator* and *non-operator* by Miller and Ervin (1964). However, despite the apparent consensus, this description rapidly lost favour when it became evident that it was inadequate both as a conventional grammatical description, because it generated utterances of the form 'my not' and 'broke come' which, as Brown (1973) admitted, had 'been mighty slow in turning up', and as a developmental description, because these two initial classes couldn't be shown to be a stage on any route to full mastery of the system.

Chomsky (1957) had argued that all attempts to write a corpus-based grammar must fail because it is impossible to derive deep structure from surface structure, and for the same reason he suggested that children must be innately pre-programmed to discover deep structure in the language(s) they learn. McNeill (1970) took the innateness hypothesis to its extreme and argued that it is the basic universal syntactic relations themselves which are innate and that the child's experience with language simply provides information about language-specific surface structures. Thus, in essence, McNeill proposed deriving a young child's utterances from an adult deep structure with extra deletions, arguing that although children are limited to *uttering* single words at the beginning of language acquisition, they are capable of conceiving of something like full sentences.

This 'solution' seemed no solution at all, and Bloom (1970) and Schlesinger (1971) approached two-word utterances in terms of the underlying deep grammar relations that they could be interpreted as realizing. Bloom suggested that to account for her data it was necessary to assume that at the two-word stage children are actually able to handle thirteen grammatical relations and that underlying structures must account for these, even though on the surface many of the differences are neutralized. Unlike the earlier work on grammar, however, Bloom was able to justify her analytic categories retrospectively by observing that as the child's utterances increase in length and complexity, the postulated underlying relations are realized in surface grammatical forms.

The early 1970s saw a sudden change of direction, with the main emphasis moving away from grammar to discourse and, as is so often the case in applied disciplines, workers in child language research discovered that the descriptive and analytic tools they wanted to use were only partially developed and often un-tested on real data. Thus there is no agreed description lying behind the research reported below, and often different papers by the same author are not directly comparable because the descriptive system has been modified in the meantime. However, the results are exciting and suggestive, and potentially much more fruitful than those produced by the earlier grammatically based investigations.

Language function

The research by Dore (1973, 1975) typifies the major change in emphasis. He argues that it is pointless to describe the utterances of young children in purely grammatical terms; the most important fact about such utterances is that the children are using them to do things and therefore a more suitable description is in terms of speech acts. Using the model outlined by Searle (1969), in which, as we saw above (p. 21), a speech act consists of a *propositional* act — referring and predicating — and an *illocutionary* act — 'stating', 'warning', 'questioning', etc. — Dore suggests that the young child's one-word utterances can be usefully characterized as *primitive speech acts*, which have no predication but consist simply of a *rudimentary referring expression*, for example 'doggie' or 'bye bye', and a *primitive force*, typically indicated by intonation. Thus the same lexical item, or rudimentary referring expression, can occur with different forces and therefore realize different primitive speech acts: ' "mama" with a falling terminal intonation contour was used in circumstances where the child merely labelled his mother or some doll as the mother; "mama" with a rising terminal contour was used to ask if an object belonged to his mother . . . and it was used with an abrupt rising-falling contour to call his mother' (p. 31).

Dore suggests that all the one-word utterances of the two children he studied were realizations of one of nine primitive speech acts:

Primitive speech act	Description of example
Labelling	M touches a doll's eyes, utters /aɪz/, then touches its nose, utters /noʊz/; she does not address her mother and her mother does not respond.
Repeating	M, while playing with a puzzle, overhears her mother's utterance of *doctor* (in a conversation with the teacher) and M utters /datə/; mother responds *Yes, that's right honey, doctor*, then continues her conversation; M resumes her play with the puzzle.
Answering	Mother points to picture of a dog and asks J *What's this?*; J responds /baʊwaʊ/.
Requesting (action)	J tries to push a peg through a hole and when he cannot succeed he looks up at his mother, keeping his finger on the peg, and utters /ʌʔʌʔʌʔ/ with constant contours and minimal pause between syllables; his mother then helps him push the peg, saying *Okay*.
Requesting (answer)	M picks up a book, looks at her mother and utters /bʊk ↑ / (where arrow indicates a rising terminal contour); mother responds *Right, it's a book*.
Calling	J, whose mother is across the room, shouts /mâma/ loudly (where ˆ indicates an abrupt rising-falling contour); his mother turns to him and says *I'm getting a cup of coffee. I'll be right there.*
Greeting	J utters /haɪ/ when teacher enters room; teacher responds *Hello*.
Protesting	J, when his mother attempts to put his shoe, utters an extended scream of varying contours, while resisting her; M, in the same circumstance, utters *No*.
Practising	M utters *daddy* when he is not present; mother often does not respond.

(Dore 1975, p. 31)

A striking feature of this descriptive system is that in fact it draws very little on Searle's own analysis — only 'requesting action' and 'requesting answer' would come into Searle's 1969 categorization and it is instructive to attempt to fit these categories into Searle's later 1976 classification. However, as we observed above, speech act analysis is not designed to handle interaction, and any adaptation of the system for this purpose must introduce alterations.

The first question one asks of any descriptive system is 'Why these categories and no others?' The most noticeable absence from the list is 'statement' or 'assertion', but Halliday (1975) notes a similar absence and goes on to suggest that in fact it should not be surprising because the idea that one can use language to convey information not known to one's audience is a sophisticated one. Of the categories Dore offers, perhaps the most contentious is that of *repeating*. Keenan (1974) argues that researchers are far too ready to classify a child's utterance simply as an imitation or a repetition, when the same phenomenon in an adult conversation, where it occurs frequently, would be felt to have some extra significance. One would not be happy with a description which simply characterized the doctor's second utterance, in the following example, as a repetition:

DOCTOR: and when did you get these
PATIENT: a week last Wednesday
DOCTOR: a week last Wednesday

As we demonstrated above (p. 118), depending on the pitch choice on 'Wednesday', the doctor will be heard as either requesting more information or indicating that he understands and acknowledges the information given. Keenan suggests that one should similarly see a child's repetition as having some function in discourse, and thus, in the example Dore offers of repeating 'doctor', the child's action may more usefully be described in Dore's terms as performing the primitive speech act of practising or requesting answer. Significantly, in Dore's own example the mother does respond 'Yes, that's right honey, doctor'.

Four of the remaining acts which Dore proposes are initiating — *requesting action, requesting answer, calling* and *greeting*; three are responding — *answering, protesting* and *greeting*; and two are non-interactive — *labelling* and *practising*. Although Dore claims that the primitive force-indicating device is 'typically an intonation pattern', in fact this is not true — all answering and protesting acts are marked as such by position in sequence, practising acts by the absence of relevant referents in the situation, while greeting acts are recognizable because there is only a closed set of items. Only three of the acts are in fact distinguished solely by intonation, *labelling, requesting answer* and *calling* — significantly, the three acts exemplified by 'mama'.

While Dore's description has moved a long way from Searle's, his proposals are intuitively acceptable if one sees them not as speakers' categories but rather as the categories that adults use to *interpret* what the child is saying, and it is interesting to compare Dore's description with that proposed from a different perspective by Halliday. Halliday (1974, 1975) reports a detailed study of the language development of one child, Nigel, from the age of nine months, before which he had no recognizable communication system, to the age of eighteen months, when he began to abandon the idiosyncratic system he had created for himself and learn the adult language. Halliday provides a description of the developing system at six-weekly intervals, and because at this age the corpus is very small, with only twelve distinct utterances or meanings at ten and a half months and fifty-two at sixteen and a half months, every meaning can be shown as an exponent of one or other of the descriptive categories. At this early stage a child's communication system is, like other animal systems, bi-stratal — 'it has a semantics and a phonology, but nothing in between' — and the only way to interpret such a system is in functional terms.

Halliday adapts a descriptive system first proposed in 1970 for adult language and argues that the very young child's language can usefully be described in terms of six functional categories:

1. *instrumental* — this is the 'I want' function of language; and it is likely to include a general expression of desire, some element meaning simply 'I want that object there (present in the context)', as well as perhaps other expressions relating to specific desires.

2. *regulatory* — the regulatory is the 'do as I tell you' function . . . in the instrumental the focus is on the goods or services required and it does not matter who provides them, whereas regulatory utterances are directed towards a particular individual.

3. *interactional* — the 'me and you' function . . . this is language used by the child to interact with those around him . . . and it includes meanings such as generalized greetings, 'Hello', 'pleased to see you' and also responses to calls, 'Yes'.

4. *personal* — this is language used to express the child's own uniqueness . . . this includes, therefore, expressions of personal feelings, of participation and withdrawal, of interest, pleasure, disgust.

5. *heuristic* — the 'tell me why' function, that which later on develops into the whole range of questioning forms that the young child uses. At this very early stage, in its most elementary form, the heuristic use of language is the demand for a name.

6. *imaginative* — the function of language whereby the child creates an environment of his own . . . a world initially of pure sound, but which gradually turns into one of story and make-believe.

(Halliday 1975)

It is instructive to compare the functions which Halliday brings to the data with the primitive speech acts which Dore derives from it:

Halliday	Dore
instrumental } regulatory }	requesting (action)
interactional	calling, greeting, answering
personal	protesting
heuristic	requesting (answer); labelling
imaginative	–

The only one of Dore's primitive speech acts to find no parallel function is practising, and this is because Halliday (1974) excluded it 'on the grounds that the learning of a system is not a function of the system', while there is only one of Halliday's functions for which Dore does not offer a parallel speech act, *imaginative*, but as the realizations are items like 'peep-o', 'cockodoodledoo' and lion noises, Dore may simply have ignored them — interestingly, in his later descriptive system (1977), for slightly older children, he does have a 'role play' category.

Just as with Dore's system, there are problems about the status of Halliday's categories; he implies that they are speaker's categories — 'these functions [are] those in respect of which the child first created a system of meanings . . . within each function the child develops a set of options' (p. 33), and 'the functions . . . emerge with remarkable clarity' (p. 40) — but there is no evidence that the child distinguishes the functions. Although Halliday asserts that 'it was possible . . . to assign . . . meanings to functions with relatively little doubt or ambiguity', the criteria are semantic and not formal and are very much the result of adult interpretation.

Further doubt is thrown on the status of the system when Halliday reveals that at about nineteen months Nigel did begin to indicate differences by using intonation systematically to make a binary distinction between two classes of utterance, *pragmatic* which required a verbal or non-verbal response and *mathetic* which were marked as 'self-sufficient': 'Nigel made the distinction between the pragmatic and mathetic function totally explicit in his own expressions because from this point on, for six months or more, he spoke all pragmatic utterances on a rising tone and all others on a falling tone' (p. 29):

mathetic   dada got scrambled egg . . .
pragmatic   mummy get foŕyou scrambled egg

Paradoxically, instead of seeing this as the child's *first* functional distinction Halliday chooses to see it as the child amalgamating the earlier distinctions, with pragmatic now subsuming the instrumental and regulatory functions and mathetic arising 'primarily from a combination . . . of the personal and the heuristic'.

Both Dore and Halliday were interested in *categorizing* utterances functionally; Bates *et al.* (1979) report a study of children aged two to eighteen months designed to discover how a child comes to produce such utterances. Their theoretical framework derives from Austin but their redefinition of his terms is so radical that they in fact no longer share the same perspective. Their aim was

> to follow the development of communication through three stages: (1) a perlocutionary stage, in which the child has a systematic effect on his listener without having an intentional, aware control over that effect; (2) an illocutionary stage, in which the child intentionally uses non-verbal signals to convey requests and to direct adult attention to objects and events; and (3) a locutionary stage, in which the child constructs propositions and utters speech sounds within the same performative sequences that he previously expressed non-verbally.   (p. 113)

The descriptive insight is a powerful and persuasive one — that the child moves from accidentally influencing parent behaviour to deliberately influencing it, to doing so linguistically — and the importance of the study is to emphasize the continuum and the fact that kinesic and vocal signals are exploited from the beginning to 'do things'.

Their observations of one child suggested that after ten months she had reached the stage of understanding 'the role of adults as agent and the role of her own signals in affecting that agency'. They proposed a binary classification system comparable to Halliday's for the child's 'illocutionary acts' — *proto-imperatives* which were items which set out to use 'adults to obtain objects' and *proto-declaratives* which were uses of 'objects to reach adults'. An example of a proto-imperative is:

> C is seated in a corridor in front of the kitchen door. She looks toward her mother and calls with an acute sound 'Ha'. M comes over to her and C looks toward the kitchen, twisting her body and upper shoulders to do so. M carries her into the kitchen and C points toward the sink. M gives her a glass of water and C drinks it eagerly.   (p. 123)

Their 'locutionary' phase covers the gradual progression from simple 'vocalization to vocalization as signal to word as signal, to word as proposition with referential value', the last of which is equivalent to Dore's primitive speech act.

In addition to proposing primitive speech acts Dore suggested an intermediary stage on the way to full adult usage:

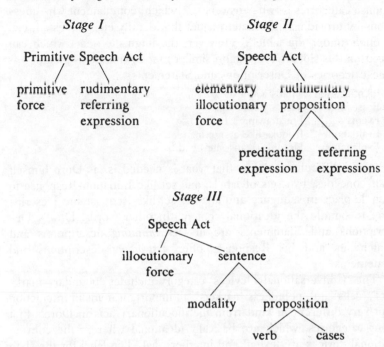

He claims from his observations of children's early two-word utterances that his characterization of Stage II is 'an adequate representation of the child's ability', but he provides no examples and, crucially, no indication of how the realization of elementary illocutionary force differs from that of primitive force. In Stage III he places the occurrence of *grammaticalization*, the process by which the illocutionary force operates to select features of the modality component, but as he exemplifies by suggesting that the illocutionary forces 'demand' and 'request' select respectively the moods imperative and declarative, it appears that the ideas have not been well thought through. Significantly, his later work makes no further reference to these suggestions.

Dore (1977), studying children aged thirty-four to forty-three months, proposes a much more detailed analytic system comprising thirty-two different illocutionary acts divided into six categories —

Requests, Responses, Descriptions, Statements, Conversational Devices and Performatives. Again, these are categories derived from rather than brought to the data, and they allow him to make interesting observations about his data, but there are problems which should make others beware of using them as they stand. Firstly, one of the Response categories is 'wh- answers . . . [which] complement wh- questions by providing information about the identity etc. requested, e.g. "John's under the table".' However, the linguistic items which can occur in this slot are remarkably similar to following items included as sub-categories of Descriptions and Statements:

Identification	That's a house
Possession	That's John's egg
Events	I'm drawing a house
Evaluation	It looks like a snowman
Explanation	He did it cause he's bad

It is not difficult to realize that what is needed is, as Dore himself half-concedes, two sets of labels: one set like Initiation-Response to handle place in sequence and another set like Request and Description to handle the ideational content. In other words, Dore's Descriptions and Statements are in fact *initiating* descriptions and statements and his Responses often *responding* descriptions and statements.

The 'Conversational Devices' category includes 'boundary markers', 'calls' and 'politeness markers', all important items in interaction but very different in kind from the illocutionary acts in Dore's first four categories, which are basically ideational whereas the conversational devices are textual and interpersonal. The label for the sixth category, Performatives, is odd but acts as a 'cover-all' and includes 'warnings', 'claims', 'protests', 'role-plays', 'jokes' and 'teases'.

Acquisition of interpretive and productive rules

As we have already seen, a major problem for discourse analysts is to relate form to function, and it therefore seems reasonable to suppose that children will have similar difficulties. Ervin-Tripp (1977) focuses on the problem of interpreting directives. Beginning with her categorization of the linguistic options open to adults in creating directives:

1. interrogative	'Gotta match'
2. imperatives	'Gimme a match'
3. imbedded imperatives	'Could you gimme a match'
4. statements of need or desire	'I need a match', 'I'm cold'
5. statements of external condition	'There aren't any matches here'

she goes on to make a prediction that a child's understanding of directives 'progresses from imperatives . . . to imbedded imperatives . . . then to need statements where the fulfilling act must be supplied. Very late would be interrogative requests and general statement-requests because of the knowledge required of implications.' In other words her expectation is that young children will decode the grammatically and lexically more explicit directives more successfully. Bellinger (1979) provides evidence to suggest that mothers work intuitively on the same linguistic hypothesis — she discovers that the grammatical form of directives used to twelve-month-old children is predominantly imperative, 74%, with 20% interrogative and 6% declarative, while to twenty-seven-month-old children the proportions are 52%, 27% and 21% respectively.

Shatz (1974), however, provides interesting evidence that at an early age children are equally happy with explicit and implicit forms of directives. Her data consists of videotapes of three two-year-olds interacting with their mothers in their own homes and playing with a 'large pre-school toy' provided by the experimenter. Shatz focused on utterances by the mothers which were directive in intent and either interrogative or imperative in form — 'suggestions implicit or explicit that the child perform an act different from the one he was performing at the time of the utterance'. The results are highly significant. Although Ervin-Tripp predicted that the explicit imperative directives would be the most successful, in fact the children responded appropriately to them in only 40% of cases while the less explicit interrogative directives were successful in 52% of cases. These interrogative directives were not all imbedded imperatives, utterances of the form 'can you shut the door': 40% were pure interrogatives like 'are there any more suitcases', where the requested action, 'find another suitcase', is not stated in the utterance.

It is, of course, always difficult to interpret data of this kind and to attempt to infer competence from performance. As Ervin-Tripp (ibid.) points out, 'failure to comply or even acknowledge may be deceptive because the child may not want to comply . . . for example when a 4-year-old hears "why are you in the garden in your socks?" and answers "because I took off my shoes", it is not clear whether he in fact understood a directive' (p. 179) but chose to reply as if it was an elicitation.

A second problem is that we may not be justified in concluding from a series of correct responses to directives of different forms that a given child is now aware that directive function can be transmitted by more than one grammatical form — the child may not be focusing on or even noticing the grammatical choices. What the Shatz data does tell us is that in occurrences where the adult analyst recognized a potential ambiguity the children chose the correct alternative with a high degree of accuracy — of all the interrogative directives to which the children actually responded, only 15% were mistakenly treated as questions, the other 85% being followed by the appropriate action.

Thus, whether one assumes the children to be blissfully unaware of grammatical structure or to be sophisticatedly discriminating, they were obviously using other, non-grammatical information and responding differentially. Shatz wondered whether the mothers were providing non-verbal indications of the directive intent of their interrogatives, but noticed that in fact all the mothers tended to use gestures more frequently with imperatives than with interrogatives. There must, therefore, be another explanation. Shatz herself proposed a basic ground rule for this type of interaction — 'Mama says; child does', and suggested that the child's strategy is to 'find some element, either action or object, in Mama's speech which you can act out or act upon; then perform some action which communicates to Mama that you have heard, are responding, are taking your turn in the interaction.' An obvious prediction from such a theory, and one on which she says she is working, is that a child will respond with an action 'even to ill-formed directives like "may you shut the door", and misinterpret questions like "can you jump" as directives even when they are intended informationally'.

In this context it is useful to recall two examples quoted in earlier chapters — on the one hand that of the five-year-old who for over a year used the formulaic 'please may you' as a generalized opening to (polite) directives and on the other Sinclair and Coulthard's 'can you play the piano' which was used to argue that, at least once they have reached school age, children work with the basic ground rule 'if the predicate describes an action which is physically possible at the time of the utterance' treat it as a directive, otherwise regard it as an elicitation requiring a verbal response.

This study by Shatz is a very useful one but, for the critical reader, there are three deficiencies: firstly, there is no indication whether interrogatives intended and heard as questions were intonationally (or gesturally) different from either those intended and heard as directives or those intended as directives but heard as questions; secondly, the ground rule 'Mama says; child does' is too powerful because it completely ignores context — for instance, it is hard to imagine that utterances of the form 'are there any more suitcases' would *invariably* be interpreted as directive; thirdly, the method followed by Shatz deduces a child's interpretation of a given utterance from his response to it, yet Reeder (1975) reports that some of his children, while understanding certain interrogatives as questions rather than directives, actually went on to act out the propositions being questioned, and thus eventually reacted *as if they had interpreted the utterance as a directive*.

Obviously what is needed is a way of discovering children's interpretations of criterial utterances. Reeder (1976) reports such an experiment with children aged thirty-eight to forty-six months, slightly older than those studied by Shatz. He provided the children with a series of tape-recorded utterances, all of the form 'would you like to do *p*' and all with rising intonation, which could be correctly interpreted as questions or directives only by reference to the context and cotext. The utterances were contextualized for the children in an ongoing interaction between a teacher and pupils in a toy playschool. Thus an utterance intended as a question would be contextualized by 'Peter, in you come and help me feed the animals . . . you choose which one you want to feed'. Peter then approaches and leaves four pets in quick succession and turns to the teacher who then asks:

would you like to feed the $\begin{cases} \text{rabbit} \\ \text{tadpoles} \\ \text{tortoise} \\ \text{mice} \end{cases}$

By contrast, for an utterance intended as a directive, the context would be 'Simon, leave the swing, Peter's on it' followed by

would you like to play on the $\begin{cases} \text{slide} \\ \text{seesaw} \\ \text{roundabout} \\ \text{climbing frame} \end{cases}$

All the 'teacher's' utterances were pre-recorded and at the appropriate time the tape-recorder was switched on, so that all the children heard exactly the same test item. The novelty of this experiment is firstly that the children were not direct participants but were being asked to interpret utterances they had 'overheard', and secondly that they were not asked to remember, repeat or paraphrase what the teacher had said but instead to choose between two alternative explicit *paraphrases* also pre-recorded. Thus the children heard utterances in form (a) below but were in fact asked to decide whether the teacher had 'said' (b) or (c):

a) would you like to do A   tone 2 (rising intonation)
b) do you want to do A   tone 1+ (high fall)
c) I want you to do A   tone 1 (mid fall)

Each child heard eight utterances intended as directives and eight intended as questions and in every case the sole disambiguating feature was contextual information — that is, in the light of what had just been said and done, the children were asked to decide whether the teacher was likely to be asking or telling the pupils. The children were 'successful' 70% of the time. These results reinforce those of Shatz in demonstrating that children do not have great difficulty with indirect realizations and in suggesting therefore that their problems may lie, rather, in interpreting the context which, as we saw in Chapter 6, can even be a problem for much older children:

T: what are you laughing at
P: nothing
T: you're laughing at nothing, nothing at all
P: no it's funny really . . .

While Shatz and Reeder discuss children's *understanding* of the directives used by others, Garvey (1975) uses videotapes of children aged three-and-a-half to five-and-a-half playing together in pairs, to discover how children *themselves* use language to direct. Interestingly, her children overwhelmingly chose the explicit form — 94%.of the younger children's directives and 89% of the older children's were imperative — despite the fact that, as we have seen, they have no difficulty in understanding less explicit forms.

Lawson (1977) reports a two-year-old with a more subtle command of directive forms — she apparently used simple imperatives almost all the time to her peers but those to three-year-olds tended to be softened by a post-posed 'please', or 'OK'; even more surprisingly, she tended to choose interrogative forms for four-year-olds while for adults she selected desire statements (56%) or interrogatives (38%). This small study is crucially important because it demonstrates that one two-year-old, and by implication many others, is aware not only that the same function has a series of possible linguistic realizations, but also that these realizations have sociolinguistic implications.

Conversational structure

Much of the early work on children's acquisition of discourse competence concentrated, as we have seen, on single utterances and even parts of utterances, examining how the child comes to be able to produce and interpret individual speech acts. Initially there was little concern with conversational structure and how a child learns to be a conversationalist — recently, however, the situation has changed dramatically.

Snow (1977) traces the roots of conversation a long way back. Examining mothers with children from the age of three months on she notices that the language used is interactional — there is a remarkably large number of questions and almost no monologue: 'essentially, all of the mothers' speech was related in content to the baby or the baby's activities and direction of attention, and much of it was directed towards eliciting responses from the baby'. She argues that there is a natural development from exchanges like the following with a three-month-old baby to cooperative two-party verbalized interaction:

Mother	*Baby*
	SMILES
Oh what a nice smile	
yes, isn't that nice	
there	
there's a nice little smile	BURPS
what a nice wind as well	

In her data every burp, yawn, sneeze, coo-vocalization, smile and laugh was picked up and commented on by the mother and she suggests that 'the mothers' attempts to maintain a conversation despite the inadequacies of their conversational partners account for the most striking characteristics of the maternal speech style — its repetitiveness'. By seven months, apparently, babies can initiate by protesting and respond by gaze and by twelve months they produce actions as responses to utterances.

Explicitly following up Snow's work, Ervin-Tripp (1979) notes that orderly dyadic interchanges occur 'at an age when adults often consider children to be quite incompetent conversationalists. By two, children are capable of replying to adjacency pairs such as greetings, yes-no questions, confirmation questions, control questions or commands and offers.' Young children are seen, however, to have more problems when they seek rather than are offered the floor — 83% of their 'anticipation or completion interruptions' and 94% of their attempted topic shifts were ignored.

The construction of coherent conversation and the ability to talk 'on topic' are skills to be acquired, and the work of Keenan on video tapes of her twin sons, recorded monthly from the age of two years nine months to three years eight months, is our main source of information about the origins of conversation.

One major feature of adult conversation is that successive utterances are closely related; as we have seen in Chapter 4, Sacks emphasizes that speakers work to achieve this coherence, while the inability to relate utterances is taken to be one of the indications of mental illness. It is therefore of interest to discover how and at what age children become able to hold a coherent conversation. Halliday (1975) notes that before the age of eighteen months Nigel had no concept of exchanging information and therefore could not indulge in dialogue, while Piaget (1926), observing children in a kindergarten, suggests that even at the age of five or six children tend not to address their speech to a co-present listener. This would suggest that the habit, if not the skills of conversation, is acquired late. However, the evidence from Keenan's children suggests just the opposite — in the earliest recordings there is strong evidence of the great importance the children attach to relevance and turn-taking. In the following example they maintain a coherent, though meaningless, interaction by focusing on the phonological shape of the previous utterance and then modifying it:

A: [ʃaː] [ʃabatʃ]
B: [ʃoːbabat]
A: [ʃoːbabat] [ʃobabatʃ] (laughs)
B: [ʃoːbababatʃ]
A: [ʃoːbatʃ] (laugh)
B: [ʃoːbatʃ]
A: [baptʃ]
B: [ʃoːbatʃ]
A: [batʃi] [bitʃi] [badi] [bidi] [babi]
B: [badi] (laughing)

(Keenan and Klein 1975)

As Keenan and Klein observe, such examples show that 'even when the child is unable to maintain a referential talk-exchange he is still willing to interact verbally'. Indeed their evidence suggests that this is a crucial development stage, for at two years nine months a third of the children's exchanges consist of sound play, while three months later it has completely disappeared.

In adult conversation questions and commands require a response from the listener; assertions, some analysts claim, do not. It is therefore interesting to discover that the twins 'observe a conversational norm which obliges the addressee routinely to acknowledge the speaker's utterance'. Keenan and Klein isolate five types of acknowledgement of relevant response:

a) basic acknowledgment	— direct repetition	A: mommy's silly B: mommy's silly
b) affirmation	— explicit agreement	A: big one B: yes

c) denial	— negation of opposition	A: Jack and Jill
		B: no Jack and Jill
d) matching	— claim to be performing a similar action	A: I find feather
		B: yes I find I get one
e) extension	— new predication to previous speaker's topic	A: flower broken
		B: many flowers broken

and they observe that the listener is expected to produce one of these
acknowledgements; if he doesn't the speaker may repeat his assertion
until it is acknowledged:

A: goosey goosey gander . . .
B: [iː] moth [iː] moth
A: goosey goosey gander where shall I wander . . .
B: [iː] moth (4 times)
A: upstairs downstairs in the lady's chamber . . .
B: [iː] moth (3 times)
A: [iː] moth
B: gone moth allgone

Keenan and Klein comment, 'in this context "goosey goosey gander"
is not a relevant response. It is not accepted by the utterer of "[iː]
moth" who, in turn, perseverates with his utterances until the other
stops singing and takes note'.

Conversation can, of course, progress only when there is an agreed
topic, and as we have seen adults have problems in introducing, maintaining and ending topics — the problem for children is even greater
as they cannot be sure that the addressee is even attending. An early
strategy is to introduce a potential new topic in one utterance, '[iː]
moth' above, and 'oh oh oh bell' below, and then following an indication of acceptance by the other child, often realized by repetition,
to predicate something about the topic:

A1: oh oh oh bell
B1: bell
A2: bell it's mommy's
B2: (unclear)
A3: was mommy's alarm clock
was mommy's alarm clock
B3: alarm clock
A4: yeah goes ding dong ding dong

(Keenan 1974)

In such cases the repetition by the second child is the indication that
he has accepted the topic and that the first speaker can go on to develop
it.

One may wonder where children get this strategy from — in fact adults interact with young children in a very similar way. Scollon (1979) noticed that around 50% of all the adult utterances in his corpus were interrogatives while Ochs *et al.* (1979) point out that very often 'the interrogative functions to draw the child's attention to something the caretaker wants noticed':

M: what's mummy have (*holding cookies*)
C: cookie
M: cookie o.k. here's a cookie for you

They go on to argue that these exchanges are crucially important because 'a child may learn to articulate propositions . . . by partici-pating in a sequence in which she contributes a component of the proposition'.

Wells *et al.* (1979) produce examples which suggest that the inter-active support from adults is not confined to helping children partici-pate in the production of isolated propositions — often mothers help build up a series of propositions which amount to a proto-conversation. There is support for this observation in Kaye and Charney (1981), who noted that the majority of mothers' turns in conversation with their two-year-olds were *turnabouts*, utterances like the third in the example below which 'unequivocally both responds to the other and expects a response from the other'. They note that the use of turnabouts is excessive compared with adult-adult conversation where the main goal 'is getting one's turn, while the main goal of an adult in adult-child conversation is getting the child to take his turn'. Wells *et al.* (ibid.) distinguish two types of mother, one that dominates the conversation choosing topics and creating the 'conversation' through a series of 'display' exchanges:

M: who came in a car
C: see Grannie Irene in a car
M: Grannie Irene's coming next weekend but who came last weekend
C: Auntie Gail in a train
M: Auntie Gail's coming . . .

Other mothers, by contrast, though still producing many of the in-itiations, ask 'real' questions intending to produce a framework to allow the child to tell his own story:

C: gone shop
M: to the shop
C: yeh
M: What's he going to buy
C: biscuits
M: what else
C: meat . . . sweeties, buy a big bag sweets

Garvey (1975) has examples which show three-and-a-half to five-and-a-half year old children still dividing what is essentially topic and comment across two utterances:

A: you see that hammer there
B: yeah
A: hand it to me

A: there's a fireman's hat
B: (*turns to hat*)
A: try it on

though she sees this as leading on to two-part utterances of the form:

A: that's where the iron belongs
    put it there

and finally to single short instructions 'hand me the truck', 'gimme the ladder'.

Second language acquisition

We now know a lot more about how a child learns to become a conversationalist, and this enables us to ask how far the process is the same in second language learning. Peck (1978), examining interaction between two seven-year-olds, one a native speaker and the other a non-native with six months' exposure to English as a second language, noted the occurrence of 'discourse patterns . . . similar to those of the 2–3 year old children that Keenan studied'. These observations are confirmed by Hatch (1978) with the following example of a five-year-old:

PAUL.: this boat
J: mmhmm boat
PAUL.: this
        my boat

Hatch goes on to show that, interestingly, the same topic-nomination strategy occurs in the conversations of adult second language learners:

RICARDO: lookit that
          this
          Empire State

RICARDO: you go
          you go
          for bicycle racing
          Los Angeles

In other words, speakers who are competent conversationalists in one language appear to return to an earlier stage of conversational structure when they are faced with situations in which they are grammatically and lexically incompetent. The implication of these observations is that as we learn more about children's acquisition of conversational competence in their first language we will gain further insight into the learning and teaching of second and foreign languages. Hatch (ibid.) has no doubts — 'only through discourse analysis can we answer the many questions that we have about second language acquisition'.

9 The analysis of literary discourse

Stylistics

Literature is the art form realized entirely through language and, al
though evaluation and interpretation is the province of the literary
critic, it is reasonable to suggest that a detailed analysis of authorial
technique and stylistic features can be more successfully achieved
within a rigorous linguistic framework.

Abercrombie (1965) uses a description of rhythm in speech to dis
cuss the difficulties inherent in certain verse forms for writers in Eng
lish and to provide persuasive solutions to some long-standing
problems in metrics. Leech (1969) draws on an analysis of English
syllable structure to show that there are only six formal options avail
able to a poet who wants to create patterns with phonemes — three
widely used across languages, alliteration, rhyme and assonance, and
three much less frequently exploited, pararhyme, consonance and re
verse rhyme. At the level of grammar Halliday (1973) demonstrates
how William Golding achieves the characterization of his Neanderthal
men in *The Inheritors* as primitive creatures rarely understanding cause
and effect, by particular choices in the transitivity network; while
Thorne (1965) works in the opposite direction and encapsulates the
oddities of an e.e. cummings poem in a unique transformational
grammar.

Like all other branches of applied linguistics, stylistics depends on
the tools provided by theoretical linguistics; as the techniques of dis
course analysis have become more sophisticated, so there has been a
growing exploitation in stylistics.

Applications of linguistic philosophy

As we saw in Chapter 2, it is very difficult to analyse real conversation
in terms of speech acts because explicit performative utterances are
rare and any attempt to expand primary performatives runs immediately
into the problem of what is/are the correct expansion(s). There is of

course a similar difficulty with utterances in novels, but sometimes the author helpfully adds a reporting verb which makes the performative significance explicit:

'I suppose it's the thing to do,' Macomber *agreed*

Indeed, one very interesting area to be investigated in detail and already touched on in Dali (1979) and Caldas (in preparation) is the stylistic significance of the marked differences between authors in their selections of reporting verbs which vary from the uninformative ('he said', 'she said') through the kinesic ('she smiled') and the interactive ('she asked', 'he replied') to the performative ('she declared/urged/invited/confessed').

Even when the author doesn't provide a performative gloss, the reader himself can. Leech and Short (1981) take a dialogue from *Pride and Prejudice* and report it using 'speech act verbs to convey roughly the interpersonal force of what is said':

Mrs Bennett TOLD Mr Bennett that he was wanted . . .
she then EXHORTED him to make Lizzy marry . . .
and she EXPLAINED to him . . .
she WARNED him . . .
Mr Bennett CLAIMED . . .   (p. 292)

They go on to argue that in fact 'we as readers must perform an analysis of this kind in order to understand what is going on in the passage'. This is a persuasive claim in view of the fact that we tend to report, if not remember, real conversations in performative terms, and a re-presentation in this form makes clear ambiguities in and differing interpretations of the text.

Ohmann (1971), in the earliest published attempt to apply speech act theory to literature, sets out to analyse not individual utterances but the whole work, which he argues consists in fact of a series of 'quasi speech acts': 'a literary work is a discourse whose sentences lack the illocutionary forces that would normally attach to them'. What he is asserting is that the felicity conditions on 'real' speech acts do not necessarily hold for speech acts in literary texts, or as Sinclair (1981) has more recently expressed it, the author of the text does not *aver* or assert the truth of any of the sentences in the text — not even in cases like the Borges story *The Shape of the Sword*, quoted in Pratt (1977), when a character 'Borges' appears in the text.

Pratt herself suggests that one can usefully apply Grice's Cooperative Principle and derived maxims to literary texts, both to writer-reader interaction and to the reported interactions within the text. In discussing writer-reader interaction she presents the opening sentences of *Tristram Shandy* and notes a series of failures to observe the maxims of Manner, Quality and Relation:

> with regard to manner the text is peppered with colloquialisms and other expressions reserved for spoken discourse . . . In addition, there are typographical abuses, notably the use of '@' and the dashes, colons and semicolons which allow a single sentence to run on for half a page. As for quantity, the passage is plagued with repetition. (p. 164)

How can one interpret this series of rule-breakings? Pratt argues, convincingly, that it can only be in terms of *flouting*, i.e. deliberate, on-record, breaking of maxims — in this case in an attempt to amuse — because none of the other real-life possibilities is possible in literary texts: there is no reason for the author to feel a *clash* or to need to *opt out* because nothing is required of him, all that he writes is volunteered; similarly it is fanciful to think of an author *violating* a maxim by lying or misrepresenting because there is, as Ohmann observed, no external truth and thus it is literally impossible to produce a violation. It is for these reasons that readers are able to treat 'an unusually wide range of deviations as floutings in literary works' (p. 173).

However, the maxims can be and are broken in all ways by characters inside literary texts — as Pratt emphasizes, returning to the same opening passage, Tristram Shandy himself, the fictional narrator, 'could be guilty of any or all of the kinds of maxim non-fulfilment' (p. 166); indeed the tradition of the unreliable narrator is as old as the novel itself.

Dali (1979), discussing a passage from Hemingway's *Ten Indians*, shows how a flouting of maxims by one character subtly controls and constrains questions by the other:

> 'What did you do this afternoon?' Nick asked.
> 'I went for a walk up by the Indian camp.'
> 'Did you see anybody?'
> 'The Indians were all in town getting drunk.'
> 5 'Didn't you see anybody at all?'
> 'I saw your friend, Prudie.'
> 'Where was she?'
> 'She was in the woods with Frank Washburn. I ran on to them. They were having quite a time.'
> 10 His father was not looking at him.
> 'What were they doing?'
> 'I didn't stay to find out.'
> 'Tell me what they were doing.'
> 'I don't know,' his father said. 'I just heard them threshing around.'

The father's reply at line 4 looks initially like a paraphrase of 'no', but as the Indians are crucially not the only people he could have seen it is designed as a flouting of the maxim of quality and intended to elicit more questioning. At lines 8 and 9 the father violates the quantity maxim providing more than was required to answer the question yet not enough to satisfy curiosity about the new topic. Again at line 12 the father violates the quality maxim and the euphemism in line 14, Dali suggests, is a 'typical violation of Grice's maxim of manner'. Thus we can see how the father is able, through the manipulation of the conversational maxims, to maintain his relationship with his son by not 'telling tales' and still pass on the information he wants to convey.

Conversational analysis

Drama texts, being scripts for the performing of pseudo-conversations, can be successfully approached with techniques originally developed to analyse real conversation. We must, of course, always remember that these are invented sequences, shaped for an artistic purpose, and that some of the rules and conventions are different — Grice's quantity maxim, 'make your contribution as informative but not more informative than is required', is frequently broken, at least from the point of view of a character's co-conversationalists, who are often told something they almost certainly know in order to indirectly inform the audience.

Burton (1980) takes a very short Pinter sketch, *Last to Go*, in which two characters are 'making conversation' to pass the time and shows that much of the humour comes from the fact that because there is nothing to talk about and virtually no new information to contribute the questions are concerned not, as one would normally expect, with Labov's B-events but rather with A–B events:

MAN: I sold my last one about then. Yes. About nine forty-five.
BARMAN: Sold your last then, did you?
MAN: Yes my last 'Evening News' it was. Went about twenty to ten.
                                  (*pause*)
BARMAN: 'Evening News' was it?   (p. 10)

As she observes, 'the characters are continually questioning and confirming matters that they both already know, that they must surely know that they both know and that the audience certainly knows that they know' (p. 13).

Burton moves on to consider Pinter's *The Dumb Waiter*, a play with only two characters, one of whom, Ben, dominates the other, Gus. She demonstrates very convincingly that the dominating/dominated relationship is achieved dramatically to a large extent through the characters' differential access to conversational options in ways typical of adult/child and teacher/pupil interaction.

As we have seen in earlier chapters, parents and teachers in the main control topic; in the play Ben's new topics are never ignored, Gus's frequently are and even when he chooses to respond Ben makes it clear that he considers Gus's contributions to be 'foolish, unfounded, uninteresting, unclear or otherwise suspect' (p. 72). Indeed Gus marks his inferior position in the discourse by frequently asking permission to introduce a topic: 'I want/wanted/was going to ask you something'.

Ben is not a cooperative conversationalist — he ignores most of the questions put to him and many of those he answers are not answered fully:

GUS: . . . have you any idea who it's going to be tonight?
BEN: Who what's going to be?
(*they look at each other*)
GUS: (*at length*) Who it's going to be.
(*silence*)
BEN: Are you feeling all right?

(ibid, p. 78)

As we noted in Chapter 5, when we first analyse a spoken text we are interested in the acts performed by those situationally defined as doctors, teachers, chairmen, patients, pupils and committee members, but ultimately we need to be able to make statements from the opposite end — in other words, being a teacher is constituted by performing the appropriate acts and this is exactly how drama works. Ben is dominating because he performs the acts that dominating participants perform: he issues more than sixty directives, receives four (and ignores three of them) and is continually evaluating Gus. Gus himself occasionally rebels:

BEN: Go and light it.
GUS: Light what?
BEN: The kettle.
GUS: You mean the gas.
BEN: Who does?

(ibid., pp. 88–9)

but in the main he accepts the role and the slots assigned to him. Stylistic analysis is very page-consuming and it has been possible to give only the flavour of Burton's analysis; what I want to do for the remainder of the chapter is to focus in detail on one aspect, questions and answers, of one text, *Othello*.

Questions and answers in 'Othello'

Every time a speaker asks a question there is a set of underlying assumptions, all of which must be true if he is to receive the answer he seeks. At times, of course, some of the assumptions may not hold and the response may consist of a challenge or a denial. There follows a list of eight assumptions with examples from *Othello* of responses which deny them:

Assumption	*Response denying assumption*	
1. Addressee is listening.		–
2. Speaker questions at an appropriate time.	OTHELLO:	Not now sweet Desdemona, some other time. (III iii 56)
3. Addressee hears the question.	IAGO: RODERIGO:	Go to, farewell . . . do you hear Roderigo? What say you? (I iii 376–7)
4. Addressee understands the question.	OTHELLO: IAGO:	Is he not honest? Honest my lord? (III iii 104–5)
5. Addressee accepts speaker as a person allowed or empowered to ask the question.	IAGO:	Though I am bound to every act of duty I am not bound to that all slaves are free to: utter my thoughts. (III iii 139–41)
6. Addressee thinks the speaker does not know the answer.	RODERIGO: IAGO:	Wilt thou be fast to my hopes? Thou art sure of me . . . I have told thee often and I tell thee again and again. (I iii 363–5)
7. Addressee is willing to answer.	IAGO: BRABANTIO:	Are all doors locked? Why, wherefore ask you this? (I i 85)
8. Addressee knows the answer.	IAGO: CASSIO:	What had he done to you? I know not (II iii 277–8)

There are, of course, certain situations in which the assumptions are different, or apply differentially. Thus in a classroom only pupils are likely to question at inappropriate times, while it is commonplace for teachers to ask questions to which they *do* know the answer, and sometimes they also ask questions, for particular purposes, which they know the addressees are unable to answer.

Sacks suggests that the first question we must always ask about any utterance is whether it is intended seriously; perhaps the second is whether the speaker is lying. A speaker always has the option of creating a false impression, or, in the restricted terms of this discussion, of falsely denying an assumption. As always, a particular linguistic option can be exploited. Parents know from long experience that children frequently 'fail' to hear utterances like

Simon, it's bath time.

and therefore resort to presequences which establish the first assumption — that the addressee is listening:

Simon.
Yes.
It's bath time.

Similarly most people have at some time pretended not to hear or not to understand difficult or embarrassing questions in order to give themselves time to think. However, the success of such manoeuvres depends on the skill with which they are carried out — if the responder is suspected of violating the quality maxim 'make your contribution one that is true', all is lost.

One of the major cruces in any literary discussion of *Othello* is how he comes to be so easily and quickly convinced in one central scene, Act III iii, of his wife's adultery — Muir (1968) observes that at the beginning of the scene

> Othello is perfectly happy in his marriage; at the end he has decided to murder Desdemona and Cassio. Unless we realise the extent to which Shakespeare has telescoped the action, we shall be bound to think that Othello was absurdly prone to jealousy, instead of 'not easily jealous' as he claims at the end of the play.

I want to suggest that Iago rouses Othello's suspicion by a sequence of unanswered questions, not simply because the questions are unanswered but because they are avoided clumsily and in fact deliberately so, in order to suggest to Othello that Iago is concealing something.

In order to establish that for most of the play question-answer pairs occur quite naturally, let us glance at this unremarkable extract from Act II iii:*

IAGO: What was he, that you followed with your sword?
        What had he done to you?
CASSIO: I know not.
IAGO: Is't possible?
CASSIO: I remember a mass of things, but nothing distinctly; a quarrel,   280
        but nothing wherefore. O God, that men should put an
        enemy in their mouths, to steal away their brains; that we
        should with joy, revel, pleasure, and applause, transform
        ourselves into beasts!
IAGO: Why, but you are now well enough: how came you thus
        recovered?
CASSIO: It hath pleas'd the devil drunkenness to give place to the
        devil wrath; one unperfectness shows me another, to make
        me frankly despise myself.

Cassio's answer to Iago's first question denies our eighth assumption, that the addressee knows the answer; Iago expresses surprise if not disbelief but Cassio explains how he comes to 'know not'. Iago asks another question and Cassio answers perfectly satisfactorily. Here, as in most other places in the play, the conventions governing questions in conversation are carried over into the simulated conversation.

However, when we come to examine the crucial Act III iii there are marked differences. At the beginning of the scene Cassio, disgraced and relieved of his command after a drunken brawl, comes to Desdemona, on Iago's advice, to ask her to intercede on his behalf. Meanwhile Iago has brought Othello to see the two together; Cassio, seeing Othello approach, takes his leave and as he does so Iago observes

IAGO: Ha, I like not that.   35
OTHELLO: What dost thou say?
IAGO: Nothing, my lord, or if — I know not what.

Here we see Othello ask for a repetition, or more likely a clarification of what Iago has said — why does he not like it? — and Iago refuses, then hesitates, then refuses again. This is the first time Iago has declined to answer a question in the play, let alone a question from Othello, but in isolation it might not be significant.

Othello asks another question, or perhaps uses an interrogative to express surprise, for there is no doubt in his mind, as his third utterance shows:

---

* Line references are to the Arden edition by M. R. Ridley.

OTHELLO: Was not that Cassio parted from my wife?
IAGO: Cassio, my lord? . . . no, sure, I cannot think it,
          That he would sneak away so guilty-like,   40
          Seeing you coming.
OTHELLO: I do believe 'twas he.

Othello presents Cassio's departure as an AB event and it is therefore
surprising that Iago does not confirm but questions. Having questioned such an obvious fact Iago must offer a reason, and so he does
with a sting in the tail — having apparently dissociated the departing
figure from the still 'honest' though disgraced Cassio, Iago is able to
suggest that he departed 'guiltily'

The oddness of these two unanswered questions is emphasized as
the play returns to normal question-answer conventions with Desdemona replying to Othello and incidentally confirming the fact which
Iago had questioned:

DESDEMONA: How now, my lord?
            I have been talking with a suitor here,
            A man that languishes in your displeasure.
OTHELLO: Who is't you mean?   45
DESDEMONA: Why, your lieutenant, Cassio, good my lord,
            If I have any grace or power to move you,
            His present reconciliation take:
            For if he be not one that truly loves you,
            That errs in ignorance, and not in cunning,   50
            I have no judgement in an honest face,
            I prithee call him back.
OTHELLO: Went he hence now?
DESDEMONA: Yes, faith, so humbled,
            That he has left part of his griefs with me,
            I suffer with him; good love, call him back.   55

Forty lines further on Desdemona and Emilia depart leaving Othello
and Iago together. Iago immediately returns to the topic of Cassio but
he still must tread warily — the status difference is strongly marked
by the asymmetrical use of the personal pronouns, 'you' and 'thou',
and Iago 'bids' to speak in the same way that children do to manoeuvre
his discourse superior into asking him to ask him a question:

IAGO: My noble lord,   94
OTHELLO: What does thou say, Iago?
IAGO: Did Michael Cassio, when you woo'd my lady,
          Know of your love?

The question he asks is amazing when one considers that twenty
lines earlier Desdemona had referred to Cassio 'that came a-wooing
with you', but in fact at this point the topic of the discourse is not

particularly important. The crucial feature is the way in which Iago represents himself as highly reluctant to answer any questions and trades on his reputation.

Othello sees 'honest Iago', the blunt, unsubtle, outspoken soldier apparently attempting clumsily and with increasing desperation to avoid committing himself to any opinion about 'honest Cassio'. In quick succession Iago avoids six questions:

IAGO:	Did Michael Cassio, when you woo'd my lady,	95
	Know of your love?	
OTHELLO:	He did, from first to last . . . why dost thou ask?	
IAGO:	But for a satisfaction of my thought.	
	No further harm.	
OTHELLO:	Why of thy thought, Iago?	
IAGO:	I did not think he had been acquainted with her.	100
OTHELLO:	O yes, and went between us very often.	
IAGO:	Indeed?	
OTHELLO:	Indeed? Indeed: discern'st thou aught in that?	
	Is he not honest?	
IAGO:	Honest, my lord?	105
OTHELLO:	Honest? ay, honest.	
IAGO:	My lord, for aught I know.	
OTHELLO:	What does thou think?	
IAGO:	Think, my lord?	

Iago's first answer, 'But for satisfaction of my thought', is the politest of possible refusals, denying assumption 7, and also allowing Iago to drop another stone into the pond — 'no further harm'. His second answer, to the insistent 'Why of thy thought', is patently untrue — had he assumed a negative answer the question wouldn't have been asked in that form. The following sequence

IAGO:	Did Michael Cassio, when you woo'd my lady,
	Know of your love?
OTHELLO:	He did not.
IAGO:	As I thought.

would have been very odd, particularly if Iago had, as he claims, no particular reason for asking the question. As Sacks reminds us, a speaker must make his utterances obviously relevant.

Iago creates more confusion or suspicion by his interested or even surprised 'indeed' and subsequent lack of response to 'discern'st thou aught in that?', and to the AB event question 'Is he not honest?' he apparently can only lamely pretend he hasn't understood and return 'Honest, my lord?', before producing the noncommittal 'My lord, for aught I know'. Iago here succeeds in presenting the image of a man wriggling and twisting not to lie but also not to tell a damaging truth.

By the time we reach the last pair

OTHELLO: What dost thou think?
IAGO: Think, my lord?

Iago has apparently run out of invention and is seen to be desperately pretending that he does not understand the question.

Othello thinks aloud, showing Iago the inferences he is making from this peculiar performance, and then pleads for clarification:

OTHELLO: Think, my lord? By heaven, he echoes me,   110
         As if there were some monster in his thought,
         Too hideous to be shown: thou didst mean something:
         I heard thee say but now, thou lik'st not that,
         When Cassio left my wife: what didst not like?
         And when I told thee he was of my counsel,   115
         In my whole course of wooing, thou criedst 'Indeed?'
         And didst contract and purse thy brow together,
         As if thou then hadst shut up in thy brain
         Some horrible conceit: if thou dost love me,
         Show me thy thought.
IAGO: My lord, you know I love you.   120
OTHELLO: I think thou dost.

Iago neatly sidesteps Othello's request 'show me thy thought' and focuses on the subordinate clause which he re-affirms — 'you know I love you'.

The cumulative effect of this series of unanswered questions is to convince Othello that Iago is not being truthful and to search for a reason. Iago is able to build on the foundations of his suspicious question-avoiding and gradually become more specific in his accusations until he can warn

Look to your wife, observe her well with Cassio.   201

The structure of the discourse has returned to normality and the dramatic development is once again being carried by the content rather than the form of the discourse.

Later scenes

Many people, on reflection, consider parts of the plot of *Othello* unconvincing. Why, they ask, does Desdemona not confess to having lost her handkerchief, and why at a later stage does she not force Othello to detail his accusations and 'ocular proof'? On stage, however, in the moment by moment development of the play, the events are utterly convincing. Sacks frequently observes that topic is a joint production, and at those points in the play when Desdemona could have cleared herself there is marked topic conflict and as a result normal interaction breaks down.

The following extract comes from Act III iv and is the first meeting between Othello and Desdemona after Iago has aroused 'the green-eyed monster', jealousy. Desdemona is anxious to continue the topic of their last meeting, the reinstatement of Cassio; Othello wants to check that she has indeed lost the handkerchief. However, Othello doesn't simply ask whether she has lost the handkerchief but prefaces it by a twenty-line disquisition on its magical properties and the dangers of losing it. Small wonder she should wish she 'had never seen it', but in the context this is for Othello the first hint of confirmation and he demands an explanation:

```
DESDEMONA: Then would to God that I had never seen it!          75
OTHELLO:   Ha, wherefore?
DESDEMONA: Why do you speak so startingly and rash?
OTHELLO:   Is't lost? is't gone? speak, is it out o' the way?
DESDEMONA: Heaven bless us!
OTHELLO:   Say you?                                             80
DESDEMONA: It is not lost, but what an if it were?
OTHELLO:   Ha!
DESDEMONA: I say it is not lost.
OTHELLO:                          Fetch't, let me set it.
```

For Desdemona the remarkable thing is his tone — she of course does not know what he has suffered in the short time since she last saw him — so she responds with surprise, 'Why do you speak so startingly and rash?' To Othello this seems like a deliberate avoidance of the question and his repeated question is similarly parried with an expression of concerned surprise. Othello has been through this before — the last time someone avoided his questions it later transpired that he was covering up untold horrors; this time he will not be put off.

Desdemona is unable to understand the overriding importance which Othello attaches to the handkerchief and suspects that he is manipulating the conversation to avoid talking about Cassio. She fears Cassio will not arise naturally as a topic and therefore determinedly reintroduces him. However, she is only partly successful and from this point on they both stick stubbornly to their own topic, 'skip-connecting' in Sacks' terms, until Othello explodes and leaves the stage:

```
DESDEMONA: Why, so I can sir, but I will not now,
           This is a trick, to put me from my suit,            85
           I pray let Cassio be receiv'd again.
OTHELLO:   Fetch me that handkerchief, my mind misgives.
```

```
DESDEMONA: Come, come,
           You'll never meet a more sufficient man.
OTHELLO:   The handkerchief!
DESDEMONA:                      I pray, talk me of Cassio.          90
OTHELLO:   The handkerchief!
DESDEMONA:                      A man that all his time
           Hath founded his good fortunes on your love,
           Shar'd dangers with you, —
OTHELLO:   The handkerchief!
DESDEMONA:                      I' faith, you are to blame.
OTHELLO:   Zounds!                              (Exit)             95
```

Desdemona and Othello meet only once more in private before the
scene in which he stifles her and this time it is Othello who is un-
willing to answer questions — there is no pretence, no attempt to deny
presuppositions, he simply acts as if he hasn't heard her questions.
He won't tell her what his 'pleasure' is; what 'horrible fancy' grips
him; what his words mean; with whom she is 'false'. This is obviously
dramatically necessary — any accusation at this stage would offer
Desdemona the chance to reply and demonstrate her innocence:

```
DESDEMONA: My lord, what is your will?
OTHELLO:                    Pray, chuck, come hither.
DESDEMONA: What is your pleasure?
OTHELLO:                    Let me see your eyes, . . .            25
           Look in my face.
DESDEMONA: What horrible fancy's this?
OTHELLO:   (to Emilia) Some of your function, mistress,
           Leave procreants alone, and shut the door,
           Cough, or cry hem, if anybody come;
           Your mystery, your mystery: nay dispatch.               30
                        (Exit Emilia)
DESDEMONA: Upon my knees, what does your speech import?
           I understand a fury in your words,
           But not the words.
OTHELLO:   Why, what art thou?
DESDEMONA: Your wife, my lord, your true and loyal wife.           35
OTHELLO:   Come, swear it, damn thyself,
           Lest, being like one of heaven, the devils themselves
           Should fear to seize thee, therefore be double-damn'd,
           Swear thou art honest.
DESDEMONA:                    Heaven doth truly know it.
OTHELLO:   Heaven truly knows, that thou art false as hell.        40
DESDEMONA: To whom, my lord? with whom? how am I false?
OTHELLO:   O Desdemona away! away! away!        (Act IV ii)
```

Othello is half-crazed with anger and grief and this is both re-
flected in and transmitted by the jerky semi-coherent discourse. Desdemona finds it difficult to contribute relevantly, let alone defend

herself. She makes one last attempt:

Alas, what ignorant sin have I committed?

but this merely evokes a rambling series of insults; finally he accuses
her of being a 'strumpet' and 'whore', ignores her denials, and storms
out.

Only in Act V ii, when it is too late and he has already resolved
to murder her, does Othello answer Desdemona's questions and reveal his evidence:

DESDEMONA: What's the matter?
OTHELLO: That handkerchief which I so lov'd, and gave thee,
            Thou gavest to Cassio.
DESDEMONA: No, by my life and soul,
            Send for the man and ask him.   50
OTHELLO: Sweet soul, take heed, take heed of perjury,
            Thou art on thy death-bed.

Thirty-five lines later he murders her.

Concluding remarks

Most of the work described in earlier chapters has been concerned
with spoken interaction, and this particular chapter has applied insights derived from conversational analysis to illuminate technique in
simulated interaction. Those working on written discourse have
tended to analyse it as monologue and to ignore the fact that as he
reads the reader interacts with the text and thus an interactive model
might also be appropriate for written discourse.

As you close this book you might like to speculate on the function
of full stops. Are they perhaps interaction points, places where the
writer thinks the reader needs to stop and ask questions about the
previous sentence, questions whose range I initially restrict by the
structuring of my argument and which I subsequently answer in the
next or later sentences?

But now, for me,
                            the rest is silence.

Further reading

In some areas it is possible to write sequels: *Português Contemporâneo 1* and *Português Contemporâneo 2; Good English* and *Better English*. However, it is hard to imagine the content or even the structure of *An Introduction to Discourse Analysis II*. Nevertheless, most readers need something to bridge the gap between the introductory chapters in a book like this and articles in research journals. With this in mind, I offer the following suggestions for further reading:

Chapter 2: Speech acts and conversational maxims
Labov and Fanshel 1977: *29–111*
Leech 1983
Levinson 1983: *97–166, 226–83*

Chapter 3: The ethnography of speaking
Saville-Troike 1982

Chapter 4: Conversational analysis
Levinson 1983: *284–370*
Richards and Schmidt 1983: *117–54*
Schenkein 1978a

Chapter 5: Intonation
Brazil 1985
Brazil, Coulthard and Johns 1980

Chapter 6: A linguistic approach
Coulthard and Montgomery 1981
Sinclair and Brazil 1982
Stubbs 1983

Chapter 7: Discourse analysis and language teaching
Finocchiario and Brumfit 1983
Larsen-Freeman 1980

Chapter 8: The acquisition of discourse
Hatch 1980
Ochs and Schiefflin 1979
Ochs and Schiefflin 1983

Chapter 9: The analysis of literary discourse
Carter 1982: *41–52, 65–77, 179–89*
Leech and Short 1981: *288–351*
Pratt 1977

Bibliography

Abbs, B, Ayton, A and Freebairn, I 1975 *Strategies.* Longman
Abbs, B, Cook, V and Underwood, M 1969 *Realistic English.* Oxford University Press
Abercrombie, D 1965 *Studies in phonetics and linguistics.* Oxford University Press
Albert, E M 1972 Culture patterning of speech behaviour in Burundi. In Gumperz and Hymes 1972
Allen, J P B and Widdowson, H G 1974a Teaching the communicative use of English. *International Review of Applied Linguistics in Language Teaching*: 1–21
Allen, J P B and Widdowson, H G 1974b *English in physical science.* Oxford University Press
Arewa, E O and Dundes, A 1964 Proverbs and the ethnography of speaking folklore. In Gumperz, J J and Hymes, D (eds.) The ethnography of communication, *American Anthropologist* 66(6): 70–85
Aston, G Birmingham song sheet (handout for unpublished lecture)
Atkinson, J M and Drew, P 1979 *Order in court.* Macmillan
Austin, J L 1962 *How to do things with words.* Oxford University Press

Barnes, D 1969 Language in the secondary classroom. In Barnes, D, Britton, J and Rosen, H *Language, the learner and the school.* Penguin
Bates, E 1974 The acquisition of pragmatic competence. *Journal of Child Language* 1: 277–81
Bates, E, Camaioni, L and Volterra, V 1979 The acquisition of performatives prior to speech. In Ochs and Schiefflin 1979: 185–201
Bellack, A A, Kliebard, H M, Hyman, R T and Smith, F L 1966 *The language of the classroom.* Teachers College Press, New York
Bellinger, D 1979 Changes in the explicitness of mothers' directives as children age. *Journal of Child Language* 6: 443–58
Bereiter, C and Engelmann, S 1966 *Teaching disadvantaged children in the pre-school.* Prentice Hall, New York
Bernstein, B B 1962 Linguistic codes, hesitation phenomena and intelligence. *Language and Speech* 5: 31–46
Berry, M 1981 Systemic linguistics and discourse analysis: a multi-layered approach to exchange structure. In Coulthard and Montgomery 1981: 120–45
Bever, T G and Ross, J R 1966 Underlying structures in discourse. Unpublished paper quoted in Labov 1972a.
Biddle, B J 1967 Methods and concepts in classroom research. *Review of Educational Research* 37: 337–57

Blom, J-P and Gumperz, J J 1972 Social meaning in linguistic structures: code-switching in Norway. In Gumperz and Hymes 1972: 407–34

Bloom, L 1970 *Language development: form and function in emerging grammars*. MIT Press, Cambridge, Massachusetts

Bloomfield, L 1933 *Language*. Holt, Rinehart and Winston, New York

Bolinger, D 1964 Around the edge of language: intonation. *Harvard Educational Review*, 34: 282–96

Borges, J L 1964 The shape of the sword. In Yates, D A and Irby, J E (eds.) *Labyrinths*. New Directions, New York

Boyd, J and Thorne, J P 1969 The deep grammar of modal verbs. *Journal of Linguistics* 5(1): 57–74

Braine, M 1963 The ontogeny of English phrase structure: the first phase. *Language* 39: 1–13

Brazil, D C 1973 *Intonation*. Working Papers in Discourse Analysis No. 2. Mimeo, English Language Research, Birmingham

Brazil, D C 1975 *Discourse Intonation*. Discourse Analysis Monographs No. 1. English Language Research, Birmingham

Brazil, D C 1978 *Discourse Intonation*. Unpublished Ph.D. thesis, University of Birmingham

Brazil, D C 1981 Intonation. In Coulthard and Montgomery 1981: 39–50

Brazil, D C 1985 *The communicative value of intonation*. English Language Research, Birmingham

Brazil, D C, Coulthard, R M and Johns, C M 1980 *Discourse intonation and language teaching*. Longman

Bricker, V R 1974 The ethnographic context of some traditional Mayan speech genres. In Bauman, R and Sherzer, J (eds.) *Explorations in the ethnography of speaking*: 368–88. Cambridge University Press

Brown, P and Levinson, S 1978 Universals in language usage: politeness phenomena. In Goody, E (ed.) *Questions and politeness: strategies in social interaction*: 56–311. Cambridge University Press

Brown, R 1973 *A first language*. Allen and Unwin

Brown, R and Bellugi, U 1964 Three processes in the child's acquisition of syntax. *Harvard Educational Review* 34: 133–51

Brumfit, C 1978 'Communicative' language teaching: an assessment. In Strevens, P (ed.) *In Honour of A.S. Hornby*: 33–44. Oxford University Press

Brumfit, C J 1979 'Communicative' language teaching: an educational perspective. In Brumfit, C J and Johnson, K (eds.) *The communicative approach to language teaching*: 183–91. Oxford University Press

Burton, D 1980 *Towards an analysis of casual conversation*. Routledge and Kegan Paul

Caldas, C R (in preparation) *Interaction in narrative*. Ph.D. thesis, University of Birmingham

Canale, M 1983 From communicative competence to communicative language pedagogy. In Richards, J and Schmidt, R (eds.) *Language and communication*: 2–27. Longman

Candlin, C N, Kirkwood, J M and Moore, H M 1973 *Study skills in English — part 1*. Mimeo, University of Lancaster

Candlin, C N, Kirkwood, J M and Moore, H M 1975 Developing study skills in English. In *English for academic study*. British Council ETIC, London

Candlin, C N, Leather, J H and Bruton, C J 1978 *Doctor patient communication skills*. Graves Audio-Visual Medical Foundation, Chelmsford

Carter, R (ed.) 1982 *Language and literature*. Allen and Unwin

Chomsky, N 1957 *Syntactic structures*. Mouton, The Hague

Cohen, L J 1969 Do illocutionary forces exist? In Fann, K T (ed.) *Symposium on J.L. Austin*: 420–44. Routledge and Kegan Paul

Cole, P (ed.) 1978 *Pragmatics*. Syntax and Semantics, vol. 9, Academic Press, New York

Cole, P and Morgan, J (eds.) 1975 *Speech acts*. Syntax and Semantics, vol. 3, Academic Press, New York

Corder, S P 1973 *Introducing applied linguistics*. Penguin

Coulthard, R M and Ashby, M C 1976 A linguistic description of doctor-patient interviews. In Wadsworth, M and Robinson, D (eds.) *Studies in everyday medical life*. Martin Robertson, London

Coulthard, R M and Brazil, D C 1981 Exchange structure. In Coulthard and Montgomery 1981: 82–106

Coulthard, R M and Brazil, D C 1982 The place of intonation in the description of interaction. In Tannen 1982

Coulthard, R M and Montgomery, M M (eds.) 1981 *Studies in discourse analysis*. Routledge and Kegan Paul

Crystal, D 1969 *Prosodic systems and intonation in English*. Cambridge University Press

Crystal, D 1975 *The English tone of voice*. Arnold, London

Dali, F 1979 *Speech in narrative*. Discourse Analysis Monographs No. 7. English Language Research, Birmingham

Dore, J 1973 *On the acquisition of speech acts: a pragmatic description of early language development*. Unpublished paper

Dore, J 1975 Holophrases, speech acts and language universals. *Journal of Child Language* 2: 21–40

Dore, J 1979 Conversational acts and the acquisition of language. In Ochs and Schiefflin 1979: 239–362

Dorian, N C 1982 Defining the speech community to include its working margins. In Romaine, S (ed.) *Sociolinguistic variation in speech communities*: 25–47. Arnold, London

Duncan, S 1972 Some signals and rules for taking speaking turns in conversation. *Journal of Personality and Social Psychology* 23(2): 283–92

Duncan, S 1973 Towards a grammar for dyadic conversation. *Semiotica* 9(1): 29–46

Duncan, S 1974 On the structure of speaker-auditor interaction during speaking turns. *Language in Society* 3(2): 161–80

Duncan, S and Niederehe, G 1974 On signalling that it's your turn to speak. *Journal of Experimental Social Psychology* 10: 234–47

Edmondson, W 1981 *Spoken discourse: a model for analysis*. Longman

Ervin-Tripp, S 1972 On sociolinguistic rules: alternation and co-occurrence. In Gumperz and Hymes 1972: 213–50

Ervin-Tripp, S 1974 The comprehension and production of requests by children. In *Papers and reports on child language development*. Stanford University

Ervin-Tripp, S 1977 Wait for me roller-skate. In Ervin-Tripp, S and Mitchell-Kernan, C (eds.) 1977: 165–88
Ervin-Tripp, S 1979 Children's verbal turn-taking. In Ochs and Schiefflin 1979: 381–414
Ervin-Tripp, S and Mitchell-Kernan, C (eds.) 1977 *Child discourse*. Academic Press, New York

Ferguson, C 1959 Diglossia. *Word* 15: 325–40
Ferguson, J 1975 *Interruptions in spontaneous dialogue*. Paper delivered at BPS conference, Stirling
Fillmore, C J 1968 The case for case. In Bach, E and Harms, R T (eds.) *Universals in linguistic theory*: 1–90. Holt, Rinehart and Winston, New York
Fillmore, C J 1972 May we come in. In Smith, D M and Shuy, R W (eds.) *Sociolinguistics in crosscultural perspective*. 97–115. Georgetown University Press, Washington
Finocchiario, M and Brumfit, C 1983 *The functional-notional approach: from theory to practice*. Oxford University Press
Firth, J R 1935 The technique of semantics. In Firth 1957: 7–33
Firth, J R 1951 Modes of meaning. In Firth 1957: 190–215
Firth, J R 1957 *Papers in linguistics 1934–51*. Oxford University Press
Flanders, N A 1970 *Analysing teaching behavior*. Addison-Wesley, Reading, Massachusetts
Forguson, L W 1973 Locutionary and illocutionary acts. In Warnock, G J (ed.) *Essays on J.L. Austin*: 60–185. Oxford University Press
Forsyth, I J (1974) Patterns in the discourse of pupils and teachers. In *The Space between . . . CILT Reports and Papers* 10: 77–99. CILT, London
Foster, M K 1974 When words become deeds: an analysis of three Iroquois longhouse speech events. In Bauman, R and Sherzer, J (eds.) *Explorations in the ethnography of speaking*: 354–67. Cambridge University Press.
Frake, C O 1972 Struck by speech: the Yakan concept of litigation. In Gumperz and Hymes 1972: 106–29

Gallagher, J J and Aschner, M J 1963 A preliminary report on analyses of classroom interaction. *Merrill-Palmer Quarterly* 9: 183–94
Garfinkel, H 1967 *Studies in ethnomethodology*. Prentice-Hall, Englewood Cliffs, NJ
Garvey, C 1975 Requests and responses in children's speech. *Journal of Child Language* 2: 41–63
Garvey, C 1979 Contingent queries and their relations in discourse. In Ochs and Schiefflin 1979: 363–72
Geertz, C 1960 *The religion of Java*. The Free Press, New York
Geertz, C 1968 Linguistic etiquette. In Fishman, J A (ed.) *Readings in the sociology of language*: 282–95 Mouton, The Hague (being pages 248–60 from Geertz 1960)
Goffman, E 1975 *Interaction ritual: essays on force-to-force behaviour*. Anchor/Doubleday, New York
Goffman, E 1976 Replies and responses. *Language in Society* 5: 257–313
Goffman, E 1979 *Forms of talk*. Blackwell, Oxford
Goldberg, J A 1978 Amplitude shift: a mechanism for the affiliation of utterances in conversational interaction. In Schenkein 1978: 99–218

Goodwin, C 1981 *Conversational organisation*. Academic Press, New York

Gordon, D and Lakoff, G 1971 Conversational postulates. In *Papers from the seventh regional meeting of the Chicago Linguistic Society*: 63–84

Gosling, J (in preparation) *Interaction in seminars: a discourse analysis approach*. Ph.D. thesis, University of Birmingham

Grice, H P 1975 Logic and conversation. In Cole and Morgan 1975: 41–58

Grice, H P 1978 Further notes on logic and conversation. In Cole 1978: 113–28

Gumperz, J J 1964 Hindi-Punjabi code-switching in Delhi. In Lunt, H G (ed.) *Proceedings of the ninth congress of linguists*: 1115–1124. Mouton, The Hague.

Gumperz, J J and Herasimchuk, E 1972 The conversational analysis of social meaning: a study of classroom interaction. In Shuy, R W (ed.) *Sociolinguistics: current trends and prospects*. Georgetown University Press, Washington

Gumperz, J J and Hymes, D (eds.) 1972 *Directions in sociolinguistics*. Holt, Rinehart and Winston, New York

Halliday, M A K 1961 Categories of the theory of grammar. *Word* 17: 241–92

Halliday, M A K 1967 *Intonation and grammar in British English*. Mouton, The Hague

Halliday, M A K 1970 *A course in spoken English: intonation*. Oxford University Press

Halliday, M A K 1973 *Explorations in the functions of language*. Arnold, London

Halliday, M A K 1974 A sociosemiotic perspective on language development. *Bulletin of the School of Oriental and African Studies* 37(1): 98–118

Halliday, M A K 1975 *Learning how to mean*. Arnold, London

Halliday, M A K and Hasan, R 1976 *Cohesion in English*. Longman

Halliday, M A K, McIntosh, A and Strevens, P 1964 *The linguistic sciences and language teaching*. Longman

Harmer, J 1982 What is communicative? *ELT Journal* 36(3): 164–8

Harris, Z 1952 Discourse analysis. *Language* 28: 1–30

Hatch, E 1978 Discourse analysis and second language acquisition. In Hatch, E (ed.) *Second language acquisition*: 401–35. Newbury House, Rowley, Massachusetts

Hoey, M 1979 *Signalling in Discourse*. Discourse Analysis Monographs No. 6. English Language Research, Birmingham

Hoey, M 1983 *On the surface of discourse*. Allen and Unwin

Huddleston, R D, Hudson, R A, Winter, E O and Henrici, A 1968 *Sentence and clause in scientific English*. OSTI report no. 5030

Hyland, K 1984 *An analysis of presuppositions in casual conversation*. Unpublished M.A. thesis, University of Birmingham

Hymes, D 1964 Introduction: towards ethnographies of communication. In Gumperz, J J and Hymes, D (eds.) *The ethnography of communication. American Anthropologist* 66(6): 1–34

Hymes, D 1971 Sociolinguistics and the ethnography of speaking. In Ardener, E (ed.) *Social anthropology and linguistics*: 47–93. Association of Social Anthropologists, monograph no. 10, Tavistock, London

Hymes, D 1972a Models of the interaction of language and social life. In Gumperz and Hymes 1972: 35–71

Hymes, D 1972b On communicative competence. In Pride, J B and Holmes, J (eds.) *Sociolinguistics*: 269–85. Penguin.

Hymes, D 1974 Ways of speaking. In Bauman, R and Sherzer, J (eds.) *Explorations in the ethnography of speaking*: 433–52. Cambridge University Press

Hymes, D 1982a postscript to *Towards linguistic competence*. Mimeo, University of Pennsylvania

Hymes, D 1982b *Ethnolinguistic study of classroom discourse*. Final report to NIE, mimeo

Irvine, J T 1974 Strategies of status manipulation in the Wolof-greeting. In Bauman, R and Sherzer, J (eds.) *Explorations in the ethnography of speaking*: 167–91. Cambridge University Press

Jakobovitz, L A and Gordon, B 1974 *The context of foreign language teaching*. Newbury House, Rowley, Massachusetts

Jefferson, G 1972 Side sequences. In Sudnow, D (ed.) *Studies in social interaction*: 294–338. The Free Press, New York

Jefferson, G 1973 A case of precision timing in ordinary conversation: overlapped tag-positioned address terms in closing sequences. *Semiotica* 9(1): 47–96

Jefferson, G 1974 Error correction as an interactional resource. *Language in Society* 3(2): 181–99

Jefferson, G 1978 Sequential aspects of storytelling in conversation. In Schenkein 1978: 219–48

Jefferson, G and Schenkein, J 1978 Some sequential negotiations in conversation. In Schenkein 1978: 155–72

Johns, T F 1976 Seminar discussion strategies: problems and principles in role simulation. *Pariser Werkstattgesprach* (Goethe Institut, Munich, 1977)

Joos, M 1967 *The five clocks*. Harbinger Books, New York

Jupp, T C and Hodlin, S 1975 *Industrial English*. Heinemann

Kaye, K and Charney, R 1981 Conversational asymmetry between mothers and children. *Journal of Child Language* 8: 35–49

Keenan, E O 1974 *Again and again: the pragmatics of imitation in child language*. Paper presented to the annual meeting of the American Anthropological Association, Mexico City, revised in Ervin-Tripp and Mitchell-Kernan 1977: 125–38

Keenan, E O 1975 Conversational competence in children. *Journal of Child Language* 1(2): 163–83

Keenan, E O and Klein, E 1975 Coherency in children's discourse. *Journal of Psycholinguistic Research* 4(4): 365–80

Keenan, E and Schiefflin, B 1976 Topic as a discourse notion. In Li, C (ed.) *Subject and topic*: 335–84. Academic Press, New York

Kendon, A 1967 Some functions of gaze direction in social interaction. *Acta Psychologica* 26: 22–63

Kendon, A 1972 Some relationships between body motion and speech: an analysis of an example. In Siegman and Pope 1972: 177–210

Kendon, A 1973 The role of visible behavior in the organisation of face-to-face interaction. In von Cranach, M and Vine, I (eds.) *Social communication and movement: studies of interaction and expression in man and chimpanzee* 29–74. Academic Press, London

Kendon, A and Ferber, A 1973 A description of some human greetings. In Michael, R P and Crook, J H (eds.) *Comparative ecology and behaviour of primates*: 591–668. Academic Press, London

Kliebard, H M 1966 The observation of classroom behaviour. In Hitchcock, C (ed.) *The way teaching is*. Association for Supervision and Curriculum Development and Centre for the Study of Instruction, Washington DC

Labov, W 1968 The reflection of social processes in linguistic structures. In Fishman, J (ed.) *Readings in the Sociology of Language*: 240–51. Mouton, The Hague

Labov, W 1969 The logic of non-standard English, *Georgetown Monographs on Language and Linguistics* 22: 1–31

Labov, W 1970 The study of language in its social context. *Studium Generale* 23: 30–87

Labov, W 1972a Rules for ritual insults. In Sudnow, D (ed.) *Studies in social interaction*: 120–69. Free Press, New York

Labov, W 1972b *Sociolinguistic patterns*. University of Pennsylvania Press, Philadelphia

Labov, W and Fanshel, D 1977 *Therapeutic discourse: psychotherapy as conversation*. Academic Press, New York

Labov, W and Waletsky, J 1966 Narrative analysis: oral versions of personal experience. In Helm, J (ed.) *Essays on the verbal and visual arts*: 12–44. University of Washington Press, Seattle

Lakoff, R 1972 Language in context. *Language* 48(4): 907–27

Larsen-Freeman, D 1980 *Discourse analysis in second language research*. Newbury House, Rowley, Massachusetts

Laver, J 1970 The production of speech. In Lyons, J (ed.) *New horizons in linguistics*: 53–77. Penguin

Laver, J 1980 *The phonetic description of voice quality*. Cambridge University Press

Lawson, C 1977 *Request patterns in a two-year-old*. Unpublished manuscript quoted in Ervin-Tripp 1977

Leech, G N 1969 *A linguistic guide to English poetry*. Longman

Leech, G N 1983 *Principles of pragmatics*. Longman

Leech, G N and Short, M 1981 *Style in fiction*. Longman

Levinson, S C 1979 Activity types and language. *Linguistics* 17(5–6): 365–99

Levinson, S C 1980 Speech act theory: the state of the art. *Language and Linguistics Abstracts* 13(1): 5–24

Levinson, S C 1983 *Pragmatics*. Cambridge University Press

Lieberman, P 1960 Some acoustic correlates of word stress in American English. *Journal of the Acoustical Society of America* 32: 451–4

de Long, A J 1974 Kinesic signals at utterance boundaries in preschool children. *Semiotica* 11(1): 43–73

Lyons, J 1968 *An introduction to theoretical linguistics*. Cambridge University Press

McNeill, D 1970 *The acquisition of language: the study of developmental psycholinguistics*. Harper and Row, New York

Mansfield, G 1983 Discourse intonation in English and Italian: a first contrastive analysis. *Analysis: Quaderni di Anglistica* 1(1): 179–89

Medley, D M and Mitzel, H E 1963 Measuring classroom behavior by systematic observation. In Gage, (ed.) *Handbook of research on teaching*. Rand McNally, Chicago

Merritt, M 1976 On questions following questions in service encounters. *Language in Society* **5**: 315–55

Meux, M D 1967 Studies of learning in the school setting. *Review of Educational Research* **37**: 539–62

Miller, W and Ervin, S 1964 The development of grammar in child language. In Bellugi, U and Brown, R (eds.) *The acquisition of language*: 9–34. Monographs of the Society for Research in Child Development, **29**

Mitchell, T F 1957 The language of buying and selling in Cyrenaica. *Hesperis* **44**: 31–71

Montgomery, M M 1977 *The structure of lectures*. Unpublished M.A. thesis, University of Birmingham

Montgomery, M M 1981 The structure of monologue. In Coulthard and Montgomery 1981: 33–39

Morgan, J L 1977 Conversational postulates revisited. *Language* **53**: 277–84

Morgan, J L 1978 Two types of convention in indirect speech acts. In Cole 1978: 261–80

Mountford, A 1975 *Discourse analysis and the simplification of reading material for English for Special Purposes*. Unpublished M. Litt. thesis, University of Edinburgh

Muir, K (ed.) 1968 *Othello*. Penguin

Ochs, E and Schiefflin, B (eds.) 1979 *Developmental pragmatics*. Academic Press, New York

Ochs, E and Schiefflin, B 1983 *Acquiring conversational competence*. Routledge and Kegan Paul

Ochs, E, Schiefflin, B and Platt, M 1979 Presuppositions across utterances and speakers. In Ochs and Schiefflin 1979: 251–68

O'Connor, D J and Arnold, G F 1959 *Intonation of colloquial English*. Longman

Ohmann, R 1971 Speech acts and the definition of literature. *Philosophy and Rhetoric* **4**: 1–19

Pearce, R D 1973 *The structure of discourse in broadcast interviews*. Unpublished M.A. thesis, University of Birmingham

Peck, S 1978 Child-child discourse in second language acquisition. In Hatch, E (ed.) *Second language acquisition*: 383–400. Newbury House, Rowley, Massachusetts

Piaget, J 1926 *The language and thought of the child*. Harcourt Brace, New York

Pike, K L 1948 *Tone languages* University of Michigan Press, Ann Arbor

Polgar, S A 1960 Biculturation of Mequaki teenage boys. *American Anthropologist* **62**: 217–35

Pomerantz, A 1978 Compliment responses: notes on the co-operation of multiple constraints. In Schenkein 1978a: 79–112. Academic Press, New York

Pomerantz, A 1984 Agreeing and disagreeing with assessments: some features of preferred/dispreferred turn shapes. In Atkinson, J and Heritage, J (eds.) *Structures of social action*: 57–101. Cambridge University Press

Pratt, M L 1977 *Towards a speech act theory of literary discourse.* Indiana University Press, Bloomington, Indiana

Reeder, K F 1975 *Preschool children's comprehension of illocutionary force: an experimental psycholinguistic study.* Unpublished Ph.D. thesis, University of Birmingham
Reeder, K F 1976 *On young children's discrimination of illocutionary force: a report on work in progress* Unpublished paper
Reisman, K 1974 Contrapuntal conversations in an Antiguan village. In Bauman, R and Sherzer, J (eds.) *Explorations in the ethnography of speaking:* 110–24. Cambridge University Press
Richards, J C and Schmidt, R W 1983 Conversational analysis. In Richards, J C and Schmidt, R W (eds.) *Language and communication:* 117–54. Longman
Ross, J R 1979 On declarative sentences. In Jacobs, R A and Rosenbaum, P S (eds.) *Readings in English transformational grammar:* 226–56. Ginn, Waltham, Massachusetts
Ryave, A 1978 On the achievement of a series of stories. In Schenkein 1978a: 113–32

Sacks, H 1967–71 Mimeo lecture notes
Sacks, H 1972a On the analysability of stories by children. In Gumperz and Hymes 1972: 325–45
Sacks, H 1972b An initial investigation of the usability of conversational data for doing sociology. In Sudnow, D (ed.) *Studies in social interaction:* 31–74. Free Press, New York
Sacks, H (MS) *Aspects of the sequential organisation of conversation.*
Sacks, H 1978 Some technical considerations of a dirty joke. In Schenkein 1978: 249–70
Sacks, H, Schegloff, E A and Jefferson, G 1974 A simplest systematics for the organisation of turn-taking for conversation. *Language* 50(4): 696–735
Sadock, J M 1974 *Towards a linguistic theory of speech acts.* Academic Press, New York
Sadock, J M 1975 The soft interpretive underbelly of generative semantics. In Cole and Morgan 1975: 383–96
Sadock, J M 1978 On testing for conversational implicature. In Cole 1978: 281–98
Salmond, S 1974 Rituals of encounter among the Maori: sociolinguistic study of a scene. In Bauman, R and Sherzer, J (eds.) *Explorations in the ethnography of speaking:* 192–212. Cambridge University Press
Sankoff, D 1974 A quantitative paradigm for the study of communicative competence. In Bauman, R and Sherzer, J (eds.) *Explorations in the ethnography of speaking:* 18–49. Cambridge University Press
Saville-Troike, M 1982 *The ethnography of communication.* Blackwell, Oxford
Scheflen, A E 1964 The significance of posture in communication systems. *Psychiatry* 27: 316–31
Schegloff, E A 1968 Sequencing in conversational openings. *American Anthropologist* 70(6): 1075–95
Schegloff, E A 1972 Notes on a conversational practice: formulating place.

In Sudnow, D (ed.) *Studies in social interaction*: 75-119. Free Press, New York

Schegloff, E A and Sacks, H 1973 Opening up closings. *Semiotica* 8(4): 289-327

Schegloff, E A, Jefferson, G and Sacks, H 1977 The preference for self-correction in the organisation of repair in conversation. *Language* 53: 361-82

Schenkein, J (ed.) 1978a *Studies in the organisation of conversational interaction.* Academic Press, New York

Schenkein, J 1978b Sketch of an analytic mentality for the study of conversational interaction. In Schenkein 1978a: 1-6

Schenkein, J 1978c Identity negotiations in conversation. In Schenkein 1978a: 57-78

Schlesinger, I M 1971 Production of utterances and language acquisition. In Slobin, D I (ed.) *The ontogenesis of grammar.* 63-101. Academic Press, New York

Schmidt, R and Richards, J (1980) Speech acts and second language learning. *Applied Linguistics* 1(2): 129-257

Scollon, R 1979 A real early stage: an unzippered condensation of a dissertation on child language. In Ochs and Schiefflin 1979: 215-28

Searle, J R 1965 What is a speech act? In Black, M (ed.) *Philosophy in America*: 221-39. Cornell University Press, Ithaca, New York

Searle, J R 1969 *Speech acts.* Cambridge University Press

Searle, J R 1975 Indirect speech acts. In Cole and Morgan 1975: 59-82

Searle, J R 1976 The classification of illocutionary acts. *Language in Society* 5: 1-24. Reprinted in Searle, J R *Expression and meaning*: 1-29. Cambridge University Press

Searle, J P, Kiefer, F and Bierwish, M (eds.) 1980 *Speech act theory and pragmatics*, Synthese Language Library, Vol. 10. Reidel, Dordrecht

Sharrock, W W and Turner, R 1978 On a conversational environment for equivocality. In Schenkein 1978a: 173-98

Shatz, M 1974 The comprehension of indirect directives: can two-year-olds shut the door? Paper presented to the summer meeting of the LSA, Amherst, Massachusetts

Sherzer, J 1974 Namakke, Summakke, Kormakke: three types of Cuna speech event. In Bauman, R and Sherzer, J (eds.) *Explorations in the ethnography of speaking*: 262-82. Cambridge University Press

Siegman, A W and Pope, B (eds.) 1972 *Studies in dyadic communication.* Pergamon, New York

Sinclair, A *The sociolinguistic significance of the form of requests used in service encounters.* Unpublished diploma dissertation, University of Cambridge

Sinclair, J McH 1966 Taking a poem to pieces. In Fowler, R (ed.) *Essays on style and language*: 68-81. Routledge and Kegan Paul

Sinclair, J McH 1971 Lines about lines. In Kachru, B B and Stahlke, H F W (eds.) *Current trends in stylistics*: 251-61. Mouton, The Hague

Sinclair, J McH 1972 *A course in spoken English: grammar.* Oxford University Press

Sinclair, J McH 1973 Linguistics in colleges of education. *Dudley Journal of Education* 3: 17-25

Sinclair, J McH 1983 Planes of discourse. In Ritzvi, S N A (ed.) *The twofold*

voice: essays in honour of Ramesh Mohan: 70–91 Pitambur Publishing Company, India
Sinclair, J McH and Brazil, D 1982 *Teacher talk*. Oxford University Press
Sinclair, J McH and Coulthard, R M 1975 *Towards an analysis of discourse.* Oxford University Press
Sinclair, J McH, Forsyth, I J, Coulthard, R M and Ashby, M C 1972 *The English used by teachers and pupils*. Final report to SSRC, mimeo, University of Birmingham
Snow, C 1977 The development of conversation between mothers and babies. *Child Language* 4: 1–22
Stenst.öm, A-B 1984 *Questions and responses*. Liber Förlag Malmö
Stiles, W B 1981 Classification of intersubjective illocutionary acts. *Language in Society* 10: 227–49
Straker-Cook, R H 1975 *A communicative approach to the analysis of extended monologue discourse and its relevance to the development of teaching materials for English for special purposes*. Unpublished M. Litt, thesis, University of Edinburgh
Strawson, P F 1964 Intention and convention in speech acts. *Philosophical Review* 73: 439–60
Strawson, P F 1973 Austin and 'locutionary meaning'. In Warnock 1973 *Essays on J.L. Austin*: 46–68. Oxford University Press
Stubbs, M 1981 Motivating analyses of exchange structure. In Coulthard and Montgomery 1981: 107–19
Stubbs, M 1983 *Discourse analysis*. Blackwell, Oxford
Stubbs, M 1984 review of *Teacher talk. Applied Linguistics* 5(1): 71–4
Sturtridge, G 1981 Role playing and simulation. In Johnson, K and Morrow, K (eds.) *Communication in the classroom*: 59–66. Longman
Sweet, H 1906 *A primer of phonetics*. Oxford University Press

Taba, H, Levine, S and Elsey, F F 1964 *Thinking in elementary school children*. US Department of Health, Education and Welfare, Office of Education; Cooperative project no. 1574, San Francisco State College
Tannen, D 1981 New York Jewish conversational style. *International Journal of the Sociology of Language* 30: 133–9
Tannen, D (ed.) 1982 *Analysing discourse: text and talk, Georgetown University Round Table on Languages and Linguistics 1981*. Georgetown University Press, Washington
Thorne, J P 1965 Stylistics and generative grammars. *Journal of Linguistics* 1: 49–59
Trager, G and Smith, H 1951 *An outline of English structure*. American Council of Learned Societies, Washington DC
Turner, R 1972 Some formal properties of therapy talk. In Sudnow, D (ed.) *Studies in social interaction*: 267–96. Free Press, New York

Walker, R 1975 Conversational implicatures. In Blackburn, S (ed.) *Meaning, reference and necessity*: 133–81 Cambridge University Press
Warnock, G J 1973 Some types of performative utterance. In Warnock, G J (ed.) *Essays on J.L. Austin*: 69–89. Oxford University Press
Watson, J 1984 *A comparison of native speaker/non-native speaker interaction in casual conversation and Cambridge First Certification oral interviews*. Unpub-

lished M.A. dissertation, English Language Research, University of Birmingham

Watson, O M and Graves, T D 1966 Quantitative research in proxemic behavior. *American Anthropologist* **68**: 971–85

Weick, K E 1968 Systematic observational methods. In Lindzey, G and Aronson, E (eds.) *Handbook of social psychology*, vol. 2. Addison-Wesley, Reading, Massachusetts

Wells, G, Montgomery, M and MacLure, M 1979 Adult-child discourse: an outline of a model of analysis. *Journal of Pragmatics* **3**: 337–80

Widdowson, H G 1971 The deep structure of discourse and the use of translation. In Corder, S P and Roulet, E (eds.) *Linguistic insights in applied linguistics* (Second Neuchâtel Colloquium in Applied Linguistics, Brussels, AIMAV). Didier, Paris

Widdowson, H G 1973 *An applied linguistic approach to discourse analysis*. Unpublished Ph.D. thesis, University of Edinburgh

Widdowson, H G 1974 An approach to the teaching of scientific English discourse. *RELC Journal* **5**: 27–40

Widdowson, H G 1975 EST in theory and practice. In Jones, K and Roe, P (eds.) *English for academic study* (ETIC occasional paper). British Council, London

Widdowson, H G 1978 *Teaching language as communication*. Oxford University Press

Widdowson, H G 1979 *Explorations in applied linguistics*, Oxford University Press

Wilkins, D 1972a *An investigation into the linguistic and situational content of the common core in a unit/credit system*. Mimeo, Council of Europe, Strasbourg

Wilkins, D 1972b *Grammatical, situational and notional syllabuses*. Paper presented to the third International Congress of Applied Linguistics, Copenhagen, August 1972

Wilkins, D 1974 Notional syllabuses and the concept of a minimum adequate grammar. In Corder, S P and Roulet, E (eds.) *Linguistic insights in applied linguistics* (Second Neuchâtel Colloquium in Applied Linguistics, Brussels, AIMAV). Didier, Paris

Wilkins, D 1976 *Notional syllabuses*. Oxford University Press

Williams, S 1974 *A sociolinguistic analysis of the general practice interview*. Unpublished M.A. thesis, University of Birmingham

Willis, J D 1983 *The implications of discourse analysis for the teaching of oral communication*. Unpublished Ph.D. thesis, University of Birmingham

Willis, J R 1981 *Spoken discourse in the ELT classroom: a system of analysis and a description*. Unpublished M.A. thesis, University of Birmingham

Winter, E O 1977 A clause-relational approach to English texts. *Instructional Science* **6**(1) (special issue)

Woolard, G 1984 *Communicative functions and language teaching with particular reference to the Malaysian English language syllabus (122) for forms 4 and 5*. Unpublished M.A. thesis, University of Birmingham

Index